Taste *of* Home

BLUE RIBBON WINNERS

© 2022 RDA Enthusiast Brands, LLC.
1610 N. 2nd St., Suite 102, Milwaukee, WI 53212-3906
All rights reserved. Taste of Home is a registered trademark
of RDA Enthusiast Brands, LLC.

Visit us at **tasteofhome.com** for other Taste of Home
books and products.

International Standard Book Number:
Retail: 978-1-62145-779-4
DTC: 978-1-62145-780-0

Executive Editor: Mark Hagen
Senior Art Director: Raeann Thompson
Editor: Hazel Wheaton
Art Director: Maggie Conners
Designer: Carrie Peterson
Deputy Editor, Copy Desk: Dulcie Shoener
Copy Editor: Sara Strauss
Contributing Designer: Jennifer Ruetz

Cover:
Photographer: Dan Roberts
Set Stylist: Melissa Franco
Food Stylist: Shannon Norris

Pictured on front cover:
Golden Peach Pie, p. 246; S'Mores on a Stick, p. 41;
Ginger Blueberry Jam, p. 208

Pictured on back cover:
Spicy Corn Kabobs, p. 41

INSTANT POT is a trademark of Double Insight Inc.
This publication has not been authorized, sponsored
or otherwise approved by Double Insight Inc.

Printed in USA
1 3 5 7 9 10 8 6 4 2

TABLE OF CONTENTS

TAKE ME TO THE FAIR!

There's no food quite like fair food. Every year, people of all ages stream to fairgrounds across the country to see the sights, ride the rides and sample the oh-so-tasty offerings—from tried-and-true classic fare to fun and adventurous new culinary inventions.

Freshly made funnel cakes and elephant ears still warm and crusted with sugar, corn on the cob cooked on a grill and dipped in herbs and butter, corn dogs, sweet and crunchy caramel corn, deep-fried cheese (deep-fried anything, really!), piping hot french fries—fairgoers line up to get these and other festival favorites.

Beyond the food vendors, there are the competitions, as cooks and bakers present their most-prized creations for the judges to taste. Desserts and main dishes, breads and sides—the competitors wait breathlessly for the results. Which dishes will be worthy of the blue ribbon? Which talented cooks will win bragging rights for the next year?

With the **275+ recipes** in the all-new *Taste of Home Blue Ribbon Winners*, you can bring the fair to your own home any time of year. No need to wait in line for a decadent cream puff or an electric-blue snow cone! We've included decorated dishes from state and county fairs as well as from all kinds of recipe contests— chili cook-offs, baking challenges, barbecue competitions and more. These recipes have won acclaim and been proven winners, so you can be sure they'll win over your family!

You'll also enjoy...
- Dozens of tips, hints and inside secrets from our Test Kitchen to speed dinner prep and ensure success.

- A complete set of nutrition facts with every recipe so you can plan a healthy meal for your family.

- Heartwarming stories shared by fairgoers of every age, with photos that bring the fair to life again.

So step right up and dig right in to the best food you'll find anywhere. Best of all, you'll find it right in your own kitchen!

P. 67

P. 43

P. 105

209

P. 14

P. 36

P. 17

P. 14

THE BEST FAIR FOODS

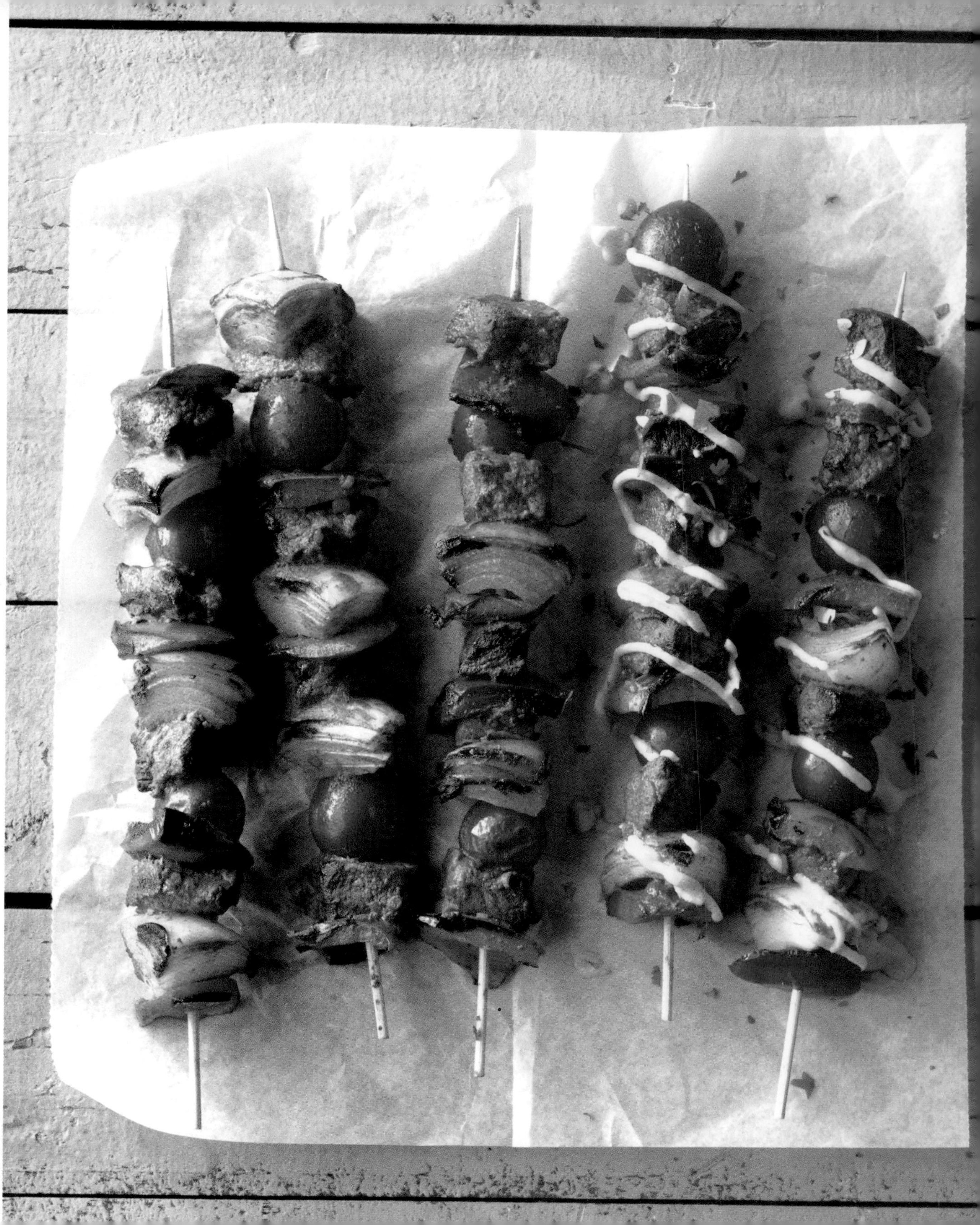

TACOS ON A STICK

Kids like assembling these creative kabobs almost as much as they like devouring them. The whole family is sure to love the sensational southwestern flavor of this twist on beef shish kabobs.
—Dixie Terry, Goreville, IL

Prep: 15 min. + marinating • **Grill:** 15 min.
Makes: 6 servings

- 1 envelope taco seasoning
- 1 cup tomato juice
- 2 Tbsp. canola oil
- 2 lbs. beef top sirloin steak, cut into 1-in. cubes
- 1 medium green pepper, cut into chunks
- 1 medium sweet red pepper, cut into chunks
- 1 large onion, cut into wedges
- 16 cherry tomatoes
  Optional: Salsa con queso or sour cream

1. In a large shallow dish, combine taco seasoning, tomato juice and oil; mix well. Remove ½ cup for basting; refrigerate. Add beef and turn to coat. Cover; refrigerate for at least 5 hours.
2. Drain and discard marinade from beef. On metal or soaked wooden skewers, alternately thread beef, peppers, onion and tomatoes. Grill, uncovered, over medium heat for 3 minutes on each side. Baste with the reserved marinade.
3. Continue turning and basting until the meat reaches desired doneness, 8-10 minutes. If desired, serve with salsa con queso or sour cream.

1 taco stick: 277 cal., 10g fat (3g sat. fat), 61mg chol., 665mg sod., 12g carb. (4g sugars, 2g fiber), 34g pro. **Diabetic exchanges:** 4 lean meat, 2 vegetable, 1 fat.

OLD-FASHIONED LEMONADE

This sweet-tart lemonade is a traditional part of Memorial Day and Fourth of July menus. Folks can't get enough of the fresh-squeezed flavor.
—Tammi Simpson, Greensburg, KY

Prep: 10 min. • **Cook:** 5 min. + chilling
Makes: 7 servings

- 1⅓ cups sugar
- 5 cups water, divided
- 1 Tbsp. grated lemon zest
- 1¾ cups lemon juice (about 10 large lemons)

In a large saucepan, combine sugar, 1 cup water and the lemon zest. Cook and stir over medium heat until sugar is dissolved, about 4 minutes. Remove from heat. Stir in lemon juice and remaining 4 cups water; refrigerate until cold. Serve over ice.

1 cup: 142 cal., 0 fat (0 sat. fat), 0 chol., 1mg sod., 37g carb. (35g sugars, 0 fiber), 0 pro.

BRATS IN BEER

Make these juicy brats at your next barbecue. The flavor of the beer-based marinade really comes through in the grilled onions.
—Jill Hazelton, Hamlet, IN

....

Prep: 10 min. + marinating • **Grill:** 15 min.
Makes: 8 servings

1 can (12 oz.) beer or nonalcoholic beer
2 Tbsp. brown sugar
2 Tbsp. soy sauce
1 Tbsp. chili powder
1 Tbsp. prepared mustard
⅛ tsp. garlic powder
8 uncooked bratwurst links
1 large onion, thinly sliced
8 brat or hot dog buns, split

1. In a small bowl, combine the first 6 ingredients. Pour 1¾ cups into a shallow dish. Add brats and turn to coat. Cover; refrigerate 4 hours or overnight. Cover and refrigerate the remaining marinade.
2. Add sliced onion to the remaining marinade; toss to coat. Place on a double thickness of heavy-duty foil (about 18 in. square). Fold foil around onion mixture and seal tightly.
3. Drain and discard marinade from bratwurst. Grill bratwurst and onion packets, covered, over medium heat or broil 4 in. from the heat 15-20 minutes or until meat is no longer pink and onion is tender, turning frequently. Open foil carefully to allow steam to escape. Serve brats in buns with onion mixture.
1 bratwurst: 510 cal., 29g fat (10g sat. fat), 63mg chol., 1209mg sod., 41g carb. (7g sugars, 2g fiber), 20g pro.

MINI NUTELLA DOUGHNUTS

These crispy bites can be made in advance and refrigerated before frying. Pop them into your mouth while they're still warm for maximum flavor.
—Renee Murphy, Smithtown, NY

....

Prep: 30 min. • **Cook:** 5 min./batch
Makes: 32 doughnuts

1 large egg, room temperature
1 Tbsp. water
1 tube (16.3 oz.) large refrigerated flaky biscuits (8 count)
⅔ cup Nutella
Oil for deep-fat frying
Confectioners' sugar

1. Whisk egg with water. On a lightly floured surface, roll each biscuit into a 6-in. circle; cut each circle into 4 wedges. Brush lightly with egg mixture; top each wedge with 1 tsp. Nutella. Bring corners up over filling; pinch edges firmly to seal.
2. In a large cast-iron or electric skillet, heat oil to 350°. In small batches, place doughnuts in hot oil, seam side down; fry until golden brown, 1-2 minutes per side. Drain on paper towels. Dust with confectioners' sugar; serve warm.
1 doughnut: 99 cal., 6g fat (1g sat. fat), 6mg chol., 142mg sod., 10g carb. (5g sugars, 0 fiber), 2g pro.

ORANGE FRITTERS

My daughter made a citrusy version of apple fritters for 4-H demonstrations at our county and state fair. This crowd-size recipe yields 11 dozen but can easily be cut in half.
—Debbie Johnson, Centertown, MO

Prep: 15 min. • **Cook:** 5 min./batch
Makes: about 11 dozen

- 6 **cups all-purpose flour**
- 6 **cups biscuit/baking mix**
- 2 **cups sugar**
- 2 **Tbsp. baking powder**
- 6 **large eggs, room temperature**
- 2 **to 3 Tbsp. grated orange zest**
- 4 **cups orange juice**
  Oil for deep-fat frying
  Confectioners' sugar

1. In a large bowl, whisk the flour, biscuit mix, sugar and baking powder. In another bowl, whisk eggs, orange zest and orange juice until blended. Add to the dry ingredients, stirring just until moistened.
2. In an electric skillet or deep fryer, heat oil to 375°. Drop batter by rounded tablespoonfuls, a few at a time, into hot oil. Fry for about 1-2 minutes on each side or until golden brown. Drain on paper towels; cool slightly. Dust with confectioners' sugar.

1 fritter: 81 cal., 3g fat (0 sat. fat), 8mg chol., 88mg sod., 12g carb. (4g sugars, 0 fiber), 1g pro.

THE BEST FAIR FOODS

STATE FAIR SUBS

My college roommate and I first ate these meaty sandwiches at the Iowa State Fair. After a little experimenting, we re-created the recipe. We ate the subs often because they were fast to fix between classes and didn't break our next-to-nothing grocery budget.
—Christi Ross, Mill Creek, OK

Prep: 20 min. • **Bake:** 20 min.
Makes: 6 servings

1 loaf (1 lb. unsliced) **French bread**
2 large eggs
¼ cup whole milk
½ tsp. pepper
¼ tsp. salt
1 lb. bulk Italian sausage
1½ cups chopped onion
2 cups shredded part-skim mozzarella cheese

1. Preheat oven to 400°. Cut bread in half lengthwise; carefully hollow out top and bottom of the loaf, leaving a 1-in. shell. Cube the removed bread. In a large bowl, beat the eggs, milk, pepper and salt. Add bread cubes and toss to coat.

2. In a skillet over medium heat, cook the sausage and onion until the meat is no longer pink; drain. Add to the bread mixture.

3. Spoon filling into bread shells; sprinkle with cheese. Wrap each in foil. Bake for 20-25 minutes or until cheese is melted. Cut into serving-size slices.

1 piece: 622 cal., 36g fat (15g sat. fat), 159mg chol., 1280mg sod., 45g carb. (5g sugars, 3g fiber), 28g pro.

APPLE-RAISIN EGG ROLLS

Tender apples are rolled inside crisp egg roll wrappers for a deliciously different dessert. These treats look fancy, but they're quite simple to make.
—Karen Orvis, Plainville, CT

Prep: 15 min. + standing
Cook: 5 min./batch
Makes: 16 servings

- 4 medium tart apples, peeled and sliced
- ¼ cup raisins
- ½ tsp. ground cinnamon
- 2 Tbsp. butter
- 1 Tbsp. cornstarch
- 1 cup unsweetened apple juice
- 3 Tbsp. honey
- 16 egg roll wrappers
    Oil for deep-fat frying
    Vanilla ice cream

1. In a large skillet, saute the apples, raisins and cinnamon in butter until tender. Combine cornstarch, juice and honey until smooth; stir into the apple mixture. Bring to a boil over medium heat. Cook and stir for 1-2 minutes or until thickened. Remove from heat; cool.
2. Place ¼ cupful of the apple mixture in the center of 1 egg roll wrapper. Fold bottom corner over the filling. Fold sides toward center over the filling. Moisten remaining corner with water; roll up tightly to seal. Repeat with the remaining apple mixture and wrappers. Let stand for 15 minutes.
3. In an electric skillet, heat 1 in. of oil to 375°. Fry turnovers, a few at a time, for 1-2 minutes on each side or until golden brown. Drain on paper towels. Serve with ice cream.

1 egg roll: 228 cal., 11g fat (2g sat. fat), 7mg chol., 194mg sod., 30g carb. (10g sugars, 1g fiber), 3g pro.

LOADED WAFFLE FRIES

Make any meal better with these special fries. I top them with a savory blend of cheese, scallions and bacon. They're great with hot dogs or burgers or by themselves.
—Jeffrey Viccone, Decatur, IL

Takes: 30 min. • **Makes:** 4 servings

- 4 cups frozen waffle-cut fries
- ½ to 1½ tsp. steak seasoning
- 1 cup shredded cheddar cheese
- 2 Tbsp. chopped green onions
- 2 Tbsp. real bacon bits

1. Arrange waffle fries in a greased 15x10x1-in. baking pan. Bake at 450° for 20-25 minutes or until lightly browned.
2. Sprinkle with steak seasoning; toss to combine. Top with remaining ingredients. Bake 2-3 minutes longer or until cheese is melted.
1 cup: 261 cal., 14g fat (8g sat. fat), 33mg chol., 404mg sod., 25g carb. (1g sugars, 2g fiber), 10g pro.

BLUE-RIBBON TIP

Swap out cheddar for another cheese if you like; go gooey with Muenster, or spicy with pepper jack. This recipe also works great with curly fries!

DEEP-FRIED COOKIES

My kids love this delicious, indulgent treat. I like to give the batter a kick by adding a pinch of cinnamon and a teaspoon of vanilla extract.
—Margarita Torres, Bayamon, Puerto Rico, AE

Prep: 10 min. + freezing • **Cook:** 15 min.
Makes: 1½ dozen

- 18 Oreo cookies
    Oil for deep-fat frying
- 1 cup biscuit/baking mix
- 1 large egg, room temperature
- ½ cup 2% milk
    Confectioners' sugar

1. On each of eighteen 4-in. wooden skewers, thread 1 cookie, inserting pointed end of the skewer into the filling. Freeze until firm, about 1 hour.
2. In a deep cast-iron skillet or deep fryer, heat oil to 375°. Place biscuit mix in a shallow bowl. In another bowl, combine egg and milk; whisk into the biscuit mix just until moistened.
3. Holding the skewer, dip cookies into the biscuit mixture to coat both sides; shake off excess.
4. Fry cookies, a few at a time, until golden brown, 1-2 minutes on each side. Drain on paper towels. Dust with confectioners' sugar before serving.
1 cookie: 100 cal., 5g fat (1g sat. fat), 11mg chol., 123mg sod., 13g carb. (5g sugars, 1g fiber), 1g pro.

FUNNEL CAKES

These are much simpler to make than doughnuts but taste just as good. They have been a regular treat of ours since we came across them at a fair when we lived in the Ozarks.
—Mary Faith Yoder, Unity, WI

Prep: 15 min. • **Cook:** 5 min./batch
Makes: 8 cakes

- 2 **large eggs, room temperature**
- 1 **cup 2% milk**
- 1 **cup water**
- ½ **tsp. vanilla extract**
- 3 **cups all-purpose flour**
- ¼ **cup sugar**
- 3 **tsp. baking powder**
- ¼ **tsp. salt**
  Oil for deep-fat frying
  Confectioners' sugar

1. In a large bowl, beat eggs. Add milk, water and vanilla until well blended. In another bowl, whisk flour, sugar, baking powder and salt; beat into egg mixture until smooth. In a deep cast-iron or electric skillet, heat oil to 375°.
2. For each cake: Cover bottom of a funnel spout with your finger; ladle ½ cup batter into funnel. Holding funnel several inches above oil, release your finger and move funnel in a spiral motion until all batter is released; scrape with a rubber spatula if needed.
3. Fry until golden brown, 2 minutes on each side. Drain on paper towels. Dust with confectioners' sugar; serve warm.
Note: The batter can be poured from a liquid measuring cup instead of a funnel.
1 funnel cake: 316 cal., 12g fat (2g sat. fat), 50mg chol., 256mg sod., 44g carb. (8g sugars, 1g fiber), 7g pro.

FAIR-FAVORITE CORN DOGS

Bring the county fair home to your kitchen with these summer-ready corn dogs. A tip for dipping: Pour the batter into a tall Mason jar and dunk your dogs for an even, all-over coating.
—*Taste of Home* Test Kitchen

Prep: 15 min. + standing
Cook: 5 min./batch • **Makes:** 10 corn dogs

- 1 **pkg. (8½ oz.) cornbread/muffin mix**
- ⅔ **cup all-purpose flour**
- 1 **tsp. ground mustard**
- ½ **tsp. onion powder**
- ½ **tsp. chili powder**
- ½ **tsp. paprika**
- ⅛ **tsp. ground cumin**
- 1 **cup 2% milk**
- 1 **large egg**
- 10 **hot dogs**
- 10 **wooden skewers**
  Oil for deep-fat frying

1. In a large bowl, combine the first 7 ingredients. In another bowl, whisk the milk and egg; stir into the dry ingredients just until moistened. Let stand 15 minutes. Insert skewers into hot dogs; dip into batter.
2. In an electric skillet or deep-fat fryer, heat oil to 375°. Fry corn dogs, a few at a time, until golden brown, 2-3 minutes, turning occasionally. Drain the dogs on paper towels.
1 corn dog: 352 cal., 23g fat (7g sat. fat), 53mg chol., 682mg sod., 26g carb. (7g sugars, 1g fiber), 9g pro.

BLUE-RIBBON TIP

Don't forget to let the batter stand before coating the hot dogs. It thickens up a bit and clings better after 15 minutes. Make sure the oil temperature returns to 375° between batches.

MAPLE-BACON DOUGHNUT BITES

While these delicious bite-size treats are ready in minutes, they disappear in a flash. And don't relegate the deep-fried goodness to the breakfast nook; I've never had anyone turn these down no matter the time of day.
—Chelsea Turner, Lake Elsinore, CA

Prep: 20 min. • **Cook:** 5 min./batch
Makes: about 2 dozen

- 1½ **cups all-purpose flour**
- ½ **cup sugar**
- 2 **tsp. baking powder**
- ½ **tsp. salt**
- 1 **large egg, room temperature**
- ½ **cup 2% milk**
- 1 **Tbsp. butter, melted**
  Oil for deep-fat frying

GLAZE

- 1 **cup confectioners' sugar**
- 3 **Tbsp. maple syrup**
- 1 **Tbsp. 2% milk**
- 1 **tsp. vanilla extract**
- 7 **maple-flavored bacon strips, cooked and crumbled**

1. In a large bowl, whisk flour, sugar, baking powder and salt. In another bowl, whisk egg, milk and melted butter until blended. Add to flour mixture; stir just until moistened.

2. Heat oil to 350° in an electric skillet or deep fryer. Drop tablespoonfuls of batter, a few at a time, into the hot oil. Fry 3-4 minutes or until golden brown, turning often. Drain on paper towels.

3. In a small bowl, mix confectioners' sugar, maple syrup, milk and vanilla until smooth. Dip warm doughnuts into glaze; sprinkle tops with bacon.

1 doughnut: 101 cal., 3g fat (1g sat. fat), 12mg chol., 115mg sod., 16g carb. (10g sugars, 0 fiber), 2g pro.

SPICY TURKEY LEGS

Your guests are sure to get a kick out of these delicious turkey legs. For less spicy flavor, reduce the amount of hot sauce and inject ½ ounce into each leg.
—Steven Schend, Grand Rapids, MI

Prep: 20 min. • **Bake:** 1¼ hours
Makes: 6 servings

- ⅔ **cup Louisiana-style hot sauce**
- 5 **Tbsp. canola oil**
- 1 **Tbsp. chili powder**
- 1 **Tbsp. soy sauce**
- 2 **tsp. ground mustard**
- 1 **tsp. garlic powder**
- 1 **tsp. poultry seasoning**
- 1 **tsp. onion powder**
- 1 **tsp. celery salt**
- ½ **tsp. white pepper**
- ½ **tsp. hot pepper sauce, optional**
- 6 **turkey drumsticks (1 lb. each)**

1. In a small bowl, combine first 11 ingredients; set aside ¼ cup for basting. Draw remaining marinade into a flavor injector. In several areas of each drumstick, inject a total of 2 Tbsp. (or 1 oz.) of marinade into the meat while slowly pulling out the needle.

2. Place drumsticks on a foil-lined 15x10x1-in. baking pan. Cover and bake at 375° for 30 minutes. Uncover; bake until a thermometer reads 180°, 45-55 minutes longer, basting occasionally with reserved marinade.

1 turkey leg: 680 cal., 39g fat (9g sat. fat), 228mg chol., 1489mg sod., 3g carb. (1g sugars, 1g fiber), 76g pro.

PUMPKIN PIE WHOOPIE PIES

Folks line up for these plump, yummy cookies, oozing with creamy filling. We make them for the annual Keene Pumpkin Festival.
—Volunteers Federated Church, Marlborough, NH

Prep: 30 min.
Bake: 10 min./batch + cooling
Makes: 2 dozen

- 3 cups all-purpose flour
- 1½ cups sugar
- 2 tsp. baking powder
- 2 tsp. baking soda
- 1½ tsp. ground cinnamon
- 1 tsp. ground nutmeg
- 1 tsp. ground cloves
- ½ tsp. salt
- 5 large eggs, room temperature
- 1 can (15 oz.) pumpkin
- ½ cup water
- ½ cup canola oil
- 1 tsp. vanilla extract

CREAM CHEESE FILLING
- 4 oz. cream cheese, softened
- ¼ cup butter, softened
- 2 cups confectioners' sugar
- 1 tsp. vanilla extract

1. Preheat oven to 350°. In a large bowl, combine the flour, sugar, baking powder, baking soda, cinnamon, nutmeg, cloves and salt. In another bowl, whisk eggs, pumpkin, water, oil and vanilla. Stir into the dry ingredients just until moistened.
2. Drop by 2 tablespoonfuls 2 in. apart onto greased baking sheets. Bake for 8-10 minutes. Remove to wire racks to cool.
3. In a small bowl, beat all the filling ingredients until smooth. Spread over the bottom of half of the cookies;

top with remaining cookies. Store in the refrigerator.
1 whoopie pie: 242 cal., 9g fat (3g sat. fat), 49mg chol., 241mg sod., 37g carb. (23g sugars, 1g fiber), 3g pro.

OVEN-FRIED PICKLES

Like deep-fried pickles? You'll love this unfried version even more. Dill pickle slices are coated with panko bread crumbs and spices, then baked until crispy. Dip them in ranch dressing for a fair-style treat you won't soon forget.
—Nick Iverson, Denver, CO

Prep: 20 min. + standing • **Bake:** 20 min.
Makes: 8 servings

- 32 dill pickle slices
- ½ cup all-purpose flour
- ½ tsp. salt
- 2 large eggs, lightly beaten
- 2 Tbsp. dill pickle juice
- ½ tsp. cayenne pepper
- ½ tsp. garlic powder
- ½ cup panko bread crumbs
- 1 Tbsp. snipped fresh dill

1. Preheat oven to 500°. Let pickle slices stand on a paper towel until liquid is almost absorbed, about 15 minutes.
2. Meanwhile, in a shallow bowl, combine flour and salt. In a second shallow bowl, whisk eggs, pickle juice, cayenne and garlic powder. Combine panko and dill in a third shallow bowl.
3. Dip pickles into flour mixture to coat both sides; shake off excess. Dip into egg mixture, then into crumb mixture, patting to help the coating adhere.
4. Transfer to a greased wire rack in a rimmed baking sheet. Bake until golden brown and crispy, 20-25 minutes.
4 pickle slices: 65 cal., 2g fat (0 sat. fat), 47mg chol., 421mg sod., 9g carb. (1g sugars, 1g fiber), 3g pro.

CARAMEL NUT-CHOCOLATE POPCORN CONES

These adorable treats were inspired by the chocolate-covered ice cream cones I used to beg for when I was little. These cones are even better, as there is no melting or dripping! They'll go fast at bake sales.
—Julie Beckwith, Crete, IL

....

Prep: 1 hour + cooling • **Makes:** 1 dozen

- 1 **cup semisweet chocolate chips**
- ¼ **cup heavy whipping cream**
- 12 **ice cream sugar cones**

CARAMEL CORN
- 7 **cups air-popped popcorn**
- ½ **cup semisweet chocolate chips**
- ¼ **cup chopped pecans**
- 25 **caramels**
- 2 **Tbsp. heavy whipping cream**
- ⅛ **tsp. salt**

TOPPING
- 5 **caramels**
- 2 **tsp. heavy whipping cream, divided**
- ¼ **cup semisweet chocolate chips**
- ¼ **cup chopped pecans**

1. Tightly cover a large roasting pan that is at least 3 in. deep with 2 layers of heavy-duty foil. Poke 12 holes, about 2 in. apart, in the foil to hold ice cream cones; set pan aside.

2. In a microwave-safe bowl, melt chocolate chips and cream; stir until smooth. Spoon about 2 tsp. into each cone, turning to coat the inside surface. Then dip rims of cones into chocolate, allowing excess chocolate to drip back into the bowl. Place cones in prepared pan. Let stand until chocolate is set.

3. Place popcorn, chocolate chips and pecans in a large bowl. In a microwave, melt the caramels, cream and salt on high for 2 minutes, stirring occasionally until smooth. Pour over the popcorn mixture and toss to coat.

4. Using lightly greased hands, fill cones with popcorn mixture. Shape popcorn into a 2-in.-diameter ball on top of cones, pressing down until popcorn mixture is firmly attached to cones.

5. For topping, place caramels and 1 tsp. cream in a small microwave-safe bowl. Microwave on high at 20-second intervals until the caramels are melted; stir until smooth. Drizzle over cones.

6. Microwave chocolate chips and remaining 1 tsp. cream until smooth. Drizzle over cones. Immediately sprinkle with pecans. Let stand until set. Place in bags and fasten with twist ties or ribbon if desired.

1 cone with about ½ cup popcorn mixture: 335 cal., 17g fat (7g sat. fat), 13mg chol., 125mg sod., 48g carb. (33g sugars, 3g fiber), 4g pro.

WATERMELON SHERBET

My family has been growing watermelon for generations. We often serve this refreshing treat at the town's annual watermelon festival.
—Lisa McAdoo, Rush Springs, OK

....

Prep: 10 min. + chilling
Cook: 5 min. + freezing • **Makes:** ½ gallon

  8   **cups seeded chopped watermelon**
1½ **cups sugar**
  ½ **cup lemon juice**
  2   **envelopes unflavored gelatin**
  ½ **cup cold water**
  2   **cups whole milk**

1. In a large bowl, combine watermelon, sugar and lemon juice. Chill 30 minutes; place half in a blender. Blend until smooth; pour into a large bowl. Repeat with the other half.
2. In a saucepan, cook and stir gelatin and water over low heat until gelatin dissolves. Add to the watermelon mixture; mix well. Stir in the milk until well blended.
3. Freeze in an ice cream freezer according to the manufacturer's directions. Serve immediately or freeze and allow to thaw about 20 minutes before serving.

½ cup: 120 cal., 1g fat (1g sat. fat), 4mg chol., 18mg sod., 26g carb. (25g sugars, 0 fiber), 2g pro.

STRAWBERRY-RHUBARB ICE POPS

These cool, creamy pops are a deliciously different way to use up the bounty from your rhubarb patch. They really hit the spot on a warm summer day.
—Donna Linihan, Moncton, NB

Prep: 10 min. + freezing
Cook: 15 min. + cooling • **Makes:** 8 pops

- 3 **cups chopped fresh or frozen rhubarb (½ in.)**
- ¼ **cup sugar**
- 3 **Tbsp. water**
- 1 **cup strawberry yogurt**
- ½ **cup unsweetened applesauce**
- ¼ **cup finely chopped fresh strawberries**
- 2 **drops red food coloring, optional**
- 8 **freezer pop molds or 8 paper cups (3 oz. each) and wooden pop sticks**

1. Place rhubarb, sugar and water in a large saucepan; bring to a boil. Reduce heat; simmer, uncovered, until thick and blended, 10-15 minutes. Remove ¾ cup mixture to a bowl; let cool completely. (Save the remaining rhubarb for another use.)

2. Add yogurt, applesauce and strawberries to rhubarb mixture; stir until blended. If desired, tint with food coloring.

3. Fill each mold or cup with about ¼ cup rhubarb mixture. Top molds with holders; top cups with foil and insert sticks through foil. Freeze until firm.

Note: If using frozen rhubarb, measure rhubarb while still frozen, then thaw completely. Drain in a colander, but do not press liquid out.

1 pop: 72 cal., 0 fat (0 sat. fat), 2mg chol., 18mg sod., 16g carb. (14g sugars, 1g fiber), 2g pro. **Diabetic exchanges:** 1 starch.

JELLY DOUGHNUTS

Fresh jelly doughnuts are a fair fave, but there's no need to wait for summer to roll around! These sweet treats are lighter than air. I've been fixing them for my family for years. They disappear almost as fast as I make them.
—Kathy Westendorf, Westgate, IA

Prep: 30 min. + rising • **Cook:** 10 min.
Makes: 16 doughnuts

- 2 pkg. (¼ oz. each) active dry yeast
- ½ cup warm water (110° to 115°)
- ½ cup warm 2% milk (110° to 115°)
- ⅓ cup butter, softened
- 1⅓ cups sugar, divided
- 3 large egg yolks, room temperature
- 1 tsp. salt
- 3 to 3¾ cups all-purpose flour
- 3 Tbsp. jelly or jam
- 1 large egg white, lightly beaten
  Oil for deep-fat frying

1. In a small bowl, dissolve yeast in warm water. In a large bowl, combine milk, butter, ⅓ cup sugar, egg yolks, salt, yeast mixture and 3 cups flour; beat until smooth. Stir in enough remaining flour to form a soft dough (do not knead).
2. Place in a greased bowl, turning once to grease top. Cover and let rise in a warm place until doubled, about 45 minutes.
3. Punch down dough. Turn onto a lightly floured surface; knead about 10 times. Divide the dough in half.
4. Roll each portion to ¼-in. thickness; cut with a floured 2½-in. round cutter. Place about ½ tsp. jelly in center of half of the circles; brush edges with egg white. Top with the remaining circles; press edges to seal tightly.
5. Place doughnuts on a greased baking sheet. Cover and let rise until doubled, about 45 minutes.
6. In an electric skillet or deep-fat fryer, heat oil to 375°. Fry doughnuts, a few at a time, 1-2 minutes on each side or until golden brown. Drain on paper towels. Roll warm doughnuts in remaining 1 cup sugar.

1 doughnut: 270 cal., 12g fat (3g sat. fat), 45mg chol., 188mg sod., 38g carb. (19g sugars, 1g fiber), 4g pro.

COLORFUL CANDIED APPLES

The glossy candy coating on these old-fashioned apples is hard, so it's best to lick them like a lollipop or cut them into wedges to serve. Be sure your apples are clean and dry before you dip them.
—Agnes Ward, Stratford, ON

Prep: 10 min. • **Cook:** 30 min. + standing
Makes: 4 servings

- 4   medium apples
- 4   wooden pop sticks or decorative lollipop sticks
- 2   cups sugar
- 1   cup water
- ⅔   cup light corn syrup
- 1   Tbsp. white food coloring
- 1   tsp. orange food coloring

1. Wash and thoroughly dry apples; remove stems. Insert pop sticks into apples. Place on a waxed paper-lined baking sheet.
2. In a large heavy saucepan, combine sugar, water and corn syrup. Cook and stir over medium heat until sugar is dissolved. Stir in food colorings. Bring to a boil. Cook, without stirring, until a candy thermometer reads 290° (soft-crack stage).
3. Remove from heat. Working quickly, dip apples into hot sugar mixture to completely coat. Place on prepared baking sheet; let stand until set.
1 candy apple: 634 cal., 0 fat (0 sat. fat), 0 chol., 39mg sod., 166g carb. (161g sugars, 4g fiber), 0 pro.

BACON-WRAPPED HOT DOGS

Here's a satisfying meal-in-a-bun I take to tailgate parties, cookouts, picnics and more. To transport the stuffed hot dogs, I wrap them in foil, then in paper.
—Peter Halferty, Corpus Christi, TX

Prep: 25 min. • **Grill:** 10 min.
Makes: 8 servings

- 12   bacon strips
- 8   cheese beef hot dogs
- 8   bakery hot dog buns, split and toasted
- ¼   cup chopped red onion
- 2   cups sauerkraut, rinsed and well drained
  Optional: Mayonnaise, ketchup or Dijon mustard

1. In a large skillet, cook bacon over medium heat until partially cooked but not crisp. Remove to paper towels to drain; cool slightly. Wrap 1½ strips of bacon around each hot dog, securing strips with toothpicks as needed (do not wrap tightly, or the bacon may tear during grilling).
2. Grill, covered, over medium heat or broil 4 in. from heat for 6-8 minutes or until bacon is crisp and hot dogs are heated through, turning frequently. Discard toothpicks. Serve hot dogs in buns with onion and sauerkraut; top with condiments of your choice.
1 wrapped hot dog: 360 cal., 22g fat (9g sat. fat), 47mg chol., 1119mg sod., 25g carb. (4g sugars, 2g fiber), 16g pro.

SALTED PEANUT ROLLS

A gift of homemade candy is always a hit. I dip these in chocolate, but they're yummy plain, too.
—Elizabeth Hokanson, Arborg, MB

Prep: 1 hour + freezing
Makes: about 5 dozen

- 1 jar (7 oz.) marshmallow creme
- 2 to 2¼ cups confectioners' sugar, divided
- 1 pkg. (14 oz.) caramels
- 2 Tbsp. water
- 4 cups salted peanuts, chopped
- 2 cups semisweet chocolate chips
- 2 tsp. shortening

1. Line two 15x10x1-in. pans with waxed paper. Beat marshmallow creme and 1 cup confectioners' sugar until blended. Knead in enough of the remaining confectioners' sugar until mixture is smooth and easy to handle.
2. Divide into 4 portions. Roll each into ½-in.-thick logs. Cut each log crosswise into 1½-in. pieces; place on 1 prepared pan. Freeze until firm, about 15 minutes.
3. Heat caramels and water over low heat until melted, stirring occasionally. Working with one-fourth of the candy pieces at a time, dip in melted caramel; roll in peanuts. Place on the remaining prepared pan. Freeze until set.
4. In a double boiler or metal bowl over barely simmering water, melt chocolate chips and shortening; stir until smooth. Dip bottom of candies into chocolate; let the excess drip off. Return to prepared pan. Refrigerate until set. Store between layers of waxed paper in an airtight container at room temperature.
1 piece: 154 cal., 9g fat (3g sat. fat), 0 chol., 48mg sod., 18g carb. (15g sugars, 2g fiber), 3g pro.

CHOCOLATE-COVERED BACON

It's a hit at state fairs everywhere—now you can make this salty-sweet concoction at home. Some say bacon can't get any better, but we think chocolate makes everything better!
—*Taste of Home* Test Kitchen

Prep: 20 min. • **Bake:** 20 min.
Makes: 1 dozen

- 12 thick-sliced bacon strips (about 1 lb.)
- 6 oz. white candy coating, coarsely chopped
  Optional: Chopped dried apple chips, apricots and crystallized ginger, finely chopped pecans and pistachios, toasted coconut, kosher salt, brown sugar, cayenne pepper and coarsely ground black pepper
- 1 cup semisweet chocolate chips
- 1 Tbsp. shortening

1. Preheat oven to 400°. Thread bacon strips, weaving them back and forth, onto twelve 12-in. soaked wooden skewers. Place skewers on a rack in a large baking pan. Bake until crisp, 20-25 minutes. Drain on paper towels; cool completely.
2. In a microwave, melt candy coating; stir until smooth. Brush onto both sides of 6 bacon strips; sprinkle with toppings as desired. Place on a waxed paper-lined baking sheet.
3. In a microwave, melt chocolate chips and shortening; stir until smooth. Brush onto both sides of remaining 6 bacon strips; decorate as desired.
4. Refrigerate until set. Store in refrigerator.
1 bacon strip: 212 cal., 14g fat (8g sat. fat), 10mg chol., 252mg sod., 19g carb. (17g sugars, 1g fiber), 5g pro.

OLD-FASHIONED WHOOPIE PIES

Who can resist soft chocolate sandwich cookies filled with a layer of fluffy white frosting? Mom has made these for years. They're a treat that never lasted very long with me and my brothers around.
—Maria Costello, Monroe, NC

Prep: 35 min. + chilling
Bake: 10 min./batch + cooling
Makes: 2 dozen

- ½ **cup baking cocoa**
- ½ **cup hot water**
- ½ **cup shortening**
- 1½ **cups sugar**
- 2 **large eggs, room temperature**
- 1 **tsp. vanilla extract**
- 2⅔ **cups all-purpose flour**
- 1 **tsp. baking powder**
- 1 **tsp. baking soda**
- ¼ **tsp. salt**
- ½ **cup buttermilk**

FILLING
- 3 **Tbsp. all-purpose flour**
  Dash salt
- 1 **cup 2% milk**
- ¾ **cup shortening**
- 1½ **cups confectioners' sugar**
- 2 **tsp. vanilla extract**

1. Preheat oven to 350°. In a small bowl, combine cocoa and water. Cool for 5 minutes. In a large bowl, cream shortening and sugar until light and fluffy, 5-7 minutes. Beat in the eggs, vanilla and cocoa mixture. Combine dry ingredients; gradually add to creamed mixture alternately with buttermilk, beating well after each addition
2. To form each cookie, drop 2 Tbsp. 2 in. apart onto greased baking sheets. Bake until firm to the touch, 10-12 minutes. Remove to wire racks to cool.

3. For filling, in a small saucepan, combine flour and salt. Gradually whisk in milk until smooth; cook and stir over medium-high heat until thickened, 5-7 minutes. Remove from heat. Cover and refrigerate until completely cool.
4. In a small bowl, cream the shortening, confectioners' sugar and vanilla until light and fluffy. Add the milk mixture; beat until fluffy, about 7 minutes. Spread filling on half of the cookies; top with the remaining cookies. Store in the refrigerator.

Note: To substitute for each cup of buttermilk, use 1 Tbsp. white vinegar or lemon juice plus enough milk to measure 1 cup. Stir, then let stand 5 min. Or, use 1 cup plain yogurt or 1¾ tsp. cream of tartar plus 1 cup milk.
1 whoopie pie: 244 cal., 11g fat (3g sat. fat), 19mg chol., 116mg sod., 33g carb. (20g sugars, 1g fiber), 3g pro.

EASY APPLE DUMPLINGS

Mother often prepared this special treat for us, ready to take out of the oven just as we came home from school. I remember so vividly, upon opening the door to the house, the magnificent aroma!
—Marjorie Thompson, West Sacramento, CA

Prep: 30 min. • **Bake:** 45 min.
Makes: 6 servings

1½ **cups sugar, divided**
1 **cup water**
4 **Tbsp. butter, divided**
½ **tsp. ground cinnamon, divided**
   Dough for double-crust pie
6 **small to medium apples, peeled and cored**

1. Preheat oven to 375°. For syrup, place 1 cup sugar, water, 3 Tbsp. butter and ¼ tsp. cinnamon in a saucepan; bring to a boil. Boil 3 minutes; remove from heat.
2. Mix remaining ½ cup sugar and ¼ tsp. cinnamon. On a lightly floured surface, roll dough to a 21x14-in. rectangle; cut into 6 squares. Place an apple on each square. Fill the center of each with 4 tsp. sugar mixture and ½ tsp. butter. Moisten edges of crust with water; bring up corners over the apples, pinching edges to seal. Place in an ungreased 13x9-in. baking dish.
3. Pour syrup around dumplings. Bake until golden brown and apples are tender, about 45 minutes. Serve warm.
Dough for double-crust pie: Combine 2½ cups all-purpose flour and ½ tsp. salt; cut in 1 cup cold butter until crumbly. Gradually add ⅓ to ⅔ cup ice water, tossing with a fork until dough holds together when pressed. Form into a disk. Wrap and refrigerate 1 hour.
1 dumpling: 773 cal., 39g fat (24g sat. fat), 101mg chol., 475mg sod., 104g carb. (62g sugars, 4g fiber), 6g pro.

BLUE-RIBBON TIP

Top warm apple dumplings with the dairy treat of your choice. For real farm-show authenticity, douse them with fresh, heavy cream.

HOMEMADE CHURROS

These fried cinnamon-sugar goodies are best served fresh and hot. Try them with a cup of coffee or hot chocolate. Don't be surprised if people start dunking, and then go back for more!
—*Taste of Home* Test Kitchen

....

Prep: 15 min. + cooling • **Cook:** 20 min.
Makes: about 1 dozen

- ½ cup water
- ½ cup 2% milk
- 1 Tbsp. canola oil
- ¼ tsp. salt
- 1 cup all-purpose flour
- 1 large egg, room temperature
- ¼ tsp. grated lemon zest
  Additional oil for frying
- ½ cup sugar
- ¼ tsp. ground cinnamon

1. In a large saucepan, bring the water, milk, oil and salt to a boil. Add flour all at once and stir until a smooth ball forms. Transfer to a large bowl; let stand for 5 minutes.
2. Beat on medium-high speed for 1 minute or until the dough softens. Add egg and lemon zest; beat for 1-2 minutes. Set aside to cool.
3. In a deep cast-iron or heavy skillet, heat 1 in. oil to 375°. Insert a large star tip in a pastry bag; fill with dough. On a baking sheet, pipe dough into 4-in. strips.
4. Transfer strips to skillet; fry until golden brown on both sides. Drain on paper towels. Combine the sugar and cinnamon; sprinkle over churros. Serve warm.
1 churro: 122 cal., 5g fat (1g sat. fat), 17mg chol., 60mg sod., 17g carb. (9g sugars, 0 fiber), 2g pro.

FRENCH TOAST WITH CRUSHED APPLE SAUCE

Heading out to a morning parade or festival? These French toast sticks make great on-the-go breakfasts—complete with an apple dipping sauce. Leftovers freeze well, too.
—Cindy Kerschner, Schnecksville, PA

....

Prep: 10 min. • **Cook:** 25 min.
Makes: 8 servings (1 cup sauce)

- 1 cup unsweetened apple juice
- 1 medium apple, peeled and chopped
- ½ cup packed brown sugar
- 2 tsp. butter

FRENCH TOAST

- 3 large eggs, room temperature
- ½ cup 2% milk
- 1 tsp. vanilla extract
- 2 Tbsp. butter, divided
- ½ loaf (1 lb.) country bread, cut into 1-in. slices
  Ground cinnamon

1. In a small saucepan, combine the juice, apple, brown sugar and butter; bring to a boil. Reduce heat; simmer for 12-15 minutes or until the apple is tender, stirring occasionally. Mash apple to the desired consistency; keep warm.
2. Meanwhile, in a shallow bowl, whisk the eggs, milk and vanilla. In a large skillet, over medium heat, melt 1 Tbsp. butter. Dip both sides of the bread in the egg mixture, allowing each side to soak for 30 seconds.
3. Place in skillet; lightly sprinkle with cinnamon. Toast each side until golden brown. Repeat with the remaining butter and bread.
4. Cut French toast into 1-in. strips; serve with sauce.
1 serving: 221 cal., 7g fat (3g sat. fat), 81mg chol., 240mg sod., 35g carb. (20g sugars, 1g fiber), 6g pro.

BAKED ELEPHANT EARS

My mother-in-law handed down this recipe from her mother. They're a special treat—even better, I think, than those you get at a carnival or festival.
—Delores Baeten, Downers Grove, IL

....

Prep: 35 min. + chilling • **Bake:** 10 min.
Makes: 2 dozen

- 1 **pkg. (¼ oz.) active dry yeast**
- ¼ **cup warm water (110° to 115°)**
- 2 **cups all-purpose flour**
- 4½ **tsp. sugar**
- ½ **tsp. salt**
- ⅓ **cup cold butter, cubed**
- ⅓ **cup fat-free milk**
- 1 **large egg yolk**

FILLING
- 2 **Tbsp. butter, softened**
- ½ **cup sugar**
- 2 **tsp. ground cinnamon**

CINNAMON SUGAR
- ½ **cup sugar**
- ¾ **tsp. ground cinnamon**

1. In a small bowl, dissolve yeast in warm water. In a large bowl, mix flour, sugar and salt; cut in butter until crumbly. Stir milk and egg yolk into the yeast mixture; add to the flour mixture, stirring to form a stiff dough (dough will be sticky). Cover and refrigerate for 2 hours.

2. Preheat oven to 375°. Turn dough onto a lightly floured surface; roll into an 18x10-in. rectangle. Spread with softened butter to within ¼ in. of edges. Mix sugar and cinnamon; sprinkle over butter. Roll up dough jelly-roll style, starting with a long side; pinch seam to seal. Cut crosswise into 24 slices. Cover slices with a clean towel.

3. In a small bowl, mix ingredients for cinnamon sugar. Place a 6-in.-square piece of waxed paper on a work surface; sprinkle with ½ tsp. cinnamon sugar. Top with 1 slice of dough; sprinkle dough with an additional ½ tsp. cinnamon sugar. Roll dough to a 4-in. circle. Using waxed paper, flip dough onto a baking sheet coated with cooking spray. Repeat with the remaining ingredients, placing slices 2 in. apart. Bake 7-9 minutes or until golden brown. Cool on wire racks.

1 elephant ear: 109 cal., 4g fat (2g sat. fat), 18mg chol., 76mg sod., 18g carb. (9g sugars, 0 fiber), 1g pro. **Diabetic exchanges:** 1 starch, ½ fat.

READER RAVE...

"These take time, but they are so worth it! We like to get elephant ears at our farmers market and now I finally have a way to make them at home!"
—HKAROW9713, TASTEOFHOME.COM

DEEP-FRIED CANDY BARS ON A STICK

Why wait in line at the state fair for deep-fried candy bars when you can satisfy your curious taste buds in your very own home? Be sure to make a lot—these novelties go fast!
—*Taste of Home* Test Kitchen

Prep: 20 min. • **Cook:** 5 min./batch
Makes: 2 dozen

- 1½ cups all-purpose flour
- 4½ tsp. baking powder
- 1 Tbsp. sugar
- 1 Tbsp. brown sugar
- ⅛ tsp. salt
- ⅛ tsp. ground cinnamon
- 1 large egg
- ½ cup water
- ½ cup 2% milk
- ¼ tsp. vanilla extract
  Oil for deep-fat frying
- 24 fun-size Snickers and/or Milky Way candy bars, frozen
  Wooden skewers
  Confectioners' sugar, optional

1. Whisk together first 6 ingredients. In another bowl, whisk together egg, water, milk and vanilla; add to dry ingredients; stir just until moistened.
2. In a deep cast-iron or electric skillet, heat oil to 375°. Dip candy bars, a few at a time. into batter; fry until golden brown, about 30 seconds per side. Drain on paper towels.
3. Insert skewers into bars. If desired, dust with confectioners' sugar.

1 fried candy bar: 136 cal., 7g fat (2g sat. fat), 11mg chol., 130mg sod., 16g carb. (9g sugars, 1g fiber), 2g pro.

GIANT CINNAMON ROLLS

As a newlywed, I took it upon myself to make cinnamon rolls because I thought that was the hallmark of a good baker. The rolls were like hockey pucks and flavorless. Our dear black Lab Annie wouldn't even eat one! So I practiced for months—finally, I entered a contest at the Iowa State Fair; and I won!
—Cristen Clark, Runnells, IA

Prep: 45 min. + rising
Bake: 25 min. + cooling • **Makes:** 1 dozen

- 2 pkg. (¼ oz. each) quick-rise yeast
- ½ cup warm water (110° to 115°)
- 2 tsp. honey
- 1½ cups warm 2% milk (110° to 115°)
- ½ cup sugar
- ½ cup butter, softened
- ½ cup mashed potatoes
- 3 large eggs, room temperature, lightly beaten
- 2 tsp. salt
- 7½ to 8 cups all-purpose flour

FILLING
- 1 cup packed brown sugar
- 2 Tbsp. ground cinnamon
- 1½ tsp. all-purpose flour
  Dash salt
- ½ cup butter, softened

VANILLA ICING
- 3 cups confectioners' sugar
- ¼ cup 2% milk
- 1 tsp. vanilla bean paste or vanilla extract
  Dash salt

1. In a small bowl, dissolve yeast in warm water and honey. In a large bowl, combine milk, sugar, butter, potatoes, eggs, salt, yeast mixture and 4 cups flour; beat on medium speed until smooth. Stir in enough of the remaining flour to form a soft dough (dough will be sticky).

2. Turn dough onto a floured surface; knead until smooth and elastic, 6-8 minutes. Place in a greased large bowl, turning once to grease the top.

Cover and let rise in a warm place until doubled, about 1 hour.

3. For filling, combine brown sugar, cinnamon, flour and salt. Punch down dough. Turn onto a lightly floured surface; roll into a 24x12-in. rectangle. Spread butter to within ½ in. of edges; sprinkle with brown sugar mixture.

4. Roll up jelly-roll style, starting with a long side; pinch seam to seal. Cut into 12 slices. Place in 2 greased 13x9-in. baking pans (6 slices per pan), cut side down. Cover with kitchen towels; let rise in a warm place until doubled, about 30 minutes.

5. Preheat oven to 350°. Bake until lightly browned, 25-30 minutes, covering loosely with foil during the last 10 minutes of baking. Cool in pan 30 minutes. In a small bowl, mix icing ingredients; drizzle over rolls.

1 roll: 695 cal., 18g fat (11g sat. fat), 90mg chol., 588mg sod., 122g carb. (59g sugars, 3g fiber), 11g pro.

APPLE FRITTERS

This is an old Southern recipe. When we got home from a trip through the South years ago, I found the recipe among the brochures I brought back. I've been making these fritters ever since.
—John Robbins, Springdale, PA

Takes: 20 min. • **Makes:** 2-3 servings

- 1 cup cake flour
- 1 Tbsp. sugar
- ¾ tsp. baking powder
- ¼ tsp. salt
- 1 large egg, room temperature
- ⅓ cup whole milk
- 4 tsp. butter, melted
- 1 Tbsp. orange juice
- 2 tsp. grated orange zest
- ¼ tsp. vanilla extract
- ¾ cup chopped peeled tart apple
  Oil for frying
  Confectioners' sugar

1. In a large bowl, combine the flour, sugar, baking powder and salt. In another bowl, combine the egg, milk, butter, orange juice, zest and vanilla. Add to the dry ingredients just until moistened. Fold in apples.

2. In an electric skillet or deep-fat fryer, heat ¼ in. of oil to 375°. Drop batter by rounded tablespoons into oil. Fry until golden brown on both sides. Drain on paper towels. Dust with confectioners' sugar. Serve warm.

1 serving: 533 cal., 24g fat (3g sat. fat), 97mg chol., 530mg sod., 69g carb. (13g sugars, 2g fiber), 10g pro.

1 cup all-purpose flour
4 large eggs, room temperature
2 Tbsp. 2% milk
1 large egg yolk, lightly beaten
2 cups heavy whipping cream
¼ cup confectioners' sugar
½ tsp. vanilla extract
    Additional confectioners' sugar

1. Preheat oven to 400°. In a large saucepan, bring the water, butter and salt to a boil over medium heat. Add flour all at once; stir until a smooth ball forms. Remove from heat; let stand for 5 minutes.
2. Add eggs, 1 at a time, beating well after each addition. Continue beating until mixture is smooth and shiny.
3. Drop batter by ¼ cupfuls 3 in. apart onto greased baking sheets. Combine the milk and egg yolk; brush over puffs. Bake until golden brown, 30-35 minutes. Remove to wire racks. Immediately cut a slit in each for steam to escape; let cool.
4. In a large bowl, beat cream until it begins to thicken. Add sugar and vanilla; beat until almost stiff. Split cream puffs; discard soft dough from inside. Fill the cream puffs just before serving. Dust with confectioners' sugar. Refrigerate any leftovers.
1 cream puff: 340 cal., 29g fat (17g sat. fat), 196mg chol., 197mg sod., 14g carb. (5g sugars, 0 fiber), 5g pro.

POUTINE

The ultimate in French-Canadian comfort food, poutine commonly features french fries topped with cheese curds and gravy. This side dish is quick to fix with frozen potatoes and packaged gravy, but it has all the traditional comfort you'd expect.
—Shelisa Terry, Henderson, NV

Takes: 30 min. • **Makes:** 4 servings

4 cups frozen french-fried potatoes
1 envelope brown gravy mix
¼ tsp. pepper
½ cup white cheddar cheese curds
    or cubed white cheddar cheese

1. Prepare potatoes according to the package directions.

2. Meanwhile, prepare the gravy mix according to package directions. Stir in pepper. Place fries on a serving plate; top with cheese curds and gravy.
1 serving: 244 cal., 13g fat (4g sat. fat), 17mg chol., 465mg sod., 26g carb. (2g sugars, 2g fiber), 7g pro.

STATE FAIR CREAM PUFFS

The Wisconsin Bakers Association has been serving these treats at the Wisconsin State Fair since 1924. In recent years, more than 300,000 are sold annually!
—Ruth Jungbluth, Dodgeville, WI

Prep: 25 min. • **Bake:** 30 min. + cooling
Makes: 10 servings

1 cup water
½ cup butter
¼ tsp. salt

S'MORES ON A STICK

My kids love to take these treats everywhere. Lucky for me, they're easy to make. Aside from sprinkles, try mini candies for toppings.
—Ronda Weirich, Plains, KS

....

Prep: 15 min. + standing • **Makes:** 2 dozen

> 1 **can (14 oz.) sweetened condensed milk, divided**
> 1 **cup miniature marshmallows**
> 1½ **cups miniature semisweet chocolate chips, divided**
> 24 **whole graham crackers, broken in half**
>   **Assorted sprinkles**
> 24 **Wooden pop sticks**

1. In a small microwave-safe bowl, microwave ⅔ cup condensed milk on high for 1½ minutes. Add marshmallows and 1 cup chips; stir until smooth. Drop by tablespoonfuls onto 24 graham cracker halves; spread evenly. Top with the remaining graham cracker halves; press down gently.
2. Microwave remaining condensed milk for 1½ minutes. Add remaining chips; stir until smooth. Drizzle over cookies; decorate with sprinkles. Let stand for 2 hours before inserting a pop stick into the center of each.
1 s'more: 177 cal., 6g fat (3g sat. fat), 6mg chol., 118mg sod., 30g carb. (20g sugars, 1g fiber), 3g pro.

SPICY CORN KABOBS

Corn on the cob becomes a tangy delight when grilled, dotted with sour cream and cheese, and zinged with a splash of lime.
—Leah Lenz, Los Angeles, CA

....

Prep: 10 min. • **Grill:** 25 min.
Makes: 6 servings

> 6 **medium ears sweet corn, husked and halved**
> ¼ **cup sour cream**
> ¼ **cup mayonnaise**
> ½ **cup grated Cotija cheese or Parmesan cheese**
> 2 **tsp. chili powder**
> ¼ **tsp. cayenne pepper, optional**
> 6 **lime wedges**

1. Insert a metal or soaked wooden skewer into the cut end of each piece of corn. Grill, covered, over medium heat until tender, 25-30 minutes, turning often.
2. In a small bowl, combine sour cream and mayonnaise; spread over the corn. Sprinkle with cheese, chili powder and, if desired, cayenne. Serve with lime wedges.
2 kabobs: 205 cal., 13g fat (4g sat. fat), 20mg chol., 222mg sod., 19g carb. (3g sugars, 3g fiber), 6g pro.

FOOD AT THE FAIR

Come early and come hungry. That's the unwritten motto of America's state and county fairs, where we indulge in the sweetest, saltiest and yummiest treats. Here's a look at the origins of three all-time favorite fair foods.

MARIJA ANDRIC · EDITOR, *COUNTRY* MAGAZINE

CREAM PUFF

▲ CREAM PUFFS

In France, they are called *profiterole* or *choux a la creme*. In Wisconsin, cream puffs are the darling of the state fair. During the 11-day event, fairgoers eat about 350,000 of them. These pastries debuted at the 1924 fair to promote the state's dairy industry. They're so popular today that Wisconsinites can order them in advance, calling the cream puff hotline and picking them up at a drive-thru. (To make your own state fair cream puffs at home, see p. 38.)

CORN DOG

▲ CORN DOGS

Several people claim to have been the first to make corn dogs, but Stanley Jenkins of Buffalo, New York, actually filed a patent in 1929 for an "apparatus in which a new and novel food product may be deep fried." Jenkins went on to say that many foods, including wieners, could be "impaled on sticks and dipped in batter." (See how to make them—no special apparatus needed—on p. 17.)

▶ FUNNEL CAKES

This crispy, delicate treat is the result of pouring batter through a funnel into hot oil and deep-frying. Though funnel cake recipes appeared in medieval Europe, the Pennsylvania Dutch get credit for taking them mainstream during the Kutztown Folk Festival in 1951. Emma Miller, who had made funnel cakes as a winter treat for her family, provided that recipe, and the cakes sold for 25 cents apiece. (See our recipe on p. 17.)

FUNNEL CAKE

BEST OF SHOW

When I was a young girl, the merry tunes of lively carnival rides and the aroma of cotton candy and caramel corn always lured me to the Calhoun County Fair in Marshall, Michigan, the state's oldest fair.

At that time, my future husband, Lloyd, was busy showing his dairy cows and his woodworking and gardening skills over at the Barry County Fair in Hastings, Michigan.

Once we married and our kids, Scott and Lisa, came along, we went back to the Marshall fair. Now it was the kids showing their rabbits, woodwork and baked goods. Scott won best of show for his woodwork, and Lisa won best of class for her baked goods.

A few decades later found us at the Kalamazoo County Youth Fair, where three of our grandchildren—Morgan, Jacob and Maddy—took their turn. They vied for ribbons in woodworking and baking, but their first love was competing in the horse arena. They spent the mornings feeding, grooming, mucking out stalls, cleaning tack and checking to make sure their show clothes were accounted for and clean. The events started early to give the kids—and horses—a jump on the summer heat.

The kids competed in English and Western, including speed events such as barrel racing. Morgan also competed in dressage and won Reserve Grand Champion at the State 4-H Show at Michigan State University. Part of the fun was that Morgan's horse was a granddaughter of Seattle Slew, the 1977 Triple Crown champ!

All the hard work, joy, sights and sounds have given us happy memories over the years. The original intent of county fairs still remains: Bringing people of all ages and backgrounds together as a community to celebrate the good in our country.

SUSAN TERRY · BATTLE CREEK, MICHIGAN

Morgan and her horse, Wolfe (above, with Maddy, Jacob, Montana and Madison), won Reserve Grand Champion. Jacob cuts pieces for his first-year woodworking project, for which he later won a blue ribbon.

P. 50

P. 60

P. 55

P. 48

FRIED FAVORITES

SEASONED CRAB CAKES

These scrumptious crab cakes won first place at the National Hard Crab Derby in Crisfield, Maryland. I entered them on a whim after trying out many crab cake recipes for my family.
—Betsy Hedeman, Timonium, MD

Prep: 20 min. + chilling • **Cook:** 10 min.
Makes: 8 crab cakes

- 3 cans (6 oz. each) crabmeat, drained, flaked and cartilage removed
- 1 cup cubed bread
- 2 large eggs
- 3 Tbsp. mayonnaise
- 3 Tbsp. half-and-half cream
- 1 Tbsp. lemon juice
- 1 Tbsp. butter, melted
- 1½ tsp. seafood seasoning
- 1 tsp. Worcestershire sauce
- 1 tsp. salt
- ½ cup dry bread crumbs
- ½ cup canola oil

1. In a large bowl, combine crabmeat and bread cubes. In another bowl, whisk the eggs, mayonnaise, cream, lemon juice, butter, seafood seasoning, Worcestershire sauce and salt. Add to the crab mixture and mix gently (mixture will be moist).
2. Place bread crumbs in a shallow dish. Drop crab mixture by ⅓ cupfuls into the crumbs; shape each into a ¾-in.-thick patty. Carefully turn to coat. Cover and refrigerate for at least 2 hours.
3. In a large skillet, cook crab cakes in oil for 4-5 minutes on each side or until golden brown and crispy

1 crab cake: 197 cal., 15g fat (3g sat. fat), 81mg chol., 640mg sod., 8g carb. (1g sugars, 0 fiber), 7g pro.

CORNFLAKE FRIED ICE CREAM

This crunchy, creamy frozen treat is even better with hot fudge or caramel drizzled on top!
—Ronda Weirich, Plains, KS

Prep: 20 min. + freezing • **Cook:** 5 min.
Makes: 2 servings

- 1 cup vanilla ice cream
- ¼ cup heavy whipping cream, divided
- ¼ tsp. vanilla extract, divided
- ¾ cup crushed frosted cornflakes
- ¼ tsp. ground cinnamon
  Oil for deep-fat frying
  Whipped cream

1. Using a ½-cup ice cream scoop, form 2 balls of ice cream. Cover and freeze for 1 hour or until firm.
2. In a small bowl, whisk 2 Tbsp. cream and ⅛ tsp. vanilla. In a shallow bowl, combine cornflakes and cinnamon. Dip ice cream balls into cream mixture; then roll in cornflake mixture. Set aside remaining cornflake mixture. Cover and freeze ice cream for 1 hour or until firm.
3. In a small bowl, whisk together the remaining 2 Tbsp. cream and ⅛ tsp. vanilla. Dip ice cream balls into the cream mixture; roll in remaining cereal mixture. Cover and freeze for 1 hour or until firm.
4. In an electric skillet or deep-fat fryer, heat oil to 375°. Fry each ice cream ball for 12-15 seconds or until golden. Drain on paper towels. Serve immediately with whipped cream.

1 ice cream ball: 323 cal., 22g fat (12g sat. fat), 70mg chol., 138mg sod., 31g carb. (18g sugars, 1g fiber), 3g pro.

DEEP-FRIED MAC & CHEESE SHELLS

I created this recipe for my husband, who loves mac and cheese. He describes this recipe as unbelievably delicious because of the crispy deep-fried coating on the outside and the creamy richness on the inside.
—Shirley Rickis, The Villages, FL

Prep: 45 min. • **Cook:** 15 min.
Makes: 20 appetizers
(2½ cups dipping sauce)

- 2 **cups uncooked small pasta shells**
- 20 **uncooked jumbo pasta shells**
- 2 **Tbsp. butter**
- 1 **pkg. (16 oz.) Velveeta, cubed**
- 2 **cups shredded cheddar cheese**
- 1 **cup heavy whipping cream**
- ¾ **cup grated Parmesan cheese, divided**
- 1¼ **cups 2% milk, divided**
- 2 **large eggs**
- 2 **cups panko bread crumbs**
- ½ **cup all-purpose flour**
  Oil for deep-fat frying

1. Cook pastas separately according to their package directions for al dente; drain. Meanwhile, in a large saucepan, melt the butter over low heat. Add Velveeta, cheddar cheese, cream and ¼ cup grated Parmesan cheese. Cook and stir over low heat until blended. Remove from heat.
2. In another large saucepan, combine small pasta shells and half the cheese mixture; set aside. For dipping sauce, stir 1 cup milk into remaining cheese mixture; keep warm.
3. In a shallow bowl, whisk eggs with the remaining ¼ cup milk. In another shallow bowl, mix bread crumbs with the remaining ½ cup Parmesan cheese. Place flour in a third shallow bowl. Fill each large shell with scant ¼ cup pasta mixture. Dip in flour to coat all sides; shake off excess. Dip in egg mixture, then in bread crumb mixture, patting to help coating adhere.
4. In an electric skillet or a deep fryer, heat oil to 375°. Fry shells, a few at a time, for 1-2 minutes on each side or until dark golden brown. Drain on paper towels. Serve with dipping sauce.

1 appetizer with 2 Tbsp. dipping sauce: 340 cal., 23g fat (10g sat. fat), 72mg chol., 451mg sod., 21g carb. (3g sugars, 1g fiber), 12g pro.

READER RAVE...

"The shells come out with a good crisp, and the inner mac is really smooth. I'm going to add garlic and cayenne next time."
—ARAGORN1_1970, TASTEOFHOME.COM

SPICY FRIED OKRA

This fried veggie is a southern delicacy that's sure to add excitement to any summer meal.
—Rashanda Cobbins, Milwaukee, WI

Takes: 30 min. • **Makes:** 4 servings

3 cups sliced fresh or
    frozen okra, thawed
6 Tbsp. buttermilk
2 tsp. Louisiana-style hot sauce
¼ cup all-purpose flour
¼ cup cornmeal
½ tsp. seasoned salt
¼ tsp. cayenne pepper
    Oil for deep-fat frying
    Optional: Additional salt
    and pepper

1. Pat okra dry with paper towels. Place buttermilk and hot sauce in a shallow bowl. In another shallow bowl, combine the flour, cornmeal, salt and pepper. Dip okra in buttermilk mixture, then roll in cornmeal mixture.

2. In a cast-iron or other heavy skillet, heat 1 in. oil to 375°. Fry okra, a few pieces at a time, until golden brown, 1½-2½ minutes on each side. Drain on paper towels. If desired, season with additional salt and pepper.

¾ cup: 237 cal., 16g fat (1g sat. fat), 1mg chol., 326mg sod., 20g carb. (4g sugars, 3g fiber), 5g pro.

HOMEMADE FRY BREAD

Crispy, doughy and totally delicious, this fry bread is fantastic with nearly any sweet or savory topping you can think of. We love it with a little butter, a drizzle of honey and a squeeze of lemon.
—Thelma Tyler, Dragoon, AZ

Prep: 20 min. + standing
Cook: 15 min. • **Makes:** 12 servings

- 2 **cups unbleached flour**
- ½ **cup nonfat dry milk powder**
- 3 **tsp. baking powder**
- ½ **tsp. salt**
- 4½ **tsp. shortening**
- ⅔ **to ¾ cup water**
  Oil for deep-fat frying
  Optional: Butter, honey and fresh lemon juice

1. Combine flour, dry milk powder, baking powder and salt; cut in the shortening until crumbly. Add water gradually, mixing to form a firm ball. Divide dough into 12 portions; shape each portion into a ball. Let stand, covered, for 10 minutes.

2. Roll each ball into a 6-in. circle. With a sharp knife, cut a ½-in.-diameter hole in the center of each.

3. In a large cast-iron skillet, heat oil over medium-high heat. Fry dough circles, 1 at a time, until puffed and golden, about 1 minute on each side. Drain on paper towels. Serve warm, with butter, honey and fresh lemon juice if desired.

1 piece: 124 cal., 5g fat (1g sat. fat), 1mg chol., 234mg sod., 17g carb. (2g sugars, 1g fiber), 3g pro.

CHEESEBURGER ONION RINGS

This new take on burgers will have your family begging for seconds. Serve these juicy, savory fried treats with spicy ketchup or your favorite dipping sauce.

—*Taste of Home* Test Kitchen

Takes: 30 min. • **Makes:** 8 servings

- 1 **lb. lean ground beef (90% lean)**
- ⅓ **cup ketchup**
- 2 **Tbsp. prepared mustard**
- ½ **tsp. salt**
- 1 **large onion**
- 4 **oz. cheddar cheese, cut into squares**
- ¾ **cup all-purpose flour**
- 2 **tsp. garlic powder**
- 2 **large eggs, lightly beaten**
- 1½ **cups panko bread crumbs**
  Oil for deep-fat frying
  Spicy ketchup, optional

1. In a small bowl, combine beef, ketchup, mustard and salt, mixing lightly but thoroughly. Cut onion into ½-in. slices; separate into rings. Fill 8 slices with half the beef mixture (save remaining onion slices for another use). Top each with a piece of cheese and the remaining beef mixture.

2. In a shallow bowl, mix flour and garlic powder. Place eggs and bread crumbs in separate shallow bowls. Dip filled onion rings in flour to coat both sides; shake off excess. Dip in the egg, then in the bread crumbs, patting to help the coating adhere.

3. In an electric skillet or deep fryer, heat oil to 350°. Fry onion rings, a few at a time, until golden brown and a thermometer inserted into beef reads 160°, 2-3 minutes on each side. Drain on paper towels. If desired, serve with spicy ketchup.

1 onion ring: 367 cal., 24g fat (6g sat. fat), 96mg chol., 488mg sod., 19g carb. (4g sugars, 1g fiber), 18g pro.

GREEN CHILE CORN FRITTERS

This is a crispy side dish, appetizer or snack to add to a Mexican meal. The fritters also go well with chili or soup. I usually have all the ingredients on hand.
—Johnna Johnson, Scottsdale, AZ

Prep: 20 min. • **Cook:** 5 min./batch
Makes: 2 dozen

- 1 cup yellow cornmeal
- ½ cup all-purpose flour
- 1½ tsp. baking powder
- ¾ tsp. salt
- ½ tsp. garlic powder
- ½ tsp. onion powder
- ½ tsp. paprika
- ½ tsp. pepper
- 1 large egg, room temperature
- ⅔ cup whole milk
- 1 can (8¾ oz.) whole kernel corn, drained
- 1 can (4 oz.) chopped green chiles, drained
  Oil for deep-fat frying
  Optional: Sriracha mayonnaise or condiment of your choice

1. In a large bowl, whisk the first 8 ingredients. In another bowl, whisk egg and milk until blended. Add to the dry ingredients, stirring just until moistened. Let stand for 5 minutes. Fold in corn and green chiles.
2. In a deep cast-iron or electric skillet, heat the oil to 375°. Drop the batter by tablespoonfuls, a few at a time, into hot oil. Fry until golden brown, 1-1½ minutes on each side. Drain on paper towels. Serve with desired condiments.
1 fritter: 74 cal., 4g fat (0 sat. fat), 8mg chol., 159mg sod., 9g carb. (1g sugars, 1g fiber), 1g pro.

SUGARED DOUGHNUT HOLES

These tasty, tender doughnut bites are easy to make. Serve them warm in a small paper bag, as is done at the fair, or tucked in a small gift box wrapped with ribbon as a party favor. No matter how they arrive, they make any day special.
—Judy Jungwirth, Athol, SD

Takes: 20 min. • **Makes:** about 3 dozen

- 1½ cups all-purpose flour
- ⅓ cup sugar
- 2 tsp. baking powder
- ½ tsp. salt
- ½ tsp. ground nutmeg
- 1 large egg, room temperature
- ½ cup 2% milk
- 2 Tbsp. butter, melted
  Oil for deep-fat frying
  Confectioners' sugar

1. In a large bowl, combine the flour, sugar, baking powder, salt and nutmeg. In a small bowl, combine the egg, milk and butter. Add to dry ingredients and mix well.
2. In an electric skillet or deep-fat fryer, heat oil to 375°. Drop dough by heaping teaspoonfuls, 5 or 6 at a time, into oil. Fry until browned, 1-2 minutes, turning once. Drain on paper towels. Roll warm doughnut holes in confectioners' sugar.
1 doughnut hole: 47 cal., 2g fat (1g sat. fat), 7mg chol., 68mg sod., 6g carb. (2g sugars, 0 fiber), 1g pro.

FRIED JALAPENOS

Here's an appetizer that will heat up any gathering. Family and friends often request I make these jalapenos.
—DeLea Lonadier, Montgomery, LA

Prep: 10 min. + chilling • **Cook:** 20 min.
Makes: 2 dozen

- 2 jars (12 oz. each) whole jalapeno peppers, drained
- 1 jar (5 oz.) olive-pimiento spread
- ¾ cup all-purpose flour, divided
- 6 Tbsp. cornmeal, divided
- ¼ tsp. salt
- ¼ tsp. pepper
- 1 cup buttermilk
   Oil for deep-fat frying

1. Cut off stems and remove seeds from peppers; pat dry with a paper towel. Stuff peppers with cheese spread. Refrigerate at least 2 hours.
2. In a shallow bowl, combine ¼ cup flour, 2 Tbsp. cornmeal, salt, pepper and buttermilk until smooth; set aside. In another shallow bowl, combine remaining ½ cup flour and 4 Tbsp. cornmeal. Dip stuffed peppers into the buttermilk batter, then dredge in the flour mixture.
3. In a deep cast-iron or electric skillet, heat oil to 375°. Fry peppers, a few at a time, until golden brown. Drain on paper towels.
Note: Wear disposable gloves when cutting hot peppers; the oils can burn exposed skin. Avoid touching your face.
1 stuffed jalapeno: 90 cal., 6g fat (1g sat. fat), 4mg chol., 249mg sod., 7g carb. (1g sugars, 1g fiber), 1g pro.

MINIATURE CORN DOGS

Fun-sized corn dogs add a little "wow" factor to any cookout or get-together. Kids and adults equally love them, so expect them to disappear fast.
—Deb Perry, Bluffton, IN

Prep: 25 min. • **Cook:** 5 min./batch
Makes: about 3½ dozen

- 1 cup all-purpose flour
- 2 Tbsp. cornmeal
- 1½ tsp. baking powder
- ¼ tsp. salt
   Dash onion powder
- 3 Tbsp. shortening
- ¾ cup 2% milk
- 1 large egg
- 1 pkg. (16 oz.) miniature smoked sausages
   Oil for deep-fat frying
   Spicy ketchup

1. In a small bowl, combine the flour, cornmeal, baking powder, salt and onion powder; cut in shortening until crumbly. Whisk milk and egg; stir into the flour mixture just until moistened. Dip sausages into the batter.
2. In a cast-iron or other heavy skillet, heat oil to 375°. Fry the sausages, a few at a time, until golden brown, 2-3 minutes. Drain on paper towels. Serve with ketchup.
1 mini corn dog: 63 cal., 6g fat (1g sat. fat), 11mg chol., 136mg sod., 2g carb. (0 sugars, 0 fiber), 2g pro.

FRIED SWEET POTATO PIES

With my dad being a farmer who grew them, sweet potatoes have graced our table for as long as I can recall. This recipe, however, resulted from an experiment for a church bake sale when we had excess pastry. People couldn't get enough of these pies!
—Marilyn Moseley, Toccoa, GA

Prep: 25 min. + chilling • **Cook:** 15 min.
Makes: 25 pies

- 4½ **cups self-rising flour**
- 3 **Tbsp. sugar**
- ½ **cup shortening**
- 2 **large eggs**
- ¾ **cup 2% milk**

FILLING

- 1½ **cups mashed sweet potatoes**
- 1 **cup sugar**
- 1 **large egg, lightly beaten**
- 2 **Tbsp. 2% milk**
- 2 **Tbsp. butter, melted**
- 1½ **Tbsp. all-purpose flour**
- ½ **tsp. vanilla extract**
  Oil for deep-fat frying
  Confectioners' sugar, optional

1. In a large bowl, combine flour and sugar; cut in shortening until mixture resembles coarse crumbs. Combine eggs and milk; add to crumb mixture, tossing with a fork until a ball forms. Cover and chill for several hours.
2. In a large bowl, combine the 7 filling ingredients; stir until smooth. Divide the dough into 25 portions. On a floured surface, roll each portion into a 5-in. circle. Spoon 1½ Tbsp. filling on half of each circle. Moisten the edges of the circle with water; fold half over filling and press edges with a fork to seal.
3. In a cast-iron or an electric skillet, heat 1 in. oil to 375°. Fry pies, in batches, until golden brown, about 1 minute. Drain on paper towels. If desired, dust with confectioners' sugar. Store in the refrigerator.

1 pie: 287 cal., 17g fat (3g sat. fat), 25mg chol., 294mg sod., 31g carb. (11g sugars, 1g fiber), 4g pro.

FRIED GREEN TOMATO STACKS

This dish is for lovers of red and green tomatoes. When I ran across the recipe, I just had to try it —it proved to be so tasty!
—Barbara Mohr, Millington, MI

Prep: 20 min. • **Cook:** 15 min.
Makes: 4 servings

- ¼ cup fat-free mayonnaise
- ¼ tsp. grated lime zest
- 2 Tbsp. lime juice
- 1 tsp. minced fresh thyme or ¼ tsp. dried thyme
- ½ tsp. pepper, divided
- ¼ cup all-purpose flour
- 2 large egg whites, lightly beaten
- ¾ cup cornmeal
- ¼ tsp. salt
- 2 medium green tomatoes
- 2 medium red tomatoes
- 2 Tbsp. canola oil
- 8 slices Canadian bacon

1. Mix the first 4 ingredients and ¼ tsp. pepper; refrigerate until serving.
2. Place flour in a shallow bowl; place egg whites in a separate shallow bowl. In a third bowl, mix cornmeal, salt and remaining ¼ tsp. pepper.
3. Cut each tomato crosswise into 4 slices. Dredge 1 slice in flour to lightly coat; shake off excess flour. Dip in egg whites, then in cornmeal mixture. Repeat with the remaining tomato slices.
4. In a large nonstick skillet, heat oil over medium heat. In batches, cook the tomatoes until golden brown, 4-5 minutes per side.
5. In same pan, lightly brown Canadian bacon on both sides. For each, stack 1 slice each green tomato, bacon and red tomato. Serve with sauce.

2 stacks: 284 cal., 10g fat (1g sat. fat), 16mg chol., 677mg sod., 37g carb. (6g sugars, 3g fiber), 12g pro. **Diabetic exchanges:** 2 starch, 1½ fat, 1 vegetable, 1 lean meat.

FRIED MASHED POTATO BALLS

The key to this recipe is to start with mashed potatoes that are firm from chilling. Serve the fried treats with sour cream or ranch salad dressing.
—*Taste of Home* Test Kitchen

Prep: 25 min. + standing
Cook: 5 min./batch • **Makes:** 6 servings

- 2 cups cold mashed potatoes
- 1 large egg, lightly beaten
- ¾ cup shredded cheddar cheese
- ½ cup chopped green onions
- 4 bacon strips, cooked and crumbled
- ½ cup dry bread crumbs
  Oil for frying

1. Place mashed potatoes in a large bowl; let stand at room temperature for 30 minutes. Stir in the egg, cheese, onions and bacon. Shape mixture into 1-in. balls; roll in bread crumbs. Let stand for 15 minutes.
2. In an electric skillet, heat 1 in. oil to 375°. Fry potato balls, a few at a time, until golden brown, 2½-3 minutes. Remove with a slotted spoon to paper towels to drain. Serve warm.
5 potato balls: 290 cal., 19g fat (5g sat. fat), 55mg chol., 496mg sod., 21g carb. (1g sugars, 1g fiber), 9g pro.

LOADED STUFFED POTATO PANCAKES

When I make mashed potatoes, I always cook extra just for these over-the-top pancakes. Fill them with sour cream, ranch, melted cheese—or all three.
—Jane Whittaker, Pensacola, FL

Prep: 25 min. • **Cook:** 5 min./batch
Makes: 4 servings

- 2 cups mashed potatoes (with added milk and butter)
- ⅔ cup shredded cheddar cheese
- ⅓ cup all-purpose flour
- 1 large egg, lightly beaten
- 1 Tbsp. minced chives
- ½ tsp. salt
- ½ tsp. pepper
- ⅔ cup seasoned bread crumbs
- 1 tsp. garlic powder
- 1 tsp. onion powder
- ½ tsp. cayenne pepper
- ⅓ cup cream cheese, softened
  Oil for deep-fat frying

1. In a large bowl, combine the first 7 ingredients. In a shallow bowl, mix bread crumbs, garlic powder, onion powder and cayenne.
2. Shape 2 tsp. cream cheese into a ball. Wrap ¼ cup potato mixture around the cream cheese to cover completely. Drop into crumb mixture. Gently coat and shape into a ½-in.-thick patty. Repeat with the remaining cream cheese and potato mixture.
3. In an electric skillet or deep-fat fryer, heat oil to 375°. Fry stuffed pancakes, a few at a time, until golden brown, 1-2 minutes on each side. Drain on paper towels.
2 pancakes: 491 cal., 34g fat (12g sat. fat), 96mg chol., 987mg sod., 35g carb. (3g sugars, 2g fiber), 12g pro.

HAM CROQUETTES WITH MUSTARD SAUCE

Whenever we have ham, any leftovers are set aside to make these crispy croquettes. I shape them early in the day, then simply fry them for dinner. The mild mustard sauce pairs especially well with ham.
—Kathy Vincek, Toms River, NJ

....

Prep: 35 min. + chilling
Cook: 5 min./batch • **Makes:** 1 dozen

- 2 **cups finely chopped fully cooked ham**
- 1 **Tbsp. finely chopped onion**
- 1 **tsp. minced fresh parsley**
- ¼ **cup butter, cubed**
- ¼ **cup all-purpose flour**
- ¼ **tsp. salt**
- ⅛ **tsp. pepper**
- 1 **cup 2% milk**
- 1 **large egg**
- 2 **Tbsp. water**
- ¾ **cup dry bread crumbs**
  Oil for deep-fat frying

SAUCE
- 1½ **tsp. butter**
- 1½ **tsp. all-purpose flour**
- ¼ **tsp. salt**
  Dash pepper
- ½ **cup milk**
- 4½ **tsp. yellow mustard**

1. In a small bowl, combine the ham, onion and parsley; set aside.
2. In a small saucepan, melt butter. Stir in the flour, salt and pepper until smooth; gradually add milk. Bring to a boil; cook and stir for 1 minute or until thickened. Stir into the ham mixture.
3. Spread into an 8-in. square baking dish; cover and refrigerate for at least 2 hours.
4. In a shallow bowl, combine egg and water. Place bread crumbs in a separate shallow bowl. Shape ham mixture into 12 balls (mixture will be soft); roll each ball in the egg mixture, then in bread crumbs. Cover and refrigerate for 2 hours longer.
5. In an electric skillet or deep fryer, heat oil to 375°. Fry croquettes, a few at a time, for 2-3 minutes or until golden brown, turning once. Drain on paper towels.
6. For the sauce, melt butter in a small saucepan. Stir in the flour, salt and pepper until smooth; gradually add milk. Bring to a boil; cook and stir for 2 minutes or until thickened. Stir in mustard. Serve with croquettes.

1 croquette with 2 tsp. sauce: 188 cal., 14g fat (5g sat. fat), 44mg chol., 503mg sod., 8g carb. (2g sugars, 0 fiber), 7g pro.

BLUE-RIBBON TIP

You can also fry foods like these on the stovetop. Use a pot with deep sides to prevent excess oil splatter.

DEEP-FRIED CHEESE BITES

These beer-battered cheese curds are the ultimate in delicious comfort food. Some folks like to serve them with ranch dressing, ketchup or barbecue sauce for dipping.
—Katie Rose, Pewaukee, WI

Prep: 10 min. • **Cook:** 5 min./batch
Makes: 12 servings

1¼ cups all-purpose flour, divided
1 lb. cheese curds or cubed cheddar cheese
Oil for deep-fat frying
1 cup beer

1. Place ¼ cup flour in a shallow dish. Add cheese curds, a few pieces at a time, and turn to coat.
2. In an electric skillet or deep fryer, heat oil to 375°. Meanwhile, in a large bowl, whisk beer and remaining flour. Dip cheese curds, a few at a time, into batter and then fry for 2-3 minutes on each side or until golden brown. Drain on paper towels.
1 serving: 257 cal., 19g fat (8g sat. fat), 40mg chol., 235mg sod., 9g carb. (1g sugars, 0 fiber), 11g pro.

FIRST-PRIZE DOUGHNUTS

One year I entered 18 different treats and baked goods in the county fair and all of them won ribbons. Here is my favorite prize-winning doughnut recipe.
—Betty Claycomb, Alverton, PA

Prep: 25 min. + rising
Cook: 5 min./batch
Makes: 20 doughnuts

   2 **pkg. (¼ oz. each) active dry yeast**
   ½ **cup warm water (110° to 115°)**
   ½ **cup warm 2% milk (110° to 115°)**
   ½ **cup sugar**
   ½ **cup shortening**
   2 **large eggs**
   1 **tsp. salt**
  4½ **to 5 cups all-purpose flour**
      Oil for deep-fat frying

TOPPINGS
  1¼ **cups confectioners' sugar**
   4 **to 6 Tbsp. water**
      Colored sprinkles and/or assorted breakfast cereals

1. In a large bowl, dissolve yeast in warm water. Add the milk, sugar, shortening, eggs, salt and 2 cups flour; beat until smooth. Stir in enough of the remaining flour to form a soft dough.
2. Turn dough onto a floured surface; knead dough until smooth and elastic, 6-8 minutes. Place in a greased bowl, turning once to grease the top. Cover and let rise in a warm place until doubled, about 1 hour.
3. Punch dough down. Turn onto a floured surface; roll out to ½-in. thickness. Cut with a floured 2½-in. doughnut cutter. Place cutouts on greased baking sheets. Cover and let rise until doubled, about 1 hour.
4. In an electric skillet or deep fryer, heat oil to 375°. Fry doughnuts, a few at a time, until golden brown on both sides. Drain on paper towels.
5. In a shallow bowl, combine the confectioners' sugar and water until smooth. Dip warm doughnuts in glaze; decorate as desired with sprinkles and/or cereals.

1 doughnut: 270 cal., 11g fat (2g sat. fat), 22mg chol., 129mg sod., 39g carb. (17g sugars, 1g fiber), 4g pro.

CRISPY PUB RINGS

I created this recipe for a party we hosted for beer-tasting (my husband brews his own), and the rings were a hit. Serve them when you entertain or on those nights when you want homemade takeout food.
—Jennifer Rodriguez, West Jordan, UT

Prep: 40 min. • **Cook:** 5 min./batch
Makes: 6 servings

- ½ cup sour cream
- ½ cup mayonnaise
- ½ cup crumbled blue cheese
- 2 green onions, finely chopped
- 1 Tbsp. dried parsley flakes
- 1 garlic clove, minced
- ½ tsp. hot pepper sauce
- ¼ tsp. garlic salt

RINGS

- 1¼ cups all-purpose flour
- 1 tsp. salt
- 1 tsp. baking powder
- 1 large egg
- 1 cup 2% milk
- 1½ tsp. hot pepper sauce
- 1 garlic clove, minced
- ¾ cup dry bread crumbs
- 1 tsp. garlic powder
- 1 tsp. seasoned salt
- 1 large sweet onion, sliced and separated into rings
   Oil for deep-fat frying

1. In a small bowl, combine the first 8 ingredients; chill until serving.
2. In a large shallow bowl, combine the flour, salt and baking powder. In another shallow bowl, whisk the egg, milk, pepper sauce and minced garlic. In a third bowl, combine the bread crumbs, garlic powder and seasoned salt. Coat onions in the flour mixture, dip in egg mixture, then roll in crumbs.
3. In a deep fryer or electric skillet, heat oil to 375°. Drop onion rings, a few at a time, into hot oil. Fry for 2-3 minutes or until golden brown. Drain on paper towels. Serve with sauce.
1 serving: 401 cal., 30g fat (8g sat. fat), 50mg chol., 862mg sod., 26g carb. (5g sugars, 2g fiber), 8g pro.

QUICK JALAPENO HUSH PUPPIES

The crunchy exterior of these southern-style snacks is a nice contrast to the moist cornbread. Jalapeno peppers and hot sauce add a hint of heat.
—*Taste of Home* Test Kitchen

Prep: 15 min. • **Cook:** 5 min./batch
Makes: 2½ dozen

- 1½ cups yellow cornmeal
- ½ cup all-purpose flour
- 1 tsp. baking powder
- 1 tsp. salt
- 2 large eggs, room temperature, lightly beaten
- ¾ cup 2% milk
- 2 jalapeno peppers, seeded and minced
- ¼ cup finely chopped onion
- 1 tsp. Louisiana-style hot sauce
  Oil for deep-fat frying

1. In a large bowl, combine cornmeal, flour, baking powder and salt. In another bowl, beat the eggs, milk, jalapenos, onion and hot sauce. Stir into the dry ingredients just until combined.

2. In a cast-iron or other heavy skillet, heat oil to 375°. Drop the batter by tablespoonfuls, a few at a time, into the hot oil. Fry until golden brown on both sides. Drain on paper towels. Serve warm.

1 hush puppy: 56 cal., 3g fat (0 sat. fat), 14mg chol., 94mg sod., 7g carb. (0 sugars, 1g fiber), 1g pro.

FRIED MUSHROOMS MARINARA

Deep-fried breaded mushrooms served on a bed of spaghetti sauce are a sure crowd pleaser for any party. Get ready to hand out the recipe!
—Barbara McCalley, Allison Park, PA

Prep: 30 min. • **Cook:** 15 min.
Makes: about 2 dozen

- 1 cup all-purpose flour
- ½ tsp. salt
- ¼ tsp. pepper
- 3 large eggs
- 1 Tbsp. water
- 1 cup seasoned bread crumbs
- 1 lb. medium fresh mushrooms, stems removed
  Oil for deep-fat frying
- 1 jar (26 oz.) marinara sauce or meatless spaghetti sauce
- 1 cup shredded part-skim mozzarella cheese
- ¼ cup grated Parmesan cheese

1. Preheat oven to 350°. In a large shallow dish, combine flour, salt and pepper. In another shallow dish, beat eggs and water. Place bread crumbs in a third shallow dish. Add mushrooms to the flour mixture; turn to coat. Dip them in egg mixture, then coat with bread crumbs. Let stand for 10 minutes.

2. In a deep saucepan, electric skillet or deep-fat fryer, heat oil to 375°. Fry the mushrooms, 6-8 at a time, for 1-2 minutes or until golden brown, turning occasionally. Set on paper towels to drain.

3. Pour spaghetti sauce into an ungreased 13x9-in. baking dish. Top with the mushrooms. Sprinkle with cheeses. Bake, uncovered, for 4-6 minutes or until the cheese is melted.

1 mushroom: 111 cal., 6g fat (1g sat. fat), 28mg chol., 310mg sod., 10g carb. (2g sugars, 1g fiber), 4g pro.

A TRIP TO THE STATE OR COUNTY FAIR

Cheering on the kids in the show ring, testing your skills with a sewing needle or a canning jar in a home arts competition, volunteering as a judge, or just eating some food on a stick and riding the Ferris wheel—these experiences often lead to bright memories. If you can't get to the fair this year to make some more, come along as readers remember their favorite moments.

FERRIS WHEEL: BEVERLY LEFEVRE/GETTY IMAGES

AMBER HERSH · CARR, COLORADO

A MENTOR'S MEMORIES

As the leader of our 4-H club in northern Colorado, I have the privilege of mentoring amazing kids like Sydney Sullivan. In her last year in 4-H, her two champion market swine made it to the overall grand champion swine drive, where she took the coveted overall grand champion market swine trophy at the Larimer County Fair.

A big deal in our county, this win represented years of hard work paying off. After each competition, Sydney would ask herself, *What do I need to change to do better?*

In her winning moment, as we both shed a few tears, it was apparent what 4-H means to these kids. Farming and ranching is not just a business; it is a lifestyle one chooses. It isn't easy. There is a lot of work that goes into it. There is also a ton of heart.

CHOOSING THE BEST

A few years ago, I arrived early at the Sioux County Fair to a long line of excited and nervous kids—all dressed in the same 4-H green clover T-shirt. They were there to enter their photography into the fair's competition, and I had the honor of judging their entries.

I'll admit I started to feel a tad nervous myself as I waited for the first child to make his way to my station. But the nerves gave way to delight as I realized the skill and artistry I would see that day. I have never looked at so many photographs in my life, and the talent was extraordinary!

I was tasked with selecting only the best pictures to be sent on to the Iowa State Fair. This proved to be a challenging undertaking. There were lots of beautiful flowers, even some with a perfectly focused bee resting on a petal. One young photographer captured water droplets from the fresh morning dew.

Photographs of sunsets and rainbows were also popular. Some of the kids took portraits of their siblings—images that would have made any professional proud.

And the livestock! A lot of these 4-H'ers not only were active in photography but were showing livestock as well. Their horses, cows, lambs and hogs—and their companion pets—were all accounted for in these images.

Then there were the barns. Old, lovely, colorful, sometimes falling down—all beautifully captured by these kids.

In the end, a few different photos went off to the state fair. But seeing all the hopeful kids made me proud that the county fair is still alive and well, at least in our little corner of the world.

HAYLEY MOSS · HULL, IOWA

Hayley Moss' boys, Merritt and McCoy, compete in mutton bustin' at the Clay County Fair in Spencer, Iowa. Bottom right, McCoy enjoys the Sioux County Fair.

P. 102

P. 75

P. 79

P. 98

SNACKS & OTHER CROWD PLEASERS

GRILLED BROCCOLI

I started using this recipe in 1987 when I began cooking light, and it's been a favorite side dish ever since. With its lemon and Parmesan flavors, it once took second-place in a cooking contest.
—Alice Nulle, Woodstock, IL

Prep: 5 min. + standing
Grill: 20 min.
Makes: 6 servings

- 6 cups fresh broccoli spears
- 2 Tbsp. plus 1½ tsp. lemon juice
- 2 Tbsp. olive oil
- ¼ tsp. salt
- ¼ tsp. pepper
- ¾ cup grated Parmesan cheese
  Optional: Grilled lemon slices and red pepper flakes

1. Place broccoli in a large bowl. Combine lemon juice, oil, salt and pepper; drizzle over the broccoli and toss to coat. Let stand for 30 minutes.
2. Toss broccoli; drain broccoli, discarding marinade. Place cheese in a small shallow bowl. Add broccoli, a few pieces at a time, toss to coat.
3. Prepare grill for indirect heat using a drip pan. Place broccoli over drip pan on an oiled grill rack. Grill, covered, over indirect medium heat for 8-10 minutes on each side or until crisp-tender. If desired, garnish with grilled lemon slices and red pepper flakes.
1 cup: 107 cal., 8g fat (3g sat. fat), 8mg chol., 304mg sod., 5g carb. (2g sugars, 2g fiber), 6g pro. **Diabetic exchanges:** 1½ fat, 1 vegetable.

BEST HUSH PUPPIES

Some years ago, when I was a cook on a large cattle ranch, I thought back to the hush puppies I'd had as a child on a southern trip. I created my own version of them for the ranchers. These go well as part of an old-fashioned fried chicken dinner with mashed potatoes and gravy, buttermilk biscuits, corn on the cob and watermelon pickles!
—Karyl Goodhart, Geraldine, MT

Prep: 15 min. • **Cook:** 20 min.
Makes: 3 dozen

- 2 cups yellow cornmeal
- ½ cup all-purpose flour
- 2 Tbsp. sugar
- 2 tsp. baking powder
- 1 tsp. salt
- ½ tsp. baking soda
- 1 large egg, room temperature, lightly beaten
- ¾ cup 2% milk
- ¾ cup cream-style corn
  Oil for deep-fat frying

1. In a large bowl, whisk cornmeal, flour, sugar, baking powder, salt and baking soda. Add egg, milk and corn; stir just until combined.
2. In a deep-fat fryer, heat oil to 375°. Drop batter by tablespoonfuls, a few at a time, into the hot oil. Fry until golden brown on both sides. Drain on paper towels. Serve warm.
1 hush puppy: 66 cal., 2g fat (0 sat. fat), 6mg chol., 129mg sod., 10g carb. (1g sugars, 0 fiber), 1g pro.

SOUTHWESTERN EGG ROLLS

At my church potluck, these crispy, spicy snacks went fast thanks to the triple kick from the Italian sausage, Mexicorn and chiles. Want to balance the hot with a little cool? Sour cream and guacamole are tasty party tricks.
—Jacqueline Bower, Washington, IA

Takes: 30 min. • **Makes:** 1½ dozen

- 1 **lb. bulk hot Italian sausage**
- 1 **can (15 oz.) black beans, rinsed and drained**
- 1 **can (11 oz.) Mexicorn, drained**
- 1 **can (10 oz.) diced tomatoes and green chiles, undrained**
- 1 **pkg. (8.8 oz.) ready-to-serve Spanish rice**
- 18 **egg roll wrappers**
   Oil for frying
   Optional: Sour cream and guacamole

1. In a large skillet, cook sausage over medium heat 6-8 minutes or until no longer pink, breaking it into crumbles; drain. Stir in beans, Mexicorn, tomatoes and rice; bring to a boil. Reduce heat; simmer, uncovered, for 5 minutes, stirring occasionally.

2. With 1 corner of an egg roll wrapper facing you, place ⅓ cup filling just below center. (Cover remaining wrappers with a damp paper towel until ready to use.) Fold bottom corner over filling; moisten remaining wrapper edges with water. Fold side corners toward center over filling. Roll up tightly, pressing at tip to seal. Repeat.

3. In an electric skillet, heat 1 in. oil to 375°. Fry egg rolls, 2 at a time, 1-2 minutes or until golden brown, turning occasionally. Drain on paper towels. If desired, serve with sour cream and guacamole.

1 egg roll: 333 cal., 19g fat (4g sat. fat), 21mg chol., 643mg sod., 31g carb. (2g sugars, 2g fiber), 10g pro.

BLUE-RIBBON TIP

Keep your egg rolls crispy by letting them cool completely, uncovered, on a wire rack. Store them in the refrigerator in a lidded container lined with paper towels. Reheat and re-crisp the egg rolls in a hot skillet for 3-5 minutes per side or on a foil-lined baking sheet in a 350° oven for 10-15 minutes.

LENTIL CHICKEN SALAD

A fantastic way to use lentils is in this satisfying salad. Besides the combination of textures, the tasty ingredients blend well with the creamy dressing. It merited a blue ribbon and praise from all the tasters at our church fair.
—Margaret Pache, Mesa, AZ

Takes: 15 min. · **Makes:** 6 servings

- 2 **cups shredded iceberg lettuce**
- 1 **cup cooked lentils**
- 1 **cup diced cooked chicken**
- 1 **cup diced celery**
- ½ **cup shredded carrot**
- ½ **cup chopped pecans**
- 1 **cup mayonnaise**
- ¼ **cup chunky salsa**
- 4 **green onions, chopped**
- 1 **Tbsp. lemon juice**

In a large bowl, combine the first 6 ingredients. In a small bowl, combine the mayonnaise, salsa, onions and lemon juice. Pour over the salad; toss gently to coat. Serve immediately.
1 cup: 435 cal., 38g fat (5g sat. fat), 34mg chol., 291mg sod., 12g carb. (3g sugars 5g fiber), 11g pro.

SUMMER SQUASH & ZUCCHINI SALAD

I came up with this colorful, tasty slaw years ago for a recipe contest and was delighted when I won honorable mention! The recipe easily doubles and is the perfect dish to take to potlucks or family gatherings.
—Paula Wharton, El Paso, TX

Prep: 25 min. + chilling
Makes: 12 servings

- 4 **medium zucchini**
- 2 **yellow summer squash**
- 1 **medium sweet red pepper**
- 1 **medium red onion**
- 1 **cup fresh sugar snap peas, trimmed and halved**
- ⅓ **cup olive oil**
- ¼ **cup balsamic vinegar**
- 2 **Tbsp. reduced-fat mayonnaise**
- 4 **tsp. fresh sage or**
-    **1 tsp. dried sage leaves**
- 2 **tsp. honey**
- 1 **tsp. garlic powder**
- 1 **tsp. celery seed**
- 1 **tsp. dill weed**
- ½ **tsp. salt**
- ½ **tsp. pepper**

Thinly slice zucchini, squash, red pepper and onion; place in a large bowl. Add snap peas. In a small bowl, whisk the remaining ingredients until blended. Pour over vegetables; toss to coat. Refrigerate, covered, at least 3 hours.
¾ cup: 101 cal., 7g fat (1g sat. fat), 1mg chol., 124mg sod., 8g carb. (6g sugars, 2g fiber), 2g pro. **Diabetic exchanges:** 1½ fat, 1 vegetable.

FRENCH FRIES

One of the culinary highlights of going to the fair is also one of the simplest—fresh-cut, fresh-cooked french fries. This recipe you can make at home is so much better than any fast-food or frozen variety.
—*Taste of Home* Test Kitchen

Prep: 20 min. + soaking
Cook: 5 min./batch
Makes: 4 servings

- 1 **lb. russet potatoes**
-    **Oil for deep-fat frying**
- ¾ **tsp. salt**

1. Cut potatoes into ¼-in. julienned strips; soak strips in cold water for 30 minutes.
2. Drain potatoes; pat dry with paper towels. In an electric skillet or deep-fat fryer, heat the oil to 340°. Working in batches, fry potatoes until lightly browned, 3-4 minutes. Remove with a slotted spoon; drain on paper towels.
3. Increase heat of oil to 375°. Fry potatoes again in batches until crisp and golden brown, 1-2 minutes, turning frequently. Drain on paper towels; sprinkle with salt. Serve immediately.
¾ cup: 190 cal., 11g fat (1g sat. fat), 0 chol., 449mg sod., 20g carb. (2g sugars, 2g fiber), 2g pro.

SUNFLOWER STRAWBERRY SALAD

We have an annual strawberry festival in our town, so recipes with strawberries are popular here. I have served this salad at luncheons and have always received compliments.
—Betty Malone, Humboldt, TN

Prep: 10 min. + chilling
Makes: 6 servings

- 2 **cups sliced fresh strawberries**
- 1 **medium apple, diced**
- 1 **cup seedless green grapes, halved**
- ½ **cup thinly sliced celery**
- ¼ **cup raisins**
- ½ **cup strawberry yogurt**
- 2 **Tbsp. sunflower kernels**

In a large bowl, combine strawberries, apple, grapes, celery and raisins. Stir in the yogurt. Cover and refrigerate for at least 1 hour. Add sunflower kernels and toss.

¾ cup: 107 cal., 2g fat (0 sat. fat), 1mg chol., 43mg sod., 22g carb. (17g sugars, 3g fiber), 2g pro. **Diabetic exchanges:** 1½ fruit, ½ fat.

MINI CORN DOGS

These bite-sized corn dogs are a baked version of the deep-fried state fair favorite. I make my own by wrapping cornmeal dough around mini hot dogs. Kids and the young at heart love them.
—Geralyn Harrington, Floral Park, NY

Takes: 30 min. • **Makes:** 2 dozen

- 1²/₃ cups all-purpose flour
- ⅓ cup cornmeal
- 3 tsp. baking powder
- 1 tsp. salt
- 3 Tbsp. cold butter
- 1 Tbsp. shortening
- 1 large egg, room temperature
- ¾ cup 2% milk
- 24 miniature hot dogs

HONEY MUSTARD SAUCE

- ⅓ cup honey
- ⅓ cup prepared mustard
- 1 Tbsp. molasses

1. Preheat oven to 450°. In a large bowl, combine the first 4 ingredients. Cut in butter and shortening until the mixture resembles coarse crumbs. Beat egg and milk. Stir into dry ingredients until a soft dough forms; dough will be sticky.
2. Turn onto a generously floured surface; knead 6-8 times or until smooth, adding additional flour as needed. Roll out to ¼-in. thickness. Cut with a 2¼-in. biscuit cutter. Fold each dough circle over a hot dog and press edges to seal.
3. Place on greased baking sheets. Bake until golden brown, 10-12 minutes. In a small bowl, combine the sauce ingredients. Serve with corn dogs.
1 corn dog: 109 cal., 5g fat (2g sat. fat), 18mg chol., 306mg sod., 14g carb. (5g sugars, 0 fiber), 3g pro.

CONTEST-WINNING WATERMELON SALSA

I entered this recipe in a local fair, and it took first place! This is one of my favorite dishes because all the ingredients (except for the lime juice) came directly from my own garden and beehives.
—Carolyn Butterfield, Lake Stevens, WA

Prep: 20 min. + chilling • **Makes:** 3 cups

- 2 cups seeded finely chopped watermelon
- ½ cup peeled finely chopped cucumber
- ¼ cup finely chopped red onion
- ¼ cup finely chopped sweet red pepper
- 1 jalapeno pepper, seeded and minced
- ¼ cup minced fresh cilantro
- 1 Tbsp. minced fresh basil
- 1 Tbsp. minced fresh mint
- 2 Tbsp. honey
- 1 tsp. lime juice
  Baked tortilla chip scoops

1. In a large bowl, combine watermelon, cucumber, onion, peppers and herbs. Drizzle with honey and lime juice; gently toss to coat.
2. Refrigerate for at least 1 hour. Serve with chips.
Note: Wear disposable gloves when cutting hot peppers; the oils can burn skin. Avoid touching your face.
¼ cup: 22 cal., 0 fat (0 sat. fat), 0 chol., 1mg sod., 6g carb. (5g sugars, 0 fiber), 0 pro. **Diabetic exchanges:** ½ starch.

CARAMEL CORN

For years, I've taken several containers of this yummy snack to our church retreat. Other church members tell us that if we can't attend, we should just send the caramel corn!
—Nancy Breen, Canastota, NY

Prep: 10 min. • **Bake:** 1 hour
Makes: 12 qt.

- 12 **qt. plain popped popcorn**
- 1 **lb. peanuts**
- 2 **cups butter, cubed**
- 2 **lbs. brown sugar**
- ½ **cup dark corn syrup**
- ½ **cup molasses**

1. Preheat oven to 250°. Divide popcorn between 2 large bowls. Add ½ pound peanuts to each bowl. In a Dutch oven, combine remaining ingredients. Bring to a boil over medium heat; cook and stir for 5 minutes.
2. Pour half the syrup over each bowl of popcorn; stir to coat. Transfer to large roasting or 15x10x1-in. baking pans. Bake 1 hour, stirring every 15 minutes.
3. Remove from oven and break apart while warm. Cool completely. Store in airtight containers.

1 cup: 267 cal., 15g fat (6g sat. fat), 20mg chol., 189mg sod., 32g carb. (22g sugars, 2g fiber), 3g pro.

CRISPY OVEN-FRIED OYSTERS

These flavorful breaded and baked oysters, served with a zippy jalapeno mayonnaise, are just divine. I entered them in a seafood contest and took first place in the hors d'oeuvres category.
—Marie Rizzio, Interlochen, MI

....

Takes: 30 min.
Makes: about 2½ dozen
(about ⅔ cup jalapeno mayonnaise)

- ¾ cup all-purpose flour
- ⅛ tsp. salt
- ⅛ tsp. pepper
- 2 large eggs
- 1 cup dry bread crumbs
- ⅔ cup grated Romano cheese
- ¼ cup minced fresh parsley
- ½ tsp. garlic salt
- 1 pint shucked oysters or 2 cans (8 oz. each) whole oysters, drained
- 2 Tbsp. olive oil

JALAPENO MAYONNAISE

- ¼ cup mayonnaise
- ¼ cup sour cream
- 2 medium jalapeno peppers, seeded and finely chopped
- 2 Tbsp. 2% milk
- 1 tsp. lemon juice
- ¼ tsp. grated lemon zest
- ⅛ tsp. salt
- ⅛ tsp. pepper

1. Preheat oven to 400°. In a shallow bowl, combine flour, salt and pepper. In another shallow bowl, whisk eggs. In a third bowl, combine bread crumbs, cheese, parsley and garlic salt.

2. Coat oysters with the flour mixture, then dip in eggs and coat with crumb mixture. Place in a greased 15x10x1-in. baking pan; drizzle with oil.

3. Bake 12-15 minutes or until golden brown. Meanwhile, in a small bowl, whisk mayonnaise ingredients. Serve with oysters.

Note: Wear disposable gloves when cutting hot peppers; the oils can burn skin. Avoid touching your face.

1 oyster with about 1 tsp. jalapeno mayonnaise: 75 cal., 4g fat (1g sat. fat), 25mg chol., 146mg sod., 6g carb. (0 sugars, 0 fiber), 3g pro.

PORTOBELLO MUSHROOM & CREAM CHEESE TAQUITOS

This party appetizer was inspired by a dish I saw on an episode of *Top Chef*. I simplified it a little and tweaked the flavors a bit. The taquitos can be made ahead and reheated in a 250° oven for 10 minutes.

—Lily Julow, Lawrenceville, GA

Prep: 30 min. • **Cook:** 15 min.
Makes: 10 servings

- 2 **Tbsp. extra virgin olive oil**
- 8 **oz. large portobello mushrooms, gills discarded, finely chopped**
- 1 **tsp. dried oregano**
- 1 **tsp. dried thyme**
- ½ **tsp. crushed red pepper flakes**
- ¼ **tsp. salt**
- 1 **pkg. (8 oz.) cream cheese, softened**
- 4 **oz. whole-milk ricotta cheese**
- 10 **flour tortillas (8 in.)**
  Oil for deep-fat frying
  Major Grey's chutney

1. In a cast-iron or other heavy skillet, heat olive oil to 350°. Add mushrooms; saute 4 minutes. Add oregano, thyme, pepper flakes and salt; saute until the mushrooms are browned, 4-6 minutes. Cool. Wipe out skillet.

2. Combine cheeses; fold in the mushrooms, mixing well. Spread 3 Tbsp. mushroom mixture on bottom half of each tortilla. Roll up tightly, making sure filling isn't seeping from either end. Secure rolls with toothpicks.

3. In same skillet, heat oil to 375°. Fry taquitos, a few at a time, until golden brown, 2-4 minutes. Drain on paper towels. When taquitos are cool enough to handle, discard toothpicks. Serve with chutney.

1 appetizer: 375 cal., 25g fat (7g sat. fat), 27mg chol., 380mg sod., 30g carb. (2g sugars, 2g fiber), 8g pro.

CANDIED PECANS

I like to pack these crispy pecans in pretty jars as gifts for family and friends. My granddaughter gave some to a doctor at the hospital where she works, and he said they were too good to be true!

—Opal Turner, Hughes Springs, TX

Prep: 25 min. • **Bake:** 30 min.
Makes: about 1 lb. (8 servings)

- 2¾ cups pecan halves
- 2 Tbsp. butter, softened, divided
- 1 cup sugar
- ½ cup water
- ½ tsp. salt
- ½ tsp. ground cinnamon
- 1 tsp. vanilla extract

1. Place the pecans in a shallow baking pan in a 250° oven for 10 minutes or until warmed. Grease a 15x10x1-in. baking pan with 1 Tbsp. butter; set aside.

2. Grease the sides of a large heavy saucepan with remaining butter; add sugar, water, salt and cinnamon. Bring to a boil, stirring constantly to dissolve sugar. Cover; cook 2 minutes to dissolve any sugar crystals that may form on the sides of pan.

3. Cook, without stirring, until a candy thermometer reads 236° (soft-ball stage). Remove from the heat; add vanilla. Stir in warm pecans until evenly coated.

4. Spread onto prepared baking pan. Bake at 250° for 30 minutes, stirring every 10 minutes. Spread on a waxed paper-lined baking sheet to cool.

2 oz.: 380 cal., 30g fat (4g sat. fat), 8mg chol., 177mg sod., 30g carb. (26g sugars, 4g fiber) 3g pro.

BLUE-RIBBON TIP

We recommend that you test your candy thermometer before each use by testing the temperature of boiling water; the thermometer should read 212°. Adjust your recipe temperature up or down based on your test.

PRETZEL BREAD BOWL WITH CHEESE DIP

Our town is known as Pretzel City—even our local sports teams are known as The Pretzels. I came up with this dish for an annual community recipe contest. People couldn't believe that the delicious bread had pretzels in the mix! For variety, try using different flavors of pretzels.
—Andrea Johnson, Freeport, IL

Prep: 30 min. + rising
Bake: 30 min. + cooling
Makes: 16 servings

- 1 **cup finely crushed cheddar miniature pretzels**
- 1 **envelope ranch salad dressing mix**
- 1 **pkg. (¼ oz.) quick-rise yeast**
- 2 **tsp. sugar**
- ⅛ **tsp. baking soda**
- 2 **to 2½ cups all-purpose flour**
- 1 **cup water**
- ¼ **cup 2% milk**
- 2 **Tbsp. butter**
- 1 **cup shredded pepper jack cheese**
- 1 **tsp. yellow cornmeal**

EGG WASH
- 1 **large egg white**
- 1 **Tbsp. water**
  Kosher salt, optional

DIP
- 2 **cups sour cream**
- 1 **cup shredded pepper jack cheese**
- 1 **envelope ranch salad dressing mix**
  Optional: Chopped seeded jalapeno peppers and additional shredded pepper jack cheese
  Assorted fresh vegetables

1. Mix pretzels, dressing mix, yeast, sugar, baking soda and 1 cup flour. In a small saucepan, heat water, milk and butter to 120°-130°. Add to the dry ingredients; beat on low speed until moistened. Add cheese; beat on medium for 3 minutes. Stir in enough remaining flour to form a stiff dough.

2. Turn the dough onto a floured surface; knead until smooth and elastic, 6-8 minutes. Cover and let rest 10 minutes.

3. Grease a baking sheet; sprinkle with cornmeal. Shape dough into a round loaf; place on prepared pan. Cover and let rise in a warm place until doubled, about 1 hour.

4. Whisk egg white with water; brush over top of loaf. If desired, sprinkle with salt. Preheat oven to 375°. Bake until golden brown and bread sounds hollow when tapped, 30-35 minutes. Cool on pan 5 minutes. Remove to a wire rack to cool completely.

5. For dip, mix sour cream, pepper jack cheese and dressing mix. Refrigerate until serving.

6. To serve, cut a fourth off the top of the bread loaf. Hollow out the center of the loaf, leaving a ½-in.-thick shell. Cut removed bread into cubes. Fill bowl with dip. If desired, top with peppers and additional cheese. Serve dip with bread cubes and vegetables.

1 serving: 212 cal., 12g fat (8g sat. fat), 40mg chol., 445mg sod., 19g carb. (2g sugars, 1g fiber), 7g pro.

BLUE RASPBERRY SNOW CONE SYRUP

Imagine you're at the county fair with snow cones made in your backyard! You can create shaved ice using a blender with a "crush" setting. Slowly add water for a slushy effect; add more ice as needed.
—Amanda Kippert, Tucson, AZ

Prep: 5 min. • **Cook:** 5 min. + cooling
Makes: 1½ cups

- 1 **cup sugar**
- ¾ **cup water**
- 1 **envelope unsweetened blue raspberry Kool-Aid mix**
- 1 **tsp. lemon juice**

In a small saucepan, combine sugar and water. Cook and stir over medium heat until sugar is dissolved; remove from heat. Stir in Kool-Aid and lemon juice; cool. Cover and store in the refrigerator up to 2 weeks.

1 Tbsp.: 49 cal., 0 fat (0 sat. fat), 0 chol., 1mg sod., 13g carb. (13g sugars, 0 fiber), 0 pro.

RAVIOLI APPETIZER POPS

Ravioli on a stick is a simple and fun appetizer everyone talks about. Use packaged sauces, or make your own.
—Erika Monroe-Williams, Scottsdale, AZ

Prep: 25 min. • **Cook:** 5 min./batch
Makes: 3½ dozen

- ½ cup dry bread crumbs
- 2 tsp. pepper
- 1½ tsp. dried oregano
- 1½ tsp. dried parsley flakes
- 1 tsp. salt
- 1 tsp. crushed red pepper flakes
- ⅓ cup all-purpose flour
- 2 large eggs, lightly beaten
- 1 pkg. (9 oz.) refrigerated cheese ravioli
  Oil for frying
  Grated Parmesan cheese, optional
- 42 lollipop sticks
  Warm marinara sauce and prepared pesto

1. In a shallow bowl, mix bread crumbs and seasonings. Place flour and eggs in separate shallow bowls. Dip ravioli in the flour to coat both sides; shake off excess. Dip in egg, then in the crumb mixture, patting to help coating adhere.
2. In a large electric or cast-iron skillet, heat ½ in. oil to 375°. Fry the ravioli, a few at a time, until golden brown, 1-2 minutes each side. Drain on paper towels. Immediately sprinkle with cheese if desired. Carefully insert a lollipop stick into the back of each ravioli. Serve warm with marinara sauce and pesto.

1 appetizer: 32 cal., 1g fat (0 sat. fat), 9mg chol., 97mg sod., 4g carb. (0 sugars, 0 fiber), 1g pro.

NACHO WINGS

I love wings. I love nachos. Together, they're the perfect pairing! This recipe earned an award in a wings and ribs contest we held at our summer cottage.
—Lori Stefanishion, Drumheller, AB

Prep: 20 min. • **Cook:** 1 hour
Makes: 2 dozen

- 24 chicken wing sections
- ½ cup butter, melted
- 1 pkg. (15½ oz.) nacho-flavored tortilla chips, crushed
- 2 cups shredded Mexican cheese blend or shredded cheddar cheese
- 1 can (4 oz.) chopped green chiles
- 1 cup chopped green onions
  Optional: Seeded jalapeno slices, salsa, sour cream and guacamole

1. Preheat oven to 350°. Dip wing sections in melted butter, then roll in the crushed nacho chips. Bake in a greased 15x10x1-in. baking pan until the juices run clear, 45-50 minutes. Remove from oven.
2. Top with cheese, chiles, green onions and, if desired, jalapeno slices. Return to oven and bake until the cheese is melted, about 15 minutes. Serve with other toppings as desired.

1 wing: 188 cal., 13g fat (5g sat. fat), 45mg chol., 317mg sod., 8g carb. (1g sugars, 1g fiber), 9g pro.

BUFFALO CHICKEN WINGS

Hot wings got their start in Buffalo, New York, in the kitchen of a bar. Cayenne, red sauce and spices keep these tangy buffalo chicken wings good and hot, just like the originals.
—Nancy Chapman, Center Harbor, NH

Prep: 10 min. • **Cook:** 10 min./batch
Makes: about 4 dozen

- 5 **lbs. chicken wings**
  Oil for frying
- 1 **cup butter, cubed**
- ¼ **cup Louisiana-style hot sauce**
- ¾ **tsp. cayenne pepper**
- ¾ **tsp. celery salt**
- ½ **tsp. onion powder**
- ½ **tsp. garlic powder**
  Optional: Celery ribs and ranch or blue cheese salad dressing

1. Cut chicken wings into 3 sections; discard wing tip sections. In an electric skillet, heat 1 in. oil to 375°. Fry wings in oil, a few at a time, for 3-4 minutes on each side or until chicken juices run clear. Drain on paper towels.

2. Meanwhile, in a small saucepan, melt butter. Stir in the hot sauce and spices. Place chicken in a large bowl; add sauce and toss to coat. Remove to a serving plate with a slotted spoon. Serve with celery and ranch or blue cheese dressing if desired.

Note: Uncooked chicken wing sections (wingettes) may be substituted for whole chicken wings.

1 piece: 126 cal., 12g fat (4g sat. fat), 25mg chol., 105mg sod., 0 carb. (0 sugars, 0 fiber), 5g pro.

ZIPPY PARTY ROLL-UPS

A guaranteed crowd pleaser, these zesty appetizers are an amazing way to pep up a party! The recipe won a blue ribbon at the county fair, and even though I always double it, I never seem to make enough.
—Dana Gonzalez del Valle, Battle Ground, WA

Prep: 20 min. + chilling • **Makes:** 6 dozen

- 1 **pkg. (8 oz.) cream cheese, softened**
- 6 **flour tortillas (8 in.)**
- 36 **spinach leaves**
- 1 **pkg. (6 oz.) thinly sliced deli ham**
- 1 **can (4¼ oz.) chopped ripe olives**
- 1 **can (4 oz.) chopped green chiles, drained**

Spread about 3 Tbsp. cream cheese over each tortilla; layer each with 6 spinach leaves and 3 slices ham. Sprinkle with the olives and chiles. Roll up tightly and cover. Refrigerate until firm. Uncover and cut each roll-up into 12 slices.

1 slice: 32 cal., 2g fat (1g sat. fat), 4mg chol., 85mg sod., 3g carb. (0 sugars, 0 fiber), 1g pro.

READER RAVE...

"These are good and have nice visual appeal. I suggest making a couple of practice roll-ups to get the hang of how the meat (round slices vs. rectangular-shaped slices) and spinach (small vs. large leaves) allow you to roll the tortillas together."
—ALLISONO, TASTEOFHOME.COM

CRISPY FRIED ONION RINGS

These crispy burger toppers add an extra element to already fantastic burgers. They're also perfect for giving salads a little crunch.
—*Taste of Home* Test Kitchen

Takes: 25 min. • **Makes:** 12 servings

- ½ cup all-purpose flour
- ½ cup water
- 1 large egg, lightly beaten
- 1 tsp. seasoned salt
- ½ tsp. baking powder
- 1 large onion, very thinly sliced
  Oil for deep-fat frying

In a shallow bowl, whisk the first 5 ingredients. Separate onion slices into rings. Dip rings into batter. In a deep-fat fryer, heat 1 in. oil to 375°. In batches, fry onion rings until golden brown, 1–1½ minutes on each side. Drain on paper towels. Serve immediately.
½ cup: 71 cal., 5g fat (0 sat. fat), 16mg chol., 153mg sod., 5g carb. (1g sugars, 0 fiber), 1g pro.

Baked Onion Rings: Beat egg in a shallow bowl. In another shallow bowl, mix ⅔ cup dry bread crumbs, ½ tsp. seasoned salt and ¼ tsp. pepper. Dip onion rings into egg, then roll in the crumb mixture. Place on a baking sheet coated with cooking spray. Bake at 425° for 15-18 minutes or until golden brown, turning once.

Red Onion Rings: Substitute a red onion for the onion. With the flour mixture, whisk in ¼ tsp. cayenne.

BUFFALO CHICKEN EGG ROLLS

This crunchy delight gets its start in the slow cooker. Tuck the chicken mixture in egg roll wrappers and bake, or use smaller wonton wrappers for a bite-sized version.
—Tara Odegaard, Omaha, NE

Prep: 35 min. • **Cook:** 3 hours
Makes: 16 egg rolls

- 1½ lbs. boneless skinless chicken breasts
- 2 Tbsp. ranch salad dressing mix
- ½ cup Buffalo wing sauce
- 2 Tbsp. butter
- 16 egg roll wrappers
- ⅓ cup crumbled feta cheese
- ⅓ cup shredded part-skim mozzarella cheese
  Ranch salad dressing, optional

1. In a 3-qt. slow cooker, combine the chicken, dressing mix and wing sauce. Cook, covered, on low until chicken is tender, 3-4 hours.
2. Preheat oven to 425°. Shred chicken with 2 forks; stir in butter.
3. With a corner of an egg roll wrapper facing you, place 3 Tbsp. chicken mixture just below the center of the wrapper; top with 1 tsp. each feta and mozzarella cheeses. (Cover remaining wrappers with a damp paper towel until ready to use.) Fold bottom corner over filling; moisten remaining wrapper edges with water. Fold side corners toward center over filling; roll up tightly, pressing at the tip to seal. Place on a parchment-lined baking sheet, seam side down. Repeat, adding additional baking sheets as needed.
4. Bake until egg rolls are golden brown, 15-20 minutes. Let stand for 5 minutes before serving. Serve warm, with ranch dressing for dipping if desired.
1 egg roll: 174 cal., 4g fat (2g sat. fat), 33mg chol., 716mg sod., 21g carb. (0 sugars, 1g fiber), 13g pro.

BLUE-RIBBON TIP

If you want to make a lighter version of this recipe, serve the filling in Bibb lettuce cups instead of egg roll wrappers.

SNACKS & OTHER CROWD PLEASERS

ROASTED PEPPER SALAD WITH BALSAMIC VINAIGRETTE

I created this colorful salad for a 4-H project and took it all the way to the state competition, where I won first place! I'd love to have my own Italian restaurant someday.
—Seth Murdoch, Red Rock, TX

Prep: 20 min. + marinating
Broil: 20 min. + standing
Makes: 5 servings

- 2 each large sweet yellow, red and green peppers
- 1 small red onion, thinly sliced
- 6 Tbsp. olive oil
- 3 Tbsp. balsamic vinegar
- 1 Tbsp. each minced fresh oregano, rosemary, basil and parsley
- 1 garlic clove, minced
- ½ tsp. garlic powder
- ½ tsp. cayenne pepper
- ½ tsp. pepper
- ¼ tsp. salt
- 1 cup cherry tomatoes, halved
- 1 carton (8 oz.) fresh mozzarella cheese pearls
- 5 fresh basil leaves

1. Broil peppers 4 in. from heat until skins blister, about 5 minutes. With tongs, rotate peppers a quarter turn. Broil and rotate until all sides are blistered and blackened. Immediately place peppers in a large bowl; cover and let stand for 20 minutes.

2. Peel off and discard charred skin. Remove stems and seeds. Cut peppers into thin strips; place in a large bowl. Add onion.

3. In a small bowl, whisk the oil, vinegar, herbs, garlic, garlic powder, cayenne, pepper and salt; pour over pepper mixture and toss to coat. Cover and refrigerate for up to 4 hours.

4. Before serving, allow peppers to come to room temperature. Place on a serving plate; top with tomatoes, cheese and basil leaves.

1 serving: 346 cal., 27g fat (9g sat. fat), 36mg chol., 196mg sod., 18g carb. (10g sugars, 4g fiber), 11g pro.

BLUE-RIBBON TIP

Over the years, balsamic vinegar has gone from an exotic ingredient to a pantry staple. This dark, thick, sweet-smelling Italian vinegar adds a rich, dark color to dishes. When a dark color is undesirable, use white balsamic vinegar instead. Balsamic vinegar comes at many different price points; just as with wine, the grapes, processing and aging method, and aging time contribute to the final cost of the vinegar. The higher priced balsamic is best drizzled over cooked foods as a finishing touch rather than used in the cooking process.

CHEESE FRIES

I came up with this recipe after my daughter had cheese fries at a restaurant and couldn't stop talking about them. She loves that I can fix them so quickly at home.
—Melissa Tatum, Greensboro, NC

Takes: 20 min. • **Makes:** 8 servings

- 1 pkg. (28 oz.) frozen steak fries
- 1 can (10¾ oz.) condensed cheddar cheese soup, undiluted
- ¼ cup 2% milk
- ½ tsp. garlic powder
- ¼ tsp. onion powder
  Paprika

1. Arrange the steak fries in a single layer in 2 greased 15x10x1-in. baking pans. Bake at 450° for 15-18 minutes or until tender and golden brown.
2. Meanwhile, in a small saucepan, combine soup, milk, garlic powder and onion powder; heat through. Drizzle over fries; sprinkle with paprika.

1 serving: 129 cal., 5g fat (2g sat. fat), 5mg chol., 255mg sod., 20g carb. (1g sugars, 2g fiber), 3g pro. **Diabetic exchanges:** 1 starch, 1 fat.

MEXICAN STREET CORN BAKE

We discovered Mexican street corn at a festival. This easy one-pan version saves on prep and cleanup. Every August, I freeze a lot of our own fresh sweet corn—I use that in this recipe, but store-bought corn works just as well.
—Erin Wright, Wallace, KS

....

Prep: 10 min. • **Bake:** 35 min.
Makes: 6 servings

- 6 **cups frozen corn (about 30 oz.), thawed and drained**
- 1 **cup mayonnaise**
- 1 **tsp. ground chipotle pepper**
- ¼ **tsp. salt**
- ¼ **tsp. pepper**
- 6 **Tbsp. chopped green onions, divided**
- ½ **cup grated Parmesan cheese**
  Lime wedges, optional

1. Preheat oven to 350°. Mix the first 5 ingredients and 4 Tbsp. green onions; transfer to a greased 1½-qt. baking dish. Sprinkle with cheese.
2. Bake, covered, 20 minutes. Uncover; bake until bubbly and lightly browned, 15-20 minutes longer. Sprinkle with remaining 2 Tbsp. green onions. If desired, serve with lime wedges.
⅔ cup: 391 cal., 30g fat (5g sat. fat), 8mg chol., 423mg sod., 30g carb. (4g sugars, 3g fiber), 6g pro.

ROAST BEEF & TOMATO SANDWICH PIZZA

I developed this recipe for a 4-H food show in a category where no cooking was allowed. The judges were so impressed, they wouldn't let me leave the table until they had time to write down the recipe!
—Seth Murdoch, Red Rock, TX

....

Takes: 20 min. • **Makes:** 6 servings

- 2 **cups fresh baby spinach**
- 2 **plum tomatoes, chopped**
- ½ **cup thinly sliced red onion**
- ½ **cup thinly sliced sweet yellow or orange pepper**
- ⅓ **cup balsamic vinaigrette**
- 4 **oz. reduced-fat cream cheese**
- ¼ **cup mayonnaise**
- 2 **Tbsp. minced chives**
- 2 **Tbsp. horseradish sauce**
- 1 **prebaked 12-in. pizza crust**
- 8 **oz. sliced deli roast beef, cut into strips**
- 1 **green onion, chopped**

1. In a small bowl, combine the spinach, tomatoes, red onion and pepper. Add vinaigrette; toss to coat.
2. In a small bowl, mix cream cheese, mayonnaise, chives and horseradish sauce until blended; spread over pizza crust. Top with beef. Using a slotted spoon, place spinach mixture over beef. Sprinkle with green onion.
1 piece: 336 cal., 17g fat (5g sat. fat), 39mg chol., 738mg sod., 29g carb. (5g sugars, 2g fiber), 15g pro.

HOMEMADE POTATO CHIPS

Forget buying the bag of potato chips at the grocery store when you can make these at home. This quick and easy recipe will delight everyone in the family.
—*Taste of Home* Test Kitchen

Prep: 30 min. + soaking
Cook: 5 min./batch • **Makes:** 8½ cups

- 7 **unpeeled medium potatoes (about 2 lbs.)**
- 2 **qt. ice water**
- 5 **tsp. salt**
- 2 **tsp. garlic powder**
- 1½ **tsp. celery salt**
- 1½ **tsp. pepper**
  Oil for deep-fat frying

1. Using a vegetable peeler or metal cheese slicer, cut potatoes into very thin slices. Place in a large bowl; add ice water and salt. Soak for 30 minutes.
2. Drain potatoes; place on paper towels and pat dry. In a small bowl, combine the garlic powder, celery salt and pepper; set aside.
3. In a cast-iron or other heavy skillet, heat 1½ in. oil to 375°. Fry the potatoes in batches until golden brown, 3-4 minutes, stirring frequently.
4. Remove with a slotted spoon; drain on paper towels. Immediately sprinkle with seasoning mixture. Store in an airtight container.
¾ cup: 176 cal., 8g fat (1g sat. fat), 0 chol., 703mg sod., 24g carb. (1g sugars, 3g fiber), 3g pro.

BAKED CRAB WONTONS

These little crab bites make everyone smile. My family loves their size, texture and taste. I love that they're quick and simple to make. They even won first prize in a cooking competition. Instead of baking them in the oven, you could also deep-fry them.
—Danielle Arcadi, Peoria, AZ

Takes: 30 min. • **Makes:** 1½ dozen

- 18 **wonton wrappers**
  Cooking spray
- 4 **oz. reduced-fat cream cheese**
- ¼ **cup reduced-fat mayonnaise**
- ¼ **tsp. salt**
- ¼ **tsp. pepper**
- 1 **can (6 oz.) crabmeat, drained, flaked and cartilage removed**
- 2 **green onions, thinly sliced**
- ¼ **cup shredded carrot**
- ¼ **cup finely chopped celery**
  Sweet-and-sour sauce, optional

1. Preheat oven to 350°. Press wonton wrappers into greased mini-muffin cups. Spritz wrappers with cooking spray. Bake until lightly browned, 5-7 minutes.
2. Beat cream cheese, mayonnaise, salt and pepper until smooth. Stir in the next 4 ingredients. Spoon into the wonton cups. Bake until heated through, 9-11 minutes. If desired, serve with sweet-and-sour sauce.
1 appetizer: 62 cal., 3g fat (1g sat. fat), 16mg chol., 182mg sod., 6g carb. (0 sugars, 0 fiber), 3g pro.

POWER
TV POWER
SLEEP
ZOOM
SAP
SIGNAL
DISPLAY
MENU
EXIT
FAV
MUTE
VOL
CH

PEANUT CARAMEL CORN

A sweet, crunchy, lighter alternative to traditional caramel corn, this can't-stop-eatin'-it treat won't stick to fingers or teeth! It's wonderful for gifts, too.
—Lois Ward, Puslinch, ON

Prep: 20 min. • **Bake:** 45 min.
Makes: 2 qt.

- 8 cups air-popped popcorn
- ½ cup salted peanuts
- ½ cup packed brown sugar
- 3 Tbsp. light corn syrup
- 4½ tsp. molasses
- 1 Tbsp. butter
- ¼ tsp. salt
- ½ tsp. vanilla extract
- ⅛ tsp. baking soda

1. Preheat oven to 250°. Place popcorn and peanuts in a large bowl coated with cooking spray; set aside.
2. In a large heavy saucepan, combine brown sugar, corn syrup, molasses, butter and salt. Bring to a boil over medium heat, stirring constantly. Boil for 2-3 minutes without stirring.
3. Remove from the heat; stir in vanilla and baking soda (mixture will foam). Quickly pour over popcorn and mix well.
4. Transfer to a 15x10x1-in. baking pan coated with cooking spray. Bake for 45 minutes, stirring every 15 minutes. Remove from pan and place on waxed paper to cool. Store in an airtight container.

1 cup: 181 cal., 6g fat (2g sat. fat), 4mg chol., 155mg sod., 30g carb. (18g sugars, 2g fiber), 3g pro. **Diabetic exchanges:** 2 starch, 1 fat.

CURRY & MANGO CHUTNEY CHICKEN WINGS

We hold an annual cook-off at our cabin. The year I made these wings, I couldn't have hoped for a better reaction from the crowd. Everyone cheered!
—Lori Stefanishion, Drumheller, AB

Prep: 15 min. + marinating
Bake: 45 min.
Makes: 1 dozen (1 cup sauce)

- ¼ cup plain Greek yogurt
- ¼ cup mango chutney
- 2 Tbsp. curry paste
- 2 Tbsp. lemon juice
- 2 garlic cloves, minced
- 12 chicken wings (about 3 lbs.), wing tips removed, if desired

SAUCE
- ¾ cup plain Greek yogurt
- ½ cup finely chopped peeled English cucumber
- 3 Tbsp. minced fresh cilantro
- 1 tsp. lemon juice
- 1 garlic clove, minced
- ¼ tsp. salt

1. In a bowl or shallow dish, combine the first 5 ingredients. Add chicken wings and turn to coat. Cover and refrigerate 4 hours or overnight.
2. In a small bowl, mix the sauce ingredients until blended. Refrigerate, covered, at least 1 hour.
3. Preheat oven to 400°. Drain chicken, discarding marinade. Place wings on a rack in a foil-lined 15x10x1-in. baking pan. Bake 45-50 minutes or until juices run clear, turning every 15 minutes. Serve with sauce.

1 chicken wing with 4 tsp. sauce: 170 cal., 10g fat (4g sat. fat), 42mg chol., 207mg sod., 6g carb. (4g sugars, 0 fiber), 12g pro.

GEORGIA PEANUT SALSA

Former President Jimmy Carter gave this zippy salsa a blue ribbon at the Plains Peanut Festival in his Georgia hometown. My daughter and I came up with the recipe just days before the competition. We weren't allowed in the judging room, but we later saw a tape of President Carter tasting our salsa and saying, "Mmm...that's good." My daughter was only 9 years old, but it's a day she'll never forget!
—Lane McLoud, Siloam Springs, AR

Prep: 25 min. + chilling
Makes: about 6½ cups

- 3 plum tomatoes, seeded and chopped
- 1 jar (8 oz.) picante sauce
- 1 can (7 oz.) white or shoepeg corn, drained
- ⅓ cup Italian salad dressing
- 1 medium green pepper, chopped
- 1 medium sweet red pepper, chopped
- 4 green onions, thinly sliced
- ½ cup minced fresh cilantro
- 2 garlic cloves, minced
- 2½ cups salted roasted peanuts or boiled peanuts
  Hot pepper sauce, optional
  Tortilla chips

1. In a large bowl, combine the first 9 ingredients. Cover and refrigerate for at least 8 hours.
2. Just before serving, stir in peanuts and, if desired, pepper sauce. Serve with tortilla chips.
¼ cup: 123 cal., 9g fat (1g sat. fat), 0 chol., 207mg sod., 8g carb. (2g sugars, 2g fiber), 5g pro.

BACON CHEESEBURGER ROLL-UPS

My husband and I both love these roll-ups. I often serve them made with broccoli and cheese. They must be good, because this recipe won a first-place prize at the Iowa State Fair!
—Jessica Cain, Des Moines, IA

Prep: 25 min. • **Bake:** 20 min.
Makes: 8 servings

- 1 lb. ground beef
- 6 bacon strips, diced
- ½ cup chopped onion
- 1 pkg. (8 oz.) Velveeta, cubed
- 1 tube (16.3 oz.) large refrigerated buttermilk biscuits
- 1 large egg, beaten, optional
  Sesame seeds, optional
- ½ cup ketchup
- ¼ cup yellow mustard

1. Preheat the oven to 400°. In a large skillet, cook beef, bacon and onion over medium heat until meat is no longer pink, breaking beef into crumbles; drain. Add cheese; cook and stir until melted. Remove from heat.
2. Flatten biscuits into 5-in. circles; top each with ⅓ cup beef mixture. Fold sides and ends over filling, and roll up. Place seam side down on a greased baking sheet. If desired, brush with egg and sprinkle with sesame seeds.
3. Bake 18-20 minutes or until golden brown. In a small bowl, combine ketchup and mustard; serve with the roll-ups.
1 roll-up: 429 cal., 24g fat (10g sat. fat), 63mg chol., 1372mg sod., 32g carb. (11g sugars, 1g fiber), 21g pro.

CITRUS PINEAPPLE COLESLAW

A blue-ribbon recipe, this slaw was a winner in our state fair competition. Alaska is famous for its giant cabbages, but any garden-variety head will taste yummy dressed in citrusy pineapple and marshmallow bits.
—Carol Ross, Anchorage, AK

Prep: 30 min. + chilling
Makes: 12 servings

- ⅓ **cup sugar**
- ¼ **cup cornstarch**
- ¼ **tsp. salt**
- 1 **cup unsweetened pineapple juice**
- ¼ **cup orange juice**
- 3 **Tbsp. lemon juice**
- 2 **large eggs, lightly beaten**
- 6 **oz. cream cheese, softened**
- 1 **medium head cabbage, shredded**
- 2 **large carrots, shredded**
- 1 **can (8 oz.) crushed pineapple, drained**
- 1 **cup miniature marshmallows**
  Carrot curls, optional

1. In a saucepan, combine the first 6 ingredients until smooth. Bring to a boil over medium heat; cook and stir for 2 minutes or until thickened. Stir a small amount into the eggs. Return all to saucepan, stirring constantly. Cook and stir until mixture reaches 160°. Cool for 5 minutes. Stir in cream cheese until melted. Refrigerate.
2. In a large salad bowl, combine the cabbage, carrots, pineapple and marshmallows. Add dressing; toss to coat. Garnish with carrot curls if desired.

1 cup: 132 cal., 4g fat (2g sat. fat), 43mg chol., 101mg sod., 24g carb. (16g sugars, 2g fiber), 3g pro.

HAWAIIAN EGG ROLLS

An avid cook, I am constantly trying to come up with recipes for leftovers. This one gives a whole new twist to extra ham. My two children think these egg rolls are fabulous, and the rolls freeze well. I thaw as many as needed and then bake them.
—Terri Wheeler, Vadnais Heights, MN

Takes: 25 min. • **Makes:** 7 egg rolls

- 10 fresh spinach leaves, julienned
- ½ tsp. ground ginger
- 2 Tbsp. olive oil
- ½ lb. fully cooked ham, coarsely ground (about 2 cups)
- 4 water chestnuts, chopped
- ¼ cup crushed pineapple, undrained
- 2 Tbsp. chopped green onion
- 1 Tbsp. soy sauce
- 7 egg roll wrappers
  Canola oil for frying
  Sweet-and-sour sauce

1. In a large saucepan, saute spinach and ginger in olive oil for 1-2 minutes. In a large bowl, combine the ham, water chestnuts, pineapple, green onion and soy sauce. Stir in the spinach mixture.
2. Place 3 Tbsp. ham mixture in the center of each egg roll wrapper. Fold bottom corner over filling; fold sides of the wrapper over filling toward center. Moisten the remaining corner of the wrapper with water; roll up tightly to seal.
3. In an electric skillet, heat 1 in. canola oil to 375°. Fry egg rolls until golden brown, about 2 minutes on each side. Drain on paper towels. Serve with sweet-and-sour sauce.
1 egg roll: 311 cal., 20g fat (4g sat. fat), 21mg chol., 743mg sod., 22g carb. (2g sugars, 1g fiber), 10g pro.

CRISPY LIME CHIPS WITH CRAB

At the spur of the moment, we drove to Chincoteague, Virginia, for a seafood cooking contest. We had just enough money for ingredients and the gas to get there—our second-place prize, $100, was enough to pay our expenses! Most of this recipe can be made ahead of time and assembled when needed.
—Tracey Stone, Gettysburg, PA

Prep: 45 min. • **Broil:** 5 min.
Makes: 80 appetizers

- 1 Tbsp. kosher salt
- 2 tsp. grated lime zest
- 10 flour tortillas (10 in.)
- ¼ cup olive oil
  TOPPING
- 1 pkg. (8 oz.) cream cheese, softened
- 2 Tbsp. lime juice
- 2 tsp. seafood seasoning, divided
- 2 cans (6 oz. each) lump crabmeat, drained
- 6 green onions, finely chopped
- ½ cup shredded sharp white cheddar cheese

1. In a small bowl, combine salt and lime zest; set aside. Use a 3-in. star-shaped cookie cutter to cut 8 star shapes from each tortilla. In a large skillet over medium-high heat, heat half the oil. Fry tortilla stars in batches until golden brown on both sides. Add more oil as needed. Drain on paper towels; immediately sprinkle with salt mixture.
2. In a small bowl, beat the cream cheese, lime juice and 1 tsp. seafood seasoning until blended. Fold in crab and onions. Arrange chips on ungreased baking sheets. Top with crab mixture; sprinkle with cheddar cheese.
3. Broil 3-4 in. from the heat 1-2 minutes or until cheese is melted. Sprinkle with remaining 1 tsp. seafood seasoning. Serve immediately.
1 appetizer: 50 cal., 2g fat (1g sat. fat), 8mg chol., 163mg sod., 4g carb. (0 sugars, 1g fiber), 2g pro.

SLOW-COOKER CHEDDAR BACON BEER DIP

My tangy, smoky dip won the top prize in our office party recipe contest. Other beers can work, but steer clear of dark varieties.
—Ashley Lecker, Green Bay, WI

Prep: 15 min. • **Cook:** 3 hours
Makes: 4½ cups

- **18** oz. cream cheese, softened
- **¼** cup sour cream
- **1½** Tbsp. Dijon mustard
- **1** tsp. garlic powder
- **1** cup amber beer or nonalcoholic beer
- **2** cups shredded cheddar cheese
- **1** lb. bacon strips, cooked and crumbled, divided
- **¼** cup heavy whipping cream
- **1** green onion, thinly sliced
  Soft pretzel bites

1. In a greased 3-qt. slow cooker, combine cream cheese, sour cream, mustard and garlic powder until smooth. Stir in beer, cheese and all but 2 Tbsp. bacon. Cook, covered, on low, stirring occasionally, until heated through, 3-4 hours.
2. In the last 30 minutes, stir in heavy cream. Top with onion and remaining bacon. Serve with soft pretzel bites.
¼ cup: 213 cal., 19g fat (10g sat. fat), 60mg chol., 378mg sod., 2g carb. (1g sugars, 0 fiber), 8g pro.

BLUE-RIBBON TIP

To lighten this, use light sour cream, half-and-half, and reduced-fat cream cheese and shredded cheese.

APPLE & PECAN STUFFED SWEET POTATOES

We first made this side dish for a beef cook-off my sister-in-law entered—our beef didn't win, but we won best side!
—Jennifer Kuehn, Avon, IL

Prep: 30 min. • **Bake:** 1 hour + cooling
Makes: 6 servings

- **6** medium sweet potatoes (about 8 oz. each)
- **½** cup butter, cubed
- **¼** cup packed brown sugar
- **½** tsp. grated orange zest
- **1** medium apple, chopped
- **¼** cup chopped pecans

1. Scrub potatoes; pierce each several times with a fork. Place on a foil-lined 15x10x1-in. baking pan. Bake at 400° for 45-60 minutes or until tender.
2. When cool enough to handle, cut off a thin slice from the top of each potato; discard. Scoop out the pulp, leaving ¼-in.-thick shells; transfer pulp to a large bowl. Mash pulp with butter, adding brown sugar and orange zest. Fold in apple and pecans.
3. Spoon mixture into potato shells. Return to baking pan. Bake until heated through, 15-20 minutes longer.
1 stuffed sweet potato: 408 cal., 19g fat (10g sat. fat), 41mg chol., 143mg sod., 59g carb. (30g sugars, 7g fiber), 4g pro.

LETTING GO

A determined 4-H'er developed a special bond with her dairy steer.
—BAILEY DOLLAR, PORTLAND, IN

During the 10 years I spent as a student in 4-H, I got to work with amazing animals and supporters. But in my eighth year of showing livestock, I had a steer that topped all the others—one I'll never forget.

Ever since my earliest days of showing, I'd wanted a Brown Swiss steer. I always considered them to be the most beautiful cattle and, in my experience, they are absolute sweethearts. A couple of years ago, my dad found an ad in the newspaper from someone who was selling a Brown Swiss bull. I figured if they had a bull, then they had to have calves.

I made a reservation to pick out a calf, and eventually my dad and I made the trip. For Dad, the journey began on a frustrating note—I had told him the calf was about an hour and a half away, and the drive ended up being closer to three hours long! But I'm pretty positive my happiness was enough to ease his sense of aggravation.

When we finally got to the location, I was directed into a pen of three bull calves. Two of the calves lay on the ground and didn't acknowledge me, but the third was quickly by my side, covering my jeans in slobber. With a smile on my face, I looked at my dad, and without a word, he walked over to the trailer and grabbed the halter for me.

My new calf and I walked back to the trailer not knowing how the next two years would go, but I was beyond excited for the journey.

We got the calf home, and not two hours later, he had earned his name: Goober. Besides all that slobbering, he would get excited when he heard us come into the barn, and he threw a fit if we didn't show him attention.

He liked thinking that he could jump over fences and be rebellious. When I was nearby but not paying him any mind, Goober would dump his water bucket and kick the wall. He disliked halters and got grumpy when he was tied up or being taken for a walk.

But Goober was the biggest softie with my siblings and me—we could handle him without any problems at all. He was everything I had ever wanted in a steer, and we became best friends.

County fair time rolled around, and with it came some unusual challenges. For example, Goober refused to drink city water, so we had to go home and bring him water from the farm every day. To say he was spoiled is an understatement!

That year, Goober took third place in the heavyweight dairy feeder steer category. We also entered the showmanship class and made it to the final cut for my age group. It was a good year for us.

The next year, fair prep began as usual. Goober learned that he could put his head under Dad's behind and lift him up when he was feeding the hogs, which pushed my dad's buttons but also put a smile on his face.

Goober had grown, and my mom's fears about me handling a big steer came back like always. He tried to eat my sister's and my hair all the time and would attempt to lick us to death. But no matter how big he got, he was still a baby.

Our last event at the fair came way too soon, and my heart felt as if it would break. The idea of having to let Goober go was the only thing on my mind. Still, I hoped it would be another good year for us—but an accident at check-in nearly ruined our chances. While helping a friend check in her calf, it kicked me in the hand, and

Bailey Dollar bonded with her Brown Swiss steer named Goober. Of her many positive 4-H experiences, Bailey's time showing Goober was a highlight.

I ended up in a splint with a fractured knuckle. The doctors told me not to show Goober. They said the knuckle could end up breaking if I worked it too much.

My mom now had even more to worry about, and Dad was uneasy, too, since the injured hand was the one I needed to hold Goober's head while showing him. It would be a big challenge, but it was one I insisted on taking. I knew the only person who could show my beloved steer for the last time was me.

My dad walked Goober to the holding ring and held him until it was time to go into the show ring. It was our moment to shine.

We placed third in the finished dairy steer class and walked back into showmanship together, and with that, the part I thought was going to be the hardest was over. But then it was time to say goodbye.

Letting my friend go wasn't easy. I went with Dad to take Goober to the sale barn, and I walked him to where he needed to go. I took his halter off, got into the truck with my dad and didn't say a word.

I will never forget Goober. People often say dogs and other small pets take a piece of your heart, but it was a big dairy steer who took mine.

P. 109

P. 121

P. 118

P. 113

CHILI COOK-OFF, TEX-MEX WINNERS & MORE

CHORIZO CHILI

I modified a bean soup recipe and came up with this wonderful chili. I make it mild, since that's how my family likes it, then I just add Tabasco sauce to my bowl to spice it up. Feel free to make it vegetarian by using soy chorizo and vegetable broth.
—Jenne Delkus, Des Peres, MO

Prep: 20 min. • **Cook:** 5 hours
Makes: 8 servings (2 qt.)

- 2   cans (15 oz. each) black beans, rinsed and drained
- 1   can (16 oz.) kidney beans, rinsed and drained
- 1   jar (16 oz.) chunky salsa
- 1   can (15 oz.) whole kernel corn, drained
- 1   pkg. (12 oz.) fully cooked Spanish chorizo links, chopped
- 1   can (10 oz.) diced tomatoes and green chiles, undrained
- 1   cup reduced-sodium chicken broth
- 2   Tbsp. ground cumin
- 1   to 2 tsp. hot pepper sauce
- 1   medium ripe avocado, peeled and cubed
- 6   Tbsp. sour cream
- ¼   cup fresh cilantro leaves

Combine the first 9 ingredients in a 4- or 5-qt. slow cooker. Cook, covered, on low 5-6 hours or until the flavors are blended. Serve with avocado, sour cream and cilantro.
1 cup: 366 cal., 17g fat (6g sat. fat), 30mg chol., 1262mg sod., 37g carb. (8g sugars, 10g fiber), 18g pro.

ROOT BEER PULLED PORK NACHOS

I count on my slow cooker to do the honors when I have a house full of summer guests. Teenagers especially love DIY nachos. Try cola, ginger ale or lemon-lime soda if you're not into root beer.
—James Schend, Pleasant Prairie, WI

Prep: 20 min. • **Cook:** 8 hours
Makes: 12 servings

- 1   boneless pork shoulder butt roast (3 to 4 lbs.)
- 1   can (12 oz.) root beer or cola
- 12 cups tortilla chips
- 2   cups shredded cheddar cheese
- 2   medium tomatoes, chopped
     Optional: Pico de gallo, chopped green onions and sliced jalapeno peppers

1. In a 4- or 5-qt. slow cooker, combine pork roast and root beer. Cook, covered, on low 8-9 hours, until meat is tender.

2. Remove roast; cool slightly. When cool enough to handle, shred meat with 2 forks. Return to slow cooker; keep warm.

3. To serve, drain pork. Layer tortilla chips with pork, cheese, tomatoes and optional toppings as desired. Serve immediately.
1 serving: 391 cal., 23g fat (8g sat. fat), 86mg chol., 287mg sod., 20g carb. (4g sugars, 1g fiber), 25g pro.

BLUE-RIBBON TIP

The cooked, cooled meat can be frozen in freezer containers for up to 4 months. Just be sure the cooking liquid covers the meat so it doesn't dry out. To use, partially thaw in the refrigerator overnight, then reheat in the microwave or on the stovetop.

JUMPIN' ESPRESSO BEAN CHILI

I love experimenting with chili and creating different takes on the classic hearty dish. This meatless version is low in fat but high in flavor. Everyone tries to guess the secret ingredient, but no one ever thinks it's coffee!
—Jess Apfe, Berkeley, CA

Prep: 15 min. • **Cook:** 35 min.
Makes: 7 servings

- 3   **medium onions, chopped**
- 2   **Tbsp. olive oil**
- 2   **Tbsp. brown sugar**
- 2   **Tbsp. chili powder**
- 2   **Tbsp. ground cumin**
- 1   **Tbsp. instant espresso powder or instant coffee granules**
- 1   **Tbsp. baking cocoa**
- ¾   **tsp. salt**
- 2   **cans (14½ oz. each) no-salt-added diced tomatoes**
- 1   **can (15 oz.) black beans, rinsed and drained**
- 1   **can (15 oz.) kidney beans, rinsed and drained**
- 1   **can (15 oz.) garbanzo beans or chickpeas, rinsed and drained**

Optional: Sour cream, thinly sliced green onions, shredded cheddar cheese and pickled jalapeno slices

1. In a Dutch oven, saute the onions in oil until tender. Add brown sugar, chili powder, cumin, espresso powder, cocoa and salt; cook and stir for 1 minute.

2. Stir in tomatoes and beans. Bring to a boil. Reduce heat; cover and simmer for 30 minutes to allow the flavors to blend. If desired, serve with sour cream, onions, cheese and jalapeno slices.

1 cup: 272 cal., 6g fat (1g sat. fat), 0 chol., 620mg sod., 45g carb. (14g sugars, 12g fiber), 12g pro. **Diabetic exchanges:** 2½ starch, 2 vegetable, 1 lean meat.

READER RAVE...

"Fantastic! We kept thinking we might need to change something, but if it ain't broke, don't fix it!"
—HBURCH, TASTEOFHOME.COM

TEX-MEX PORK CHOPS

These easy, flavorful chops won a contest for me. Salsa, cumin and green chiles give these chops the kick they need to be called Tex-Mex.
—Jo Ann Dalrymple, Claremore, OK

Takes: 20 min. • **Makes:** 6 servings

    Butter-flavored cooking spray
1 **small onion, chopped**
6 **boneless pork loin chops (5 oz. each)**
1 **cup salsa**
1 **can (4 oz.) chopped green chiles**
½ **tsp. ground cumin**
¼ **tsp. pepper**

1. In a large skillet coated with butter-flavored cooking spray, saute onion until tender. Add pork chops; cook over medium heat until a thermometer reads 145°, 5-6 minutes on each side.
2. Combine the salsa, chiles, cumin and pepper; pour over pork. Bring to a boil. Reduce heat; cover and simmer until heated through.

1 pork chop: 223 cal., 8g fat (3g sat. fat), 68mg chol., 433mg sod., 9g carb. (3g sugars, 5g fiber), 32g pro. **Diabetic exchanges:** 4 lean meat, 1 vegetable.

LIMA BEAN SOUP

A yearly Lima Bean Festival in nearby West Cape May honors the many growers there and showcases different recipes using their crops. This comforting chowder was a contest winner at the festival several years ago.
—Kathleen Olsack, North Cape May, NJ

Prep: 10 min. • **Cook:** 30 min.
Makes: 12 servings (3 qt.)

- 3 cans (14½ oz. each) chicken broth
- 2 cans (15¼ oz. each) lima beans, rinsed and drained
- 3 medium carrots, thinly sliced
- 2 medium potatoes, peeled and diced
- 2 small sweet red peppers, chopped
- 2 small onions, chopped
- 2 celery ribs, thinly sliced
- ¼ cup butter
- 1½ tsp. dried marjoram
- ½ tsp. salt
- ½ tsp. pepper
- ½ tsp. dried oregano
- 1 cup half-and-half cream
- 3 bacon strips, cooked and crumbled

1. In a Dutch oven or soup kettle, combine the first 12 ingredients; bring to a boil over medium heat. Reduce heat; cover and simmer 25-35 minutes or until vegetables are tender.
2. Add cream; heat through but do not boil. Sprinkle with bacon just before serving.
1 cup: 110 cal., 7g fat (4g sat. fat), 22mg chol., 431mg sod., 9g carb. (3g sugars, 2g fiber), 3g pro.

HEARTY SAUSAGE-CHICKEN CHILI

The company I work for has an annual chili cook-off, and this unusual recipe of mine was a winner. I combined two chili recipes and then added a few extra touches of my own.
—Carolyn Etzler, Thurmont, MD

Prep: 20 min. • **Cook:** 4 hours
Makes: 11 servings (2¾ qt.)

- 1 lb. Italian turkey sausage links, casings removed
- 1 medium onion, chopped
- ¾ lb. boneless skinless chicken thighs, cut into ¾-in. pieces
- 2 cans (14½ oz. each) diced tomatoes with mild green chiles, undrained
- 2 cans (8 oz. each) tomato sauce
- 1 can (16 oz.) kidney beans, rinsed and drained
- 1 can (15 oz.) cannellini beans, rinsed and drained
- 1 can (15 oz.) pinto beans, rinsed and drained
- 1 can (15 oz.) black beans, rinsed and drained
- 1 tsp. chili powder
- ½ tsp. garlic powder
- ⅛ tsp. pepper
  Thinly sliced green onions, optional

1. Crumble sausage into a large nonstick skillet. Add onion; cook and stir over medium heat until meat is no longer pink. Drain.
2. Transfer to a 5-qt. slow cooker. Stir in remaining ingredients except green onions. Cook, covered, on low 4-5 hours or until the chicken is no longer pink. Serve with green onions if desired.
1 cup: 272 cal., 6g fat (1g sat. fat), 45mg chol., 826mg sod., 32g carb. (7g sugars, 8g fiber), 21g pro.

CHUNKY CHIPOTLE PORK CHILI

Perfect for using leftover pork roast, this tasty, easy recipe can be made ahead and reheated. It's even better the second day.
—Peter Halferty, Corpus Christi, TX

Prep: 15 min. • **Cook:** 20 min.
Makes: 4 servings

- 1 medium green pepper, chopped
- 1 small onion, chopped
- 1 chipotle pepper in adobo sauce, finely chopped
- 1 Tbsp. canola oil
- 3 garlic cloves, minced
- 1 can (16 oz.) red beans, rinsed and drained
- 1 cup beef broth
- ½ cup salsa
- 2 tsp. ground cumin
- 2 tsp. chili powder
- 2 cups shredded cooked pork
- ¼ cup sour cream
  Sliced jalapeno pepper, optional

1. In a large saucepan, saute the green pepper, onion and chipotle pepper in oil until tender. Add the garlic; cook 1 minute longer.

2. Add beans, broth, salsa, cumin and chili powder. Bring to a boil. Reduce heat; simmer, uncovered, 10 minutes or until thickened. Add pork; heat through. Serve with sour cream and, if desired, jalapeno slices.

Freeze option: Cool chili and transfer to freezer containers. Freeze up to 3 months. To use, thaw in refrigerator. Transfer to a large saucepan to heat through; add water to thin if desired.
1 cup: 340 cal., 14g fat (4g sat. fat), 73mg chol., 834mg sod., 24g carb. (3g sugars, 7g fiber), 27g pro.

BLUE-RIBBON TIP

If your grocery store doesn't carry chipotle peppers in adobo sauce, you can make do with 1-2 teaspoons of smoked paprika plus some form of tomato sauce or canned tomato (if the recipe doesn't already contain tomatoes).

CHILI CORNBREAD

Our daughter made this recipe for a 4-H food show and won a blue ribbon. It's so simple to prepare, even on hurried, hectic days. We like to eat these squares with sour cream and salsa.
—Tracy Johnson, Canyon, TX

Prep: 15 min. • **Bake:** 45 min.
Makes: 8 servings

- 1 **cup plus 3 Tbsp. cornmeal, divided**
- 1 **tsp. salt**
- ½ **tsp. baking soda**
- 4 **large eggs, room temperature**
- 1 **can (14¾ oz.) cream-style corn**
- 1 **cup whole milk**
- 2 **Tbsp. canola oil**
- 1 **lb. ground beef, cooked and drained**
- 2 **cups shredded cheddar cheese**
- 1 **can (4 oz.) chopped green chiles**
- 1 **medium onion, chopped**

1. Preheat oven to 350°. Sprinkle a greased 13x9-in. baking pan with 3 Tbsp. cornmeal; set aside. In a bowl, combine the salt, baking soda and remaining 1 cup cornmeal.
2. In another bowl, beat eggs; add corn, milk and oil. Stir into the dry ingredients just until moistened. Pour half the batter into prepared pan. Layer with the beef, cheese, chiles and onion. Top with the remaining batter.
3. Bake 45-50 minutes or until golden brown. Let stand for 5 minutes before cutting into squares.
1 piece: 420 cal., 22g fat (11g sat. fat), 178mg chol., 824mg sod., 31g carb. (5g sugars, 3g fiber), 24g pro.

CHEESY CHILI FRIES

My family is all about chili fries, but restaurant versions pile on the calories. For a healthier approach, bake the fries and serve them with green onions and avocado.
—Beverly Nowling, Bristol, FL

Takes: 30 min. • **Makes:** 4 servings

- 5 cups frozen seasoned curly fries
- 1 Tbsp. olive oil
- 1 can (15 oz.) vegetarian chili with beans
- 1 cup shredded cheddar cheese
  Optional: Sour cream, thinly sliced green onions and cubed avocado

1. Preheat oven to 450°. Place fries on an ungreased 15x10x1-in. baking pan; drizzle with oil and toss to coat. Bake according to the package directions.
2. Divide fries among four 2-cup baking dishes; top each with chili and cheese. Bake until the cheese is melted, 5-7 minutes. Serve with toppings as desired.

Note: You may use one 8-in. square baking dish instead of four 2-cup baking dishes. Bake as directed.

1 serving: 435 cal., 22g fat (8g sat. fat), 47mg chol., 1001mg sod., 44g carb. (4g sugars, 5g fiber), 17g pro.

COWBOY BEEF DIP

In a foods class, a group of us developed this recipe for the North Dakota State Beef Bash Competition. We won the contest, and now my family requests this dip for all our special gatherings!
—Jessica Klym, Dunn Center, ND

Prep: 20 min. • **Cook:** 25 min.
Makes: 12 servings (3 cups)

- 1 lb. ground beef
- 4 Tbsp. chopped onion, divided
- 3 Tbsp. chopped sweet red pepper, divided
- 2 Tbsp. chopped green pepper, divided
- 1 can (10¾ oz.) condensed nacho cheese soup, undiluted
- ½ cup salsa
- 4 Tbsp. sliced ripe olives, divided
- 4 Tbsp. sliced pimiento-stuffed olives, divided
- 2 Tbsp. chopped green chiles
- 1 tsp. chopped seeded jalapeno pepper
- ¼ tsp. dried oregano
- ¼ tsp. pepper
- ¼ cup shredded cheddar cheese
- 2 Tbsp. sour cream
- 2 to 3 tsp. minced fresh parsley
   Tortilla chips

1. In a large skillet, cook the beef, 3 Tbsp. onion, 2 Tbsp. red pepper and 1 Tbsp. green pepper over medium heat until the meat is no longer pink, breaking it into crumbles; drain.

2. Stir in the soup, salsa, 3 Tbsp. ripe olives, 3 Tbsp. pimiento-stuffed olives, chiles, jalapeno, oregano and pepper. Bring to a boil. Reduce heat; simmer, uncovered, for 5 minutes.

3. Transfer to a serving dish. Top with the cheese, sour cream and parsley; sprinkle with the remaining 1 Tbsp. each onion, peppers and olives. Serve with tortilla chips.

Note: Wear disposable gloves when cutting hot peppers; the oils can burn skin. Avoid touching your face.

¼ cup: 116 cal., 7g fat (3g sat. fat), 26mg chol., 336mg sod., 4g carb. (1g sugars, 1g fiber), 8g pro.

READER RAVE...

"Amazing flavor...a bit spicy, which I love. I made it a day ahead, then heated it in a pot and placed it in serving dish with fresh toppings. I doubled the recipe for a gathering and there were only a couple of spoonfuls left. Yum!"
—CORNWALL, TASTEOFHOME.COM

POTATO CHEESE SOUP WITH SALMON

I started cooking for a harvest crew when I was 10 years old. Now, decades later, my husband and I live in the heart of a potato-growing area. One year, this recipe won me a prize!
—Nancy Horsburgh, Everett, ON

Takes: 30 min. • **Makes:** 6 servings

1¼ cups diced celery
 1 large onion, thinly sliced
 ¼ cup butter, cubed
3½ cups sliced peeled
     uncooked potatoes
 1 cup chicken broth
 3 cups whole milk,
     room temperature, divided
 1 cup half-and-half cream
 2 cups shredded sharp
     cheddar cheese
 1 tsp. dried thyme
 1 Tbsp. Worcestershire sauce
 1 can (7½ oz.) red sockeye salmon,
     drained, bones and skin removed
     Salt and pepper to taste
     Minced fresh parsley

1. In a large saucepan, saute celery and onion in butter until tender. Add potatoes and broth; cover and cook on low heat until potatoes are tender. Cool slightly.
2. Puree potato mixture in a blender with 2 cups milk. Return to pan; add remaining 1 cup milk, cream, cheese, thyme, Worcestershire sauce and salmon; heat through. Season with salt and pepper. Garnish with parsley.
1 cup: 505 cal., 31g fat (17g sat. fat), 119mg chol., 737mg sod., 30g carb. (10g sugars, 2g fiber), 25g pro.

ANYTIME TURKEY CHILI

I created this dish to grab the voters' attention at a chili contest we held in our backyard. With pumpkin, brown sugar and cooked turkey, it's like an entire Thanksgiving dinner in one bowl.
—Brad Bailey, Cary, NC

Prep: 20 min. • **Cook:** 1¼ hours
Makes: 8 servings (2 qt.)

 ⅔ cup chopped sweet onion
 ½ cup chopped green pepper
1½ tsp. dried oregano
 1 tsp. ground cumin
 1 tsp. olive oil
 2 garlic cloves, minced
 1 can (16 oz.) kidney beans,
     rinsed and drained
 1 can (15½ oz.) great northern
     beans, rinsed and drained
 1 can (15 oz.) pumpkin
 1 can (15 oz.) crushed tomatoes
 1 can (14½ oz.) reduced-sodium
     chicken broth
 ½ cup water
 2 Tbsp. brown sugar
 2 Tbsp. chili powder
 ½ tsp. pepper
 3 cups cubed cooked turkey breast
     Shredded cheddar cheese,
     optional

1. In a large saucepan, saute the onion, green pepper, oregano and cumin in oil until vegetables are tender. Add garlic; cook 1 minute longer.
2. Stir in the beans, pumpkin, tomatoes, broth, water, brown sugar, chili powder and pepper; bring to a boil. Reduce heat; cover and simmer for 1 hour.
3. Add turkey; heat through. If desired, top with cheddar cheese.
1 cup: 241 cal., 2g fat (0 sat. fat), 45mg chol., 478mg sod., 32g carb. (7g sugars, 10g fiber), 25g pro. **Diabetic exchanges:** 3 lean meat, 1½ starch, 1 vegetable.

WALKING TACOS

These walking tacos are perfect for an on-the-go dinner, a campfire meal or an easy game-night supper. The ingredients go right into the chip bags!
—Beverly Matthews, Richland, WA

Prep: 10 min. • **Cook:** 30 min.
Makes: 5 servings

- 1 lb. ground beef
- 1 envelope reduced-sodium chili seasoning mix
- ¼ tsp. pepper
- 1 can (10 oz.) diced tomatoes and green chiles
- 1 can (15 oz.) Ranch Style beans (pinto beans in seasoned tomato sauce)
- 5 pkg. (1 oz. each) corn chips
  Toppings: Shredded cheddar cheese, sour cream and sliced green onions

1. In a large skillet, cook beef over medium heat until no longer pink, breaking into crumbles, 6-8 minutes; drain. Stir in the chili seasoning mix, pepper, tomatoes and beans; bring to a boil. Reduce heat; simmer, uncovered, until thickened, 20-25 minutes, stirring occasionally.
2. Just before serving, cut open the corn chip bags. Add beef mixture and toppings.
1 serving: 530 cal., 28g fat (6g sat. fat), 56mg chol., 1017mg sod., 44g carb. (5g sugars, 6g fiber), 24g pro.

BEEF BRISKET CHILI

My son and I concocted this beef brisket chili for a chili cook-off at his work. He proudly came home with a first-place ribbon!
—Marie Hattrup, Sonoma, CA

Prep: 30 min. • **Cook:** 3¼ hours
Makes: 10 servings (2½ qt.)

- 1 fresh beef brisket (2 lbs.), cut into ½-in. pieces
- 1 large onion, finely chopped
- 2 Tbsp. canola oil
- 2 cans (16 oz. each) kidney beans, rinsed and drained
- 1 lb. smoked kielbasa or Polish sausage, halved and sliced
- 1 jar (16 oz.) salsa
- 1 can (14½ oz.) diced tomatoes, undrained
- 1 can (8 oz.) tomato sauce
- 2 cans (4 oz. each) chopped green chiles
- 2 garlic cloves, minced
- 1 Tbsp. chili powder
- 1 Tbsp. ground cumin
- 1 tsp. celery salt
- ¼ tsp. salt
- ⅛ tsp. pepper
- 2 to 3 Tbsp. lemon juice
- 1½ tsp. grated lemon zest
  Optional: Shredded cheddar cheese and sliced green onions

1. In a Dutch oven, brown beef and onion in oil in batches; drain. Stir in the beans, kielbasa, salsa, tomatoes, tomato sauce, chiles, garlic and seasonings.
2. Bring to a boil. Reduce heat; cover and simmer for 3 hours or until meat is tender. Just before serving, stir in lemon juice and zest. If desired, top with cheddar cheese and sliced green onions.
Note: This is a fresh beef brisket, not corned beef.
1 cup: 404 cal., 19g fat (6g sat. fat), 69mg chol., 1309mg sod., 25g carb. (5g sugars, 6g fiber), 32g pro.

CARRIE'S CINCINNATI CHILI

Every time we had a gathering or company, folks would request this. My husband convinced me to enter it in a local chili contest, and I won third place! It's quick and easy. If I don't have fresh garlic, I use minced garlic from a jar.
—Carrie Birdsall, Dallas, GA

Prep: 20 min. • **Cook:** 6 hours
Makes: 6 servings (1½ qt.)

- 1½ lbs. ground beef
- 1 small onion, chopped
- 1 can (29 oz.) tomato puree
- 1 can (14½ oz.) whole tomatoes, crushed
- 2 Tbsp. brown sugar
- 4 tsp. chili powder
- 1 Tbsp. white vinegar
- 1 tsp. salt
- ¾ tsp. ground cinnamon
- ½ tsp. ground allspice
- ½ tsp. pepper
- 1 garlic clove, crushed
- 3 bay leaves
  Hot cooked spaghetti
  Optional: Shredded cheddar cheese and additional chopped onion

1. In a large skillet over medium heat, cook beef and onion until beef is no longer pink and onion is tender, 6-8 minutes, breaking meat into crumbles; drain. Transfer to a 3- or 4-qt. slow cooker. Add next 11 ingredients.

2. Cook, covered, on low 6-8 hours. Discard garlic clove and bay leaves. Serve over hot cooked spaghetti. If desired, top with shredded cheddar cheese and additional chopped onion.

Freeze option: Before adding toppings, cool chili. Freeze in freezer containers. To use, partially thaw in refrigerator overnight. Heat through in a saucepan, stirring occasionally; add water or broth if necessary. Serve as directed.

1 cup: 315 cal., 14g fat (5g sat. fat), 70mg chol., 644mg sod., 19g carb. (9g sugars, 4g fiber), 23g pro.

READER RAVE...

"I live in the Cincinnati area, and I love Cincinnati chili. But sometimes it's simply too spicy for me. This recipe provides all the taste and none of the stomach upset."
—PATRICIA, TASTEOFHOME.COM

BARBECUED TURKEY CHILI

The first time I made this, it won first prize at a chili cook-off. It takes just minutes to mix together, and the slow cooker does the rest. It's often requested by friends and family when we all get together.
—Melissa Webb, Ellsworth, SD

Prep: 5 min. • **Cook:** 4 hours
Makes: 6 servings

- 1 can (16 oz.) kidney beans, rinsed and drained
- 1 can (16 oz.) hot chili beans, undrained
- 1 can (15 oz.) turkey chili with beans
- 1 can (14½ oz.) diced tomatoes, undrained
- ⅓ cup barbecue sauce

In a 3-qt. slow cooker, combine all of the ingredients. Cover and cook on high for 4 hours or until heated through and flavors are blended.
1 cup: 215 cal., 2g fat (1g sat. fat), 10mg chol., 936mg sod., 36g carb. (7g sugars, 10g fiber), 14g pro.

BEEF TACO CHILI

This is one of my husband's absolute favorite dishes. It was voted best chili at our county's autumn harvest festival. If you like less broth, use just 1¾ cups water and 1½ tsp. bouillon.
—Dana Beery, Ione, WA

Prep: 25 min. • **Cook:** 7 hours
Makes: 6 servings (2¼ qt.)

- 1 **lb. ground beef**
- 1 **medium onion, chopped**
- 2½ **cups water**
- 2 **cans (15 oz. each) pinto beans, rinsed and drained**
- 1 **can (14½ oz.) diced tomatoes, undrained**
- 2 **cans (8 oz. each) tomato sauce**
- 2½ **tsp. beef bouillon granules**
- 2 **garlic cloves, minced**
- 1 **envelope taco seasoning**
- 2 **Tbsp. chili powder**
- 2 **tsp. dried oregano**
- 2 **tsp. baking cocoa**
- 1½ **tsp. ground cumin**
- 1 **tsp. Louisiana-style hot sauce**
- ½ **tsp. pepper**
  Optional: Sour cream, tortilla strips and sliced jalapenos

1. Cook beef and onion in a large skillet over medium heat until meat is no longer pink, 5-7 minutes, breaking beef into crumbles; drain. Transfer to a 4-qt. slow cooker. Stir in the next 13 ingredients.
2. Cover and cook on low for 7-9 hours or until heated through. Serve with toppings if desired.

1½ cups: 337 cal., 11g fat (3g sat. fat), 47mg chol., 1657mg sod., 39g carb. (7g sugars, 10g fiber), 23g pro.

CORN CHOWDER WITH POTATOES

I developed this soup out of two other recipes to create my own low-calorie marvel. It turned out so well that I entered it in my county fair and won a blue ribbon.
—Alyce Wyman, Pembina, ND

Prep: 15 min. • **Cook:** 30 min.
Makes: 6 servings (1½ qt.)

- 1 **small onion, chopped**
- 1 **garlic clove, minced**
- 1½ **cups cubed peeled potatoes**
- ¼ **cup shredded carrot**
- 2 **cups water**
- 2 **tsp. dried parsley flakes**
- 2 **tsp. reduced-sodium chicken bouillon granules**
- ¼ **tsp. salt**
- ⅛ **tsp. pepper**
- 1 **can (14¾ oz.) cream-style corn**
- 1½ **cups fat-free milk, divided**
- 3 **bacon strips, cooked and crumbled**
- 3 **Tbsp. all-purpose flour**
- ½ **cup cubed reduced-fat Velveeta**
- ½ **cup beer or nonalcoholic beer**
- ½ **tsp. liquid smoke, optional**

1. Place a large saucepan coated with cooking spray over medium heat. Add onion and garlic; cook and stir until tender. Add potatoes, carrot, water, parsley, bouillon, salt and pepper. Bring to a boil. Reduce heat; cook, covered, until potatoes are tender, 15-20 minutes.
2. Stir in corn, 1¼ cups milk and the bacon. In a small bowl, mix flour and remaining ¼ cup milk until smooth; stir into soup. Bring to a boil; cook and stir until thickened, about 2 minutes. Add cheese; stir until melted. Stir in beer and, if desired, liquid smoke; heat through.

1 cup: 179 cal., 3g fat (1g sat. fat), 9mg chol., 681mg sod., 31g carb. (8g sugars, 2g fiber), 8g pro.

STEAK & BEER CHILI

A cup of chili is always a pleasant way to warm up on a cold day. This one has a combination of budget-friendly chuck steak and brats in a spicy broth. I like to serve it with a dollop of sour cream.
—Elizabeth King, Duluth, MN

Prep: 20 min. • **Cook:** 40 min.
Makes: 10 servings (about 3½ qt.)

- 1 **boneless beef chuck steak (1 lb.), cubed**
- 2 **Tbsp. canola oil, divided**
- 1 **lb. uncooked bratwurst links, sliced**
- 1 **medium onion, chopped**
- 4 **garlic cloves, minced**
- 3 **cans (14½ oz. each) diced tomatoes with mild green chiles, undrained**
- 2 **cans (16 oz. each) hot chili beans, undrained**
- 1 **bottle (12 oz.) beer or 1½ cups beef broth**
- 1 **can (14¾ oz.) cream-style corn**
- 1 **can (8 oz.) pizza sauce**
- ½ **tsp. chili powder**
- ½ **tsp. ground cumin**
- ¼ **tsp. crushed red pepper flakes Sour cream, optional**

1. In a Dutch oven, brown steak in 1 Tbsp. oil. Remove and keep warm.
2. Add the bratwurst, onion and remaining oil to the pan; cook and stir over medium heat until the sausage is no longer pink. Add the garlic; cook 1 minute longer.
3. Return steak to the pan. Stir in tomatoes, beans, beer, corn, pizza sauce, chili powder, cumin and pepper flakes. Bring to a boil.
4. Reduce heat; simmer, uncovered, until heated through, 25-30 minutes. Serve with sour cream if desired.
1⅓ cups: 431 cal., 21g fat (7g sat. fat), 63mg chol., 1317mg sod., 39g carb. (12g sugars, 8g fiber), 23g pro.

THOMAS FELTS PHOTOGRAPHY

110

ROBIN KROGMAN · CLINTON, IOWA

53

ANNA WESTERMAN · SAUK CENTRE, MINNESOTA

1. NO ORDINARY PIG
Kansas kid Hanna Wecker was in 4-H for 10 years, and she showed pigs each of those years. Here she is with Fancy, who joined Hanna for 15 shows.

2. OFF TO A STRONG START
Our farm girl, Ciera, shows a steer at our county fair for the first time. Learning to show was new for her, but she rocked it out and won her class. Cheers to 4-H and FFA!

3. QUIET MOMENTS
Sometimes patience is exhausting! The dairy show at the Stearns County Fair was running a few hours behind, allowing the kids some time to rest before showing their animals.

P. 156

P. 145

P. 155

P. 142

PRIZE-WINNING ENTREES

HAM & SCALLOPED POTATOES

I fix this saucy skillet dish often, especially when I'm running late, because it's easy and it takes so little time to prepare. The recipe won first prize in our local paper some years back.
—Emma Magielda, Amsterdam, NY

Takes: 30 min. • **Makes:** 4 servings

- 4 medium potatoes, peeled and thinly sliced
- 2 Tbsp. butter
- ⅓ cup water
- ½ cup 2% milk
- 2 to 3 Tbsp. onion soup mix
- 3 Tbsp. minced fresh parsley
- 1 cup cubed Velveeta
- 1 cup cubed fully cooked ham

1. In a large skillet, cook potatoes in butter until lightly browned. Add water; bring to a boil. Reduce heat; cover and simmer 14-15 minutes or until tender.
2. Meanwhile in a small bowl, combine the milk, soup mix and parsley; stir in cheese. Pour over the potatoes. Add ham; cook and stir gently over medium heat until the cheese is melted and sauce is bubbly.

1 serving: 353 cal., 17g fat (10g sat. fat), 56mg chol., 1170mg sod., 36g carb. (6g sugars, 2g fiber), 16g pro.

READER RAVE...

"I was quite surprised at how fast this cooked up. Great for a busy weeknight and it was packed with lots of flavor.'
—ANGEL182009, TASTEOFHOME.COM

LAYERED PICNIC LOAVES

This big sandwich is inspired by one I fell in love with at a New York deli. It's easy to make ahead of time and cart to any party. Kids and adults alike say it's super.
—Marion Lowery, Medford, OR

Prep: 20 min. + chilling
Makes: 2 loaves (12 servings each)

- 2 unsliced loaves (1 lb. each) Italian bread
- ¼ cup olive oil
- 3 garlic cloves, minced
- 2 tsp. Italian seasoning, divided
- ½ lb. deli roast beef
- 12 slices part-skim mozzarella cheese (1 oz. each)
- 16 fresh basil leaves
- 3 medium tomatoes, thinly sliced
- ¼ lb. thinly sliced salami
- 1 jar (6½ oz.) marinated artichoke hearts, drained and sliced
- 1 pkg. (10 oz.) ready-to-serve salad greens
- 8 oz. thinly sliced deli chicken
- 1 medium onion, thinly sliced
- ¼ tsp. salt
- ⅛ tsp. pepper

1. Cut loaves in half horizontally; hollow out tops and bottoms, leaving ½-in. shells (discard removed bread or save for another use).
2. Combine oil and garlic; brush inside bread shells. Sprinkle with 1 tsp. Italian seasoning. Layer bottom of each loaf with a fourth of each of the roast beef, mozzarella, basil, tomatoes, salami, artichokes, salad greens, chicken and onion. Repeat the layers. Season with salt, pepper and the remaining 1 tsp. Italian seasoning.
3. Drizzle with remaining oil mixture if desired. Replace bread tops; wrap tightly and refrigerate at least 1 hour before slicing.

1 serving: 341 cal., 18g fat (7g sat. fat), 47mg chol., 991mg sod., 26g carb. (3g sugars, 2g fiber), 19g pro.

BEEFY EGGPLANT PARMIGIANA

I developed this recipe one summer when my husband grew eggplant in the garden. I was thrilled when the parmigiana won high honors at a national beef contest.
—Celeste Copper, Baton Rouge, LA

Prep: 50 + simmering
Bake: 35 min. + standing
Makes: 8 servings

- ⅓ cup chopped onion
- ¼ cup finely chopped celery
- ⅛ tsp. garlic powder
- 2 Tbsp. canola oil
- 1 can (14½ oz.) Italian stewed tomatoes
- ½ cup water
- ¼ cup tomato paste
- 1 tsp. dried parsley flakes
- ½ tsp. dried oregano
- 1¼ tsp. salt, divided
- ½ tsp. pepper, divided
- 1 bay leaf
- 1 lb. ground beef
- 1½ cups all-purpose flour
- 1 cup buttermilk
- 2 medium eggplants, peeled and cut into ½-in. slices
  Additional canola oil
- ½ cup grated Parmesan cheese
- 2 cups shredded part-skim mozzarella cheese, divided
  Minced fresh parsley

1. In a large saucepan, saute onion, celery and garlic powder in oil until tender. Stir in the tomatoes, water, tomato paste, parsley, oregano, ½ tsp. salt, ¼ tsp. pepper and bay leaf. Bring to a boil. Reduce heat; cover and simmer for 1 hour. Discard bay leaf.

2. In a large skillet, cook beef over medium heat until no longer pink, breaking it into crumbles; drain and set aside. In a shallow dish, combine flour and remaining ¾ tsp. salt and ¼ tsp. pepper. Place buttermilk in another shallow dish. Dip eggplant in the buttermilk, then in the flour mixture.

3. In a large skillet, cook eggplant in batches in ½ in. of hot oil until golden brown on each side; drain.

4. Place half the eggplant in a greased 13x9-in. baking dish. Top with half of each of the Parmesan cheese, beef and tomato mixture. Sprinkle with 1 cup mozzarella cheese. Top with the remaining eggplant, Parmesan cheese, beef and tomato mixture.

5. Bake, uncovered, at 350° for 30 minutes or until heated through. Sprinkle with the remaining 1 cup mozzarella cheese. Bake 5-10 minutes longer or until cheese is melted. Let stand for 10 minutes before serving. Sprinkle with parsley.

1 cup: 498 cal., 33g fat (8g sat. fat), 58mg chol., 841mg sod., 27g carb. (4g sugars, 2g fiber), 22g pro.

CARAMELIZED-ONION PORK

We live in a farming community, and one of our main crops is onion. When I competed in a cooking contest at the Idaho-Eastern Oregon Onion Festival, I was flabbergasted when I won the top three prizes. This was the first-place recipe.
—Nell Cruse, Ontario, OR

Prep: 30 min. • **Bake:** 40 min. + standing
Makes: 4 servings

- 1 **large sweet onion, thinly sliced**
- 1 **tsp. sugar**
- 2 **tsp. olive oil**
- 1 **pork tenderloin (1 lb.)**
- ¼ **tsp. salt**
- ⅛ **tsp. pepper**

1. In a large skillet, cook onion and sugar in oil over medium-low heat until the onion is tender and golden brown, about 30 minutes, stirring occasionally.
2. Preheat oven to 350°. Place the pork in a 13x9-in. baking dish coated with cooking spray. Sprinkle with salt and pepper. Top with the onion mixture.
3. Bake, uncovered, for 40-45 minutes or until a thermometer reads 160°. Let stand for 5 minutes before slicing.

3 oz. cooked pork: 191 cal., 6g fat (2g sat. fat), 74mg chol., 207mg sod., 8g carb. (0 sugars, 1g fiber), 25g pro. **Diabetic exchanges:** 3 lean meat, 1 vegetable.

BEST-EVER FRIED CHICKEN

Family reunions and neighborly gatherings will never be the same when you serve this crispy, juicy and perfectly seasoned chicken. I grew up on a farm and every year when it was time to bale hay, my dad would hire farm hands to help. The crew looked forward to it—they knew they'd be treated to my mom's fried chicken!
—Lola Clifton, Vinton, VA

Prep: 15 min. • **Cook:** 20 min.
Makes: 4 servings

1¾ **cups all-purpose flour**
  1 **Tbsp. dried thyme**
  1 **Tbsp. paprika**
  2 **tsp. salt**
  2 **tsp. garlic powder**
  1 **tsp. pepper**
  1 **large egg**
  ⅓ **cup 2% milk**
  2 **Tbsp. lemon juice**
  1 **broiler/fryer chicken (3 to 4 lbs.), cut up**
     Oil for deep-fat frying

1. In a shallow bowl, mix the first 6 ingredients. In a separate shallow bowl, whisk egg, milk and lemon juice until blended. Dip chicken in flour mixture to coat all sides; shake off excess. Dip in egg mixture, then again in flour mixture.
2. In an electric skillet or deep fryer, heat oil to 375°. Fry chicken, a few pieces at a time, 6-10 minutes on each side or until skin is golden brown and juices run clear. Drain on paper towels.

1 serving: 811 cal., 57g fat (9g sat. fat), 176mg chol., 725mg sod., 26g carb. (2g sugars, 2g fiber), 47g pro.

BLUE-RIBBON TIP

For great fried chicken, the most important factors are type of oil, oil temperature and cooking vessel. Use canola, vegetable or peanut oil and make sure it's heated properly (around 375°). Also, use an appropriate-sized pan, so the pieces are not overcrowded. If you don't have an electric skillet or deep-fat fryer, a deep-sided cast-iron skillet or Dutch oven does the trick, too.

CALGARY STAMPEDE RIBS

"More, please!" is what I hear whenever I serve these zippy, finger-licking ribs to family or guests. The first time my husband and I tried them, we pronounced them the best ever. The recipe has its roots in the Calgary Stampede, an annual Western and agricultural fair and exhibition in our province.
—Marian Misik, Sherwood Park, AB

Prep: 2¼ hours + marinating
Grill: 15 min. • **Makes:** 8 servings

- 4 **lbs. pork baby back ribs, cut into serving-size pieces**
- 3 **garlic cloves, minced**
- 1 **Tbsp. sugar**
- 2 **tsp. salt**
- 1 **Tbsp. paprika**
- 2 **tsp. ground cumin**
- 2 **tsp. chili powder**
- 2 **tsp. pepper**

BARBECUE SAUCE

- 2 **Tbsp. butter**
- 1 **small onion, finely chopped**
- 1 **cup ketchup**
- ¼ **cup packed brown sugar**
- 3 **Tbsp. lemon juice**
- 3 **Tbsp. Worcestershire sauce**
- 2 **Tbsp. cider vinegar**
- 1½ **tsp. ground mustard**
- 1 **tsp. celery seed**
- ⅛ **tsp. cayenne pepper**

1. Preheat oven to 325°. Rub ribs with garlic; place in a roasting pan. Bake, covered, until tender, about 2 hours.

2. Mix sugar, salt and seasonings; sprinkle over ribs. Remove from pan; cool slightly. Refrigerate, covered, 8 hours or overnight.

3. In a small saucepan, heat butter over medium heat; saute onion until tender. Stir in the remaining ingredients; bring to a boil. Reduce heat; cook, uncovered, until thickened, about 10 minutes, stirring frequently.

4. Brush ribs with some of the sauce. Grill, covered, over medium heat until heated through, 12-15 minutes, turning and brushing occasionally with additional sauce. Serve with the remaining sauce.

1 serving: 394 cal., 24g fat (9g sat. fat), 89mg chol., 1170mg sod., 21g carb. (18g sugars, 1g fiber), 23g pro.

LOBSTER ROLLS

Mayonnaise infused with dill and lemon lends refreshing flavor to these super sandwiches. Try pan-toasting the buns in butter for something special.
—*Taste of Home* Test Kitchen

Takes: 30 min. • **Makes:** 8 sandwiches

1	**cup chopped celery**
⅓	**cup mayonnaise**
2	**Tbsp. lemon juice**
½	**tsp. dill weed**
5	**cups cubed cooked lobster meat (about 4 small lobsters)**
8	**hoagie rolls, split and toasted**

In a large bowl, combine the celery, mayonnaise, lemon juice and dill weed. Gently stir in lobster. Serve on rolls.

1 sandwich: 354 cal., 12g fat (2g sat. fat), 133mg chol., 887mg sod., 36g carb. (5g sugars, 1g fiber), 25g pro.

RUSTIC TOMATO PIE

Perk up your plate with this humble tomato pie. We like to use fresh-from-the-garden tomatoes and herbs, but store-bought produce will work in a pinch.
—*Taste of Home* Test Kitchen

Prep: 15 min. • **Bake:** 30 min. + standing
Makes: 8 servings

      Dough for single-crust pie
1¾ **lbs. mixed tomatoes, seeded and cut into ½-in. slices**
¼ **cup thinly sliced green onions**
½ **cup mayonnaise**
½ **cup shredded cheddar cheese**
2 **Tbsp. minced fresh basil**
¼ **tsp. salt**
¼ **tsp. pepper**
2 **bacon strips, cooked and crumbled**
2 **Tbsp. grated Parmesan cheese**

1. Preheat oven to 400°. On a lightly floured surface, roll dough to a ⅛-in.-thick circle; transfer to a 9-in. pie plate. Trim crust to ½ in. beyond rim of plate.

2. Place half the tomatoes and half the onions in crust. Combine mayonnaise, cheddar cheese, basil, salt and pepper; spread over tomatoes. Top with the remaining onions and tomatoes. Fold crust edge over filling, pleating as you go and leaving an 8-in. opening in the center. Sprinkle with bacon and Parmesan cheese.

3. Bake on a lower oven rack until until the crust is golden and the filling is bubbly, 30-35 minutes. Let stand 10 minutes before cutting. If desired, sprinkle with additional basil.

1 piece: 325 cal., 25g fat (11g sat. fat), 41mg chol., 409mg sod., 19g carb. (3g sugars, 2g fiber), 6g pro.

Dough for single-crust pie: Combine 1¼ cups all-purpose flour and ¼ tsp. salt; cut in ½ cup cold butter until crumbly. Gradually add 3-5 Tbsp. ice water, tossing with a fork until dough holds together when pressed. Shape into a disk; wrap and refrigerate 1 hour.

ITALIAN SAUSAGE HOAGIES

In southeastern Wisconsin, our cuisine is influenced by both Germans and Italians who immigrated to this area. When preparing this recipe, we'll often substitute German bratwurst for the Italian sausage, so we blend the two influences with delicious results.
—Craig Wachs, Racine, WI

Prep: 15 min. • **Cook:** 4 hours
Makes: 10 servings

- 10 **Italian sausage links**
- 2 **Tbsp. olive oil**
- 1 **jar (24 oz.) meatless spaghetti sauce**
- ½ **medium green pepper, julienned**
- ½ **medium sweet red pepper, julienned**
- ½ **cup water**
- ¼ **cup grated Romano cheese**
- 2 **Tbsp. dried oregano**
- 2 **Tbsp. dried basil**
- 2 **loaves French bread (20 in.)**

1. In a large skillet over medium-high heat, brown sausage in oil; drain. Transfer to a 5-qt. slow cooker. Add the spaghetti sauce, peppers, water, cheese, oregano and basil. Cover and cook on low for 4 hours or until sausage is no longer pink.

2. Slice each French bread loaf lengthwise but not all the way through; cut each loaf widthwise into 5 pieces. Fill each with a sausage link, peppers and sauce.

1 sandwich: 509 cal., 21g fat (7g sat. fat), 48mg chol., 1451mg sod., 56g carb. (7g sugars, 5g fiber), 22g pro.

PEPPERY HERBED TURKEY TENDERLOIN

I won the North Carolina Turkey Cook-Off with these full-flavored tenderloins in rich sauce. Marinating the turkey in wine, garlic, rosemary and thyme gives it a fantastic taste.
—Virginia C. Anthony, Jacksonville, FL

Prep: 10 min. + marinating
Cook: 15 min. • **Makes:** 6 servings

- 2 **lbs. turkey breast tenderloins**
- 1 **cup dry white wine or apple juice**
- 3 **green onions, chopped**
- 3 **Tbsp. minced fresh parsley**
- 6 **tsp. olive oil, divided**
- 1 **Tbsp. finely chopped garlic**
- ¾ **tsp. dried rosemary, crushed**
- ¾ **tsp. dried thyme**
- 1 **tsp. coarsely ground pepper**
- ¾ **tsp. salt, divided**
- 4 **tsp. cornstarch**
- 1 **cup reduced-sodium chicken broth**

1. Pat tenderloins dry; flatten to ¾-in. thickness. In a small bowl, combine the wine or juice, onions, parsley, 4 tsp. oil, garlic, rosemary and thyme. Pour ¾ cup marinade into a large shallow dish; add turkey and turn to coat. Cover and refrigerate for at least 4 hours, turning occasionally. Cover and refrigerate the remaining marinade.

2. Drain turkey, discarding marinade left in dish. Sprinkle turkey with pepper and ½ tsp. salt. In a large nonstick skillet, cook turkey in remaining 2 tsp. oil for 5-6 minutes on each side or until a thermometer reads 165°. Remove and keep warm.

3. In a small bowl, combine cornstarch, broth, the reserved marinade and remaining ¼ tsp. salt until smooth; pour into skillet. Bring to a boil; cook and stir for 1-2 minutes or until thickened. Slice turkey; serve with sauce.

5 oz. cooked turkey with 2 Tbsp. sauce: 203 cal., 4g fat (0 sat. fat), 60mg chol., 479mg sod., 3g carb. (0 sugars, 0 fiber), 38g pro. **Diabetic exchanges:** 5 lean meat.

BARBECUED SHRIMP & PEACH KABOBS

Shrimp grilled with peaches and green onions really sets off fireworks! These won me a ribbon at the county fair.
—Jen Smallwood, Portsmouth, VA

Prep: 25 min. • **Grill:** 10 min.
Makes: 4 servings

- 1 Tbsp. packed brown sugar
- 1 tsp. paprika
- ½ to 1 tsp. ground ancho chile pepper
- ½ tsp. ground cumin
- ¼ tsp. salt
- ¼ tsp. freshly ground pepper
- ⅛ to ¼ tsp. cayenne pepper
- 1 lb. uncooked shrimp (16-20 per lb.), peeled and deveined
- 3 medium peaches, each cut into 8 wedges
- 8 green onions (light green and white portion only), cut into 2-in. pieces
  Olive oil-flavored cooking spray
  Lime wedges

1. Mix brown sugar and seasonings. Place shrimp, peaches and green onions in a large bowl; sprinkle with brown sugar mixture and toss to coat. On 4 or 8 metal or soaked wooden skewers, alternately thread shrimp, peaches and green onions.

2. Lightly spritz both sides of kabobs with cooking spray. Grill, covered, over medium heat or broil 4 in. from heat 3-4 minutes on each side or until the shrimp turn pink. Squeeze lime wedges over kabobs.

1 kabob: 170 cal., 2g fat (0 sat. fat), 138mg chol., 289mg sod., 18g carb. (13g sugars, 3g fiber), 20g pro. **Diabetic exchanges:** 3 lean meat, 1 fruit.

HORSERADISH-CRUSTED TURKEY TENDERLOINS

Looking for a low-carb entree ideal for company? Consider this specialty. It won a local recipe contest and was featured on a restaurant's menu. The creamy sauce adds a flavor punch.
—Ellen Cross, Hubbardsville, NY

Prep: 20 min. • **Bake:** 15 min.
Makes: 4 servings

- 2 Tbsp. reduced-fat mayonnaise
- 2 Tbsp. prepared horseradish
- ½ cup soft bread crumbs
- 1 green onion, chopped
- 2 Tbsp. minced fresh parsley
- 1 lb. turkey breast tenderloins

SAUCE
- ¼ cup reduced-fat mayonnaise
- ¼ cup fat-free plain yogurt
- 2 Tbsp. fat-free milk
- 1 Tbsp. prepared horseradish
- 1 Tbsp. Dijon mustard
- ¼ tsp. paprika

1. Preheat oven to 425°. Mix the mayonnaise and horseradish. In a shallow bowl, toss bread crumbs with green onion and parsley. Spread tenderloins with the mayonnaise mixture, then dip in crumb mixture to coat. Place in a greased 15x10x1-in. pan.

2. Bake until a thermometer reads 165°, 12-15 minutes. Let stand for 5 minutes before slicing.

3. Mix the sauce ingredients. Serve with turkey.

Note: To make soft bread crumbs, tear bread into pieces and place in a food processor or blender. Cover and pulse until crumbs form. One slice of bread yields ½ to ¾ cup crumbs.

1 serving: 230 cal., 9g fat (1g sat. fat), 53mg chol., 386mg sod., 8g carb. (3g sugars, 1g fiber), 30g pro. **Diabetic exchanges:** ½ starch, 3 lean meat, 2 fat.

CHICKEN MARSALA BOW TIES

Back in 2008, I won first place in a state fair cooking contest with this recipe. I absolutely love mushrooms, and this dish is full of them! You can substitute Italian dressing mix for the ranch with equally delicious results.
—Regina Farris, Mesquite, TX

Prep: 20 min. • **Cook:** 25 min.
Makes: 8 servings

- 2 cups uncooked bow tie pasta
- ⅓ cup all-purpose flour
- ½ tsp. salt
- ½ tsp. garlic powder
- ½ tsp. dried thyme
- 1¾ lbs. boneless skinless chicken breasts, cut into ½-in. cubes
- 3 Tbsp. olive oil
- 6 Tbsp. butter, cubed
- ½ lb. sliced baby portobello mushrooms
- 3 shallots, finely chopped
- ½ cup Marsala wine or chicken broth
- 1 can (10¾ oz.) condensed golden mushroom soup, undiluted
- 1 pkg. (3 oz.) cream cheese, cubed
- ½ cup heavy whipping cream
- 1 envelope ranch salad dressing mix
- ⅓ cup grated Parmesan cheese
  Minced fresh parsley, optional

1. Cook pasta according to the package directions. Meanwhile, combine flour and seasonings in a shallow dish. Add chicken, a few pieces at a time, tossing to coat.

2. In a Dutch oven, heat oil over medium heat. Add chicken in batches; cook and stir until no longer pink, 5-7 minutes. Remove from pot; set aside.

3. Add butter to same pot; heat over medium-high heat. Add mushrooms and shallots; cook and stir until tender, 2-3 minutes. Stir in wine; bring to a boil. Cook until liquid is reduced by half. Stir in soup, cream cheese, cream and dressing mix; stir until cream cheese is melted.

4. Drain pasta. Add pasta and chicken to the mushroom mixture; heat through, tossing to coat. Sprinkle with Parmesan cheese and, if desired, parsley.

1 cup: 468 cal., 28g fat (13g sat. fat), 108mg chol., 870mg sod., 28g carb. (3g sugars, 2g fiber), 27g pro.

INDIANA SWISS STEAK

I won first place in the Indiana State Beef Contest with this recipe. A mixture of picante sauce, ketchup, cider vinegar and veggies enhances tender slow-simmered steak. I like to serve it with bow tie pasta.
—Ann Dixon, North Vernon, IN

Prep: 20 min. • **Cook:** 1¼ hours
Makes: 6 servings

- ¼ cup all-purpose flour
- 1 tsp. salt
- ½ tsp. pepper
- 1½ lbs. boneless beef top round steak, cut into serving-size pieces
- 1 Tbsp. canola oil
- 1 medium onion, chopped
- ¾ cup grated carrot
- ¾ cup water
- ½ cup chopped celery
- ½ cup chopped green pepper
- ½ cup ketchup
- ¼ cup picante sauce
- 1 Tbsp. cider vinegar
  Hot cooked pasta

1. In a large container with a tight-fitting lid, combine the flour, salt and pepper. Add beef, a few pieces at a time, and shake to coat. In a large skillet, brown beef in oil.

2. Combine the onion, carrot, water, celery, green pepper, ketchup, picante sauce and vinegar; pour over beef. Bring to a boil. Reduce heat; cover and simmer for 60-75 minutes or until beef is tender. Serve with pasta.

1 serving: 222 cal., 6g fat (1g saturated fat), 63mg chol., 771mg sod., 14g carb. (8g sugars, 1g fiber), 26g pro. **Diabetic Exchanges:** 3 lean meat, 1 starch, ½ fat.

SLOW-COOKED REUBEN BRATS

Sauerkraut gives these beer-simmered brats a flavor boost, but the chili sauce and melted cheese put them over the top. Top your favorite burger with some of the chili sauce; you won't be sorry.
—Alana Simmons, Johnstown, PA

Prep: 30 min. • **Cook:** 7¼ hours
Makes: 10 servings

- 10 uncooked bratwurst links
- 3 bottles (12 oz. each) light beer or nonalcoholic beer
- 1 large sweet onion, sliced
- 1 can (14 oz.) sauerkraut, rinsed and well-drained
- ¾ cup mayonnaise
- ¼ cup chili sauce
- 2 Tbsp. ketchup
- 1 Tbsp. finely chopped onion
- 2 tsp. sweet pickle relish
- 1 garlic clove, minced
- ⅛ tsp. pepper
- 10 hoagie buns, split
- 10 slices Swiss cheese

1. In a large skillet, brown bratwurst in batches; drain. In a 5-qt. slow cooker, combine the beer, sliced onion and sauerkraut; add bratwurst. Cook, covered, on low 7-9 hours or until the sausages are cooked through.
2. Preheat oven to 350°. In a small bowl, mix mayonnaise, chili sauce, ketchup, chopped onion, relish, garlic and pepper until blended. Spread over cut sides of buns; top with cheese, bratwurst and sauerkraut mixture. Place on an ungreased baking sheet. Bake for 8-10 minutes or until cheese is melted.
1 sandwich: 733 cal., 50g fat (16g sat. fat), 94mg chol., 1643mg sod., 45g carb. (10g sugars, 2g fiber), 26g pro.

ITALIAN BEEF ON ROLLS

This is one of my all-time favorite slow cooker recipes! With 29 grams of protein per serving, it's a great way to meet your daily needs!
—Jami Hilker, Harrison, AR

Prep: 15 min. • **Cook:** 8 hours
Makes: 8 servings

- 1 beef sirloin tip roast (2 lbs.)
- 1 can (14½ oz.) diced tomatoes, undrained
- 1 medium green pepper, chopped
- ½ cup water
- 1 Tbsp. sesame seeds
- 1½ tsp. garlic powder
- 1 tsp. fennel seed, crushed
- ½ tsp. salt
- ½ tsp. pepper
- 8 kaiser rolls, split

1. Place the roast in a 3-qt. slow cooker. In a small bowl, combine tomatoes, green pepper, water and seasonings; pour over roast. Cover and cook on low for 8-9 hours or until meat is tender.
2. Remove roast; cool slightly. Skim fat from cooking juices; shred beef and return to the slow cooker. Serve on rolls.
1 sandwich: 333 cal., 8g fat (2g sat. fat), 72mg chol., 573mg sod., 34g carb. (3g sugars, 3g fiber), 29g pro. **Diabetic exchanges:** 2 starch, 3 lean meat.
Stovetop Italian Beef on Rolls: Place the roast in a Dutch oven. Pour tomato mixture over the top. Bring to a boil. Reduce heat; cover and simmer for 1½ to 2 hours or until meat is very tender. Proceed as directed.
Spicy Italian Beef: Add 1 chopped jalapeno pepper or ½ tsp. crushed red pepper along with the other seasoning to the slow cooker.

BLUE-RIBBON BEEF NACHOS

Chili powder and sassy salsa season a zesty mixture of ground beef and refried beans sprinkled with green onions, tomatoes and ripe olives.
—Diane Hixon, Niceville, FL

Takes: 20 min. • **Makes:** 6 servings

- 1 lb. ground beef
- 1 small onion, chopped
- 1 can (16 oz.) refried beans
- 1 jar (16 oz.) salsa
- 1 can (6 oz.) pitted ripe olives, chopped
- ½ cup shredded cheddar cheese
- 1 green onion, chopped
- 2 Tbsp. chili powder
- 1 tsp. salt
  Tortilla chips
  Optional: Sliced ripe olives, chopped green onions and diced tomatoes

In a large skillet, cook the beef and onion over medium heat until meat is no longer pink; crumble the beef; drain. Stir in next 7 ingredients; heat through. Serve over tortilla chips. Top with olives, onions and tomatoes if desired.

1 serving: 294 cal., 14g fat (6g sat. fat), 53mg chol., 1353mg sod., 19g carb. (5g sugars, 9g fiber), 20g pro.

BLUE-RIBBON TIP

You can prevent soggy nachos by adding heavy, wet toppings, like salsa or sour cream, right before you're ready to eat. Or you can serve them on the side. Using real cheese instead of processed, liquid cheese also prevents mushy chips.

GRILLED PORK TACOS

My family raves about this moist pork with smoked paprika and pineapple. I dish it up next to brown rice and a salad of avocado and tomatoes.
—E. Gelesky, Bala Cynwyd, PA

Takes: 30 min. • **Makes:** 4 servings

- 1 lb. boneless pork ribeye chops, cut into ¾-in. cubes
- 2 Tbsp. plus 2 tsp. lime juice, divided
- 1 tsp. smoked or regular paprika
- ½ tsp. salt
- ¼ tsp. pepper
- ¾ cup canned black beans, rinsed and drained
- ½ cup canned unsweetened pineapple tidbits plus 1 Tbsp. reserved juice
- 2 Tbsp. finely chopped red onion
- 2 Tbsp. chopped fresh cilantro
- 4 flour tortillas (6 to 8 in.), warmed
  Optional: Reduced-fat sour cream or plain yogurt

1. In a large bowl, toss pork with 2 Tbsp. lime juice and the seasonings; let stand 5 minutes. Meanwhile, in a small bowl, mix beans, pineapple with reserved pineapple juice, onion, cilantro and remaining 2 tsp. lime juice.

2. Thread pork onto 4 metal or soaked wooden skewers. Grill kabobs, covered, on a lightly oiled rack over medium heat for 6-8 minutes or until meat is tender, turning occasionally.

3. Remove pork from skewers; serve in tortillas. Top with bean mixture and, if desired, sour cream.

1 taco with ¼ cup salsa: 383 cal., 16g fat (6g sat. fat), 66mg chol., 636mg sod., 31g carb. (6g sugars, 4g fiber), 27g pro. **Diabetic exchanges:** 3 starch, 3 medium-fat meat.

SLOPPY JOE MEATBALL SUBS

A mashup of two favorite recipes, these meatball subs are unique because of the sloppy joe-flavored sauce. I love to make them on a lazy afternoon and freeze the leftovers for an easy weeknight meal.
—Susan Seymour, Valatie, NY

Prep: 1 hour • **Bake:** 20 min./batch
Makes: 12 servings

- 2 large eggs, lightly beaten
- ¼ cup canola oil, divided
- 2 medium onions, finely chopped, divided
- ½ cup dry bread crumbs
- 1 tsp. dried oregano
- 2 lbs. ground beef
- 1 medium green pepper, chopped
- 2 cans (15 oz. each) tomato sauce
- ¼ cup packed brown sugar
- 2 Tbsp. prepared mustard
- 2½ tsp. chili powder
- ¾ tsp. salt
- ¾ tsp. garlic powder
- ½ tsp. pepper
  Dash Louisiana-style hot sauce

ADDITIONAL INGREDIENTS (PER SERVING)
- 1 hoagie bun, split and toasted
- 2 Tbsp. shredded cheddar cheese

1. Preheat oven to 400°. In a large bowl, combine the eggs, 2 Tbsp. oil, ½ cup onion, bread crumbs and oregano. Crumble beef over mixture and mix lightly but thoroughly. With wet hands, shape into 1½-in. balls.
2. Place meatballs on greased racks in shallow baking pans. Bake, uncovered, until no longer pink, 20-25 minutes.
3. Meanwhile, in a Dutch oven, saute green pepper and remaining onion in remaining 2 Tbsp. oil until tender. Stir in the tomato sauce, brown sugar, mustard, chili powder, salt, garlic powder, pepper and hot sauce. Bring to a boil. Reduce heat; simmer, uncovered, for 5 minutes. Drain meatballs on paper towels; add to sauce and stir to coat.
4. For each sandwich, place 4 meatballs on a bun and sprinkle with cheese.

Freeze option: Cool meatballs; transfer to freezer containers. Cover and freeze for up to 3 months. To use, thaw in the refrigerator. Place in an ungreased shallow microwave-safe dish. Cover and microwave on high until heated through. Prepare sandwiches as directed above.

1 sandwich: 649 cal., 31g fat (10g sat. fat), 138mg chol., 1369mg sod., 58g carb. (17g sugars, 4g fiber), 36g pro. **Diabetic exchanges:** 1 lean meat.

PITAWURST

Every August, our town hosts a Bratwurst Festival. To celebrate the sausage season, we stuff brats and sauerkraut inside pita bread.
—Brooke Young, Bucyrus, OH

....

Takes: 30 min. • **Makes:** 4 servings

- 1 pkg. (19 oz.) uncooked bratwurst links, casings removed
- 1 medium onion, chopped
- 1 small green pepper, chopped
- 1 can (14 oz.) sauerkraut, rinsed and well drained
- ½ cup sour cream
- 2 Tbsp. stone-ground mustard
- 8 pita pocket halves, warmed

1. In a large cast-iron or other heavy skillet, cook the bratwurst, onion and pepper over medium heat until the bratwurst is no longer pink and vegetables are tender, 8-10 minutes, breaking up bratwurst into crumbles; drain. Stir in sauerkraut; heat through.
2. For sauce, in a small bowl, mix sour cream and mustard. Fill pita halves with bratwurst mixture; serve with sauce.
2 filled pita halves with about 1 Tbsp. sauce: 706 cal., 46g fat (17g sat. fat), 120mg chol., 2260mg sod., 45g carb. (6g sugars, 5g fiber), 26g pro.

HORSERADISH POT ROAST

We tasted a dish similar to this at a horseradish festival in Illinois. I like to serve it over noodles. The recipe is easily adaptable for stovetop cooking.
—Barbara White, Katy, TX

Prep: 10 min. • **Cook:** 8¼ hours
Makes: 6 servings

- 1 boneless beef chuck roast (2 to 3 lbs.)
- ½ tsp. salt
- ½ tsp. pepper
- 2 medium onions, thinly sliced into rings
- 1 jar (6 to 6½ oz.) prepared horseradish
- ¼ cup dry white wine or beef broth
- 1 Tbsp. butter, melted
- 1 garlic clove, minced
- 1 Tbsp. sugar
- 2 Tbsp. all-purpose flour
- 2 Tbsp. cold water
  Hot cooked egg noodles
  Minced fresh thyme, optional

1. Place roast in a 6-qt. slow cooker; sprinkle with salt and pepper. Top roast with onions. In a small bowl, combine the next 5 ingredients; pour over roast and onions. Cook, covered, on low until the meat is tender, 7-8 hours.
2. Remove roast; cool slightly and shred with 2 forks. Skim fat from the cooking juices. Mix flour and water until smooth; gradually stir into juices.
3. Return beef to the slow cooker. Cook, covered, on high 15-30 minutes or until sauce is thickened. Serve with noodles. If desired, top with minced thyme.
1 serving: 320 cal., 17g fat (7g sat. fat), 103mg chol., 395mg sod., 11g carb. (6g sugars, 2g fiber), 31g pro.

REUBEN PUFF PASTRY STROMBOLI

I love this quick-to-fix, layered Reuben Stromboli. I used another sandwich recipe as a guide but made it with Reuben fixings. Switch things up by using sliced turkey and coleslaw instead of corned beef and sauerkraut.
—Joan Hallford, N. Richland Hills, TX

Prep: 25 min. • **Bake:** 40 min. + standing
Makes: 6 servings

- 1 sheet frozen puff pastry, thawed
- ⅔ cup Thousand Island salad dressing, divided
- 3 Tbsp. dill pickle relish
- ½ lb. thinly sliced deli corned beef
- ½ lb. thinly sliced deli pastrami
- 4 Tbsp. spicy brown mustard
- 8 slices Swiss or fontina cheese
- 1½ cups sauerkraut, rinsed and well drained
- 1 large egg white, lightly beaten
- 2 tsp. caraway seeds or sesame seeds

1. Preheat oven to 400°. On a lightly floured surface, unfold puff pastry. Roll into a 14x11-in. rectangle. Spread ⅓ cup dressing to within ½ in. of edges. Sprinkle with relish. Layer with corned beef, pastrami, mustard, cheese and sauerkraut. Roll up jelly-roll style, starting with a long side.
2. Place roll on a parchment-lined baking sheet, seam side down; tuck ends under and press to seal. Brush with egg white and sprinkle with caraway seeds; cut small slits in top.
3. Bake until golden brown and pastry is cooked through, 40-45 minutes. Let stand 10 minutes before slicing. Serve with remaining dressing.
1 piece: 491 cal., 32g fat (10g sat. fat), 50mg chol., 1566mg sod., 32g carb. (4g sugars, 4g fiber), 18g pro.

BARBECUED BURGERS

I can't take all the credit for these burgers. My husband's uncle passed down the special barbecue sauce recipe. We love it on everything... it was only natural to try it on, and in, burgers.

—Rhoda Troyer, Glenford, OH

Prep: 25 min. • **Grill:** 15 min.
Makes: 6 servings

SAUCE

- 1 **cup ketchup**
- ½ **cup packed brown sugar**
- ⅓ **cup sugar**
- ¼ **cup honey**
- ¼ **cup molasses**
- 2 **tsp. prepared mustard**
- 1½ **tsp. Worcestershire sauce**
- ¼ **tsp. salt**
- ¼ **tsp. liquid smoke**
- ⅛ **tsp. pepper**

BURGERS

- 1 **large egg, lightly beaten**
- ⅓ **cup quick-cooking oats**
- ¼ **tsp. onion salt**
- ¼ **tsp. garlic salt**
- ¼ **tsp. pepper**
- ⅛ **tsp. salt**
- 1½ **lbs. ground beef**
- 6 **hamburger buns, split**
  Toppings of your choice

1. In a small saucepan, combine the first 10 ingredients. Bring to a boil. Remove from the heat. Set aside 1 cup barbecue sauce to serve with burgers.

2. In a large bowl, combine the egg, oats, ¼ cup of the remaining barbecue sauce, the onion salt, garlic salt, pepper and salt. Crumble beef over the egg mixture and mix well. Shape into 6 patties.

3. Grill, covered, over medium heat until a thermometer reads 160°, 6-8 minutes on each side, basting with ½ cup barbecue sauce during the last 5 minutes. Serve on buns with the toppings of your choice and reserved barbecue sauce.

1 burger: 626 cal., 19g fat (7g sat. fat), 121mg chol., 1146mg sod., 86g carb. (56g sugars, 2g fiber), 30g pro.

MY BEST-EVER JAMBALAYA

I tried to mimic jambalaya from my favorite restaurant and it turned out so well that my daughter and husband now prefer my recipe.

—Alexis Van Vulpen, St. Albert, AB

Prep: 20 min. • **Cook:** 40 min.
Makes: 10 servingsa

- 2 Tbsp. canola oil
- ½ lb. fully cooked Spanish chorizo links, sliced
- 2 cups cubed fully cooked ham
- ¾ lb. boneless skinless chicken breasts, cubed
- 1 can (28 oz.) diced tomatoes, undrained
- 3 cups chicken broth
- 2 large green peppers, chopped
- 1 large onion, chopped
- 1 Tbsp. Cajun seasoning
- 2 tsp. hot pepper sauce
- 3 cups instant brown rice
- ½ lb. uncooked medium shrimp, peeled and deveined

1. In a Dutch oven, heat oil over medium-high heat. Add chorizo and ham; cook and stir 3-4 minutes or until browned.
2. Add chicken to pan; cook 5-7 minutes or until no longer pink. Stir in tomatoes, broth, peppers, onion, Cajun seasoning and pepper sauce. Bring to a boil. Reduce heat; simmer, uncovered, for 8-10 minutes or until the peppers are crisp-tender.
3. Return to a boil; stir in the rice and shrimp. Reduce heat; simmer, covered, 7-9 minutes or until shrimp turn pink. Remove from heat; let stand, covered, 5 minutes or until rice is tender.

1⅓ cups: 323 cal., 12g fat (3g sat. fat), 79mg chol., 1124mg sod., 31g carb. (5g sugars, 3g fiber), 24g pro.

READER RAVE...

"Hands down, awesome recipe! Huge hit with my husband and stepsons. Might double the cajun seasoning and hot pepper sauce for more heat. Will make again and again! Thanks for the recipe!."

—MARIANNS, TASTEOFHOME.COM

SLOPPY JOE TATER TOT CASSEROLE

This simple casserole is an easy dinner for both you and the kids. Serve with carrot and celery sticks for a fuss-free feast. You can also stir in some spicy brown mustard if the adults want more zing.
—Laura Wilhelm, West Hollywood, CA

Prep: 20 min. • **Cook:** 4 hours + standing
Makes: 10 servings

- 1 **bag (32 oz.) frozen Tater Tots, divided**
- 2 **lbs. ground beef or turkey**
- 1 **can (15 oz.) tomato sauce**
- 1 **bottle (8 oz.) sweet chili sauce**
- 2 **Tbsp. packed brown sugar**
- 1 **Tbsp. Worcestershire sauce**
- 1 **Tbsp. dried minced garlic**
- 1 **Tbsp. dried minced onion**
- ½ **tsp. salt**
- ½ **tsp. pepper**
- 1¼ **cups shredded Colby-Monterey Jack cheese**
- ¼ **tsp. paprika**

1. Place half the Tater Tots in bottom of 5-qt. slow cooker. In a large skillet, cook beef over medium-high heat until no longer pink, 5-6 minutes, breaking into crumbles. Drain. Stir in the next 8 ingredients; reduce heat and simmer 2-3 minutes.
2. Place beef mixture in slow cooker; top with the remaining Tater Tots. Cook, covered, on low 4 hours. Top with cheese. Sprinkle with paprika. Let stand, uncovered, 15 minutes before serving.
1 cup: 466 cal., 24g fat (9g sat. fat), 69mg chol., 1332mg sod., 41g carb. (18g sugars, 4g fiber), 22g pro.

BUTTERY HERB ROASTED CHICKEN

Roasting chicken is always such a comforting thing, especially when you can pick the herbs right from your garden and pair them with some fresh citrus to smear across the bird! My family can't get enough of this herb-roasted chicken dish.
—Jenn Tidwell, Fair Oaks, CA

Prep: 15 min. • **Bake:** 1½ hours + standing
Makes: 6 servings

- 1 **roasting chicken (5 to 6 lbs.)**
- ½ **cup unsalted butter, softened, divided**
- 1 **cup chicken broth**
- ¾ **cup orange juice**
- ½ **cup white wine or additional chicken broth**
- 2 **garlic cloves, minced**
- 1 **tsp. salt**
- ½ **tsp. pepper**
- 2 **fresh rosemary sprigs**
- 2 **fresh thyme sprigs**
- 2 **fresh sage sprigs**

1. Preheat oven to 350°. With fingers, carefully loosen skin from chicken; rub ¼ cup butter under skin. Secure skin to underside of breast with toothpicks. Place chicken on a rack in a shallow roasting pan, breast side up. Tuck wings under chicken; tie drumsticks together. Pour broth around chicken.
2. Melt remaining ¼ cup butter; brush over chicken. Drizzle with orange juice and wine. Combine garlic, salt and pepper; rub over skin. Place rosemary, thyme and sage in roasting pan.
3. Roast until thermometer inserted in thickest part of thigh reads 170°-175°, 1½ to 2 hours (Cover loosely with foil if chicken browns too quickly.) Remove chicken from oven; tent with foil. Let stand for 15 minutes before carving; remove toothpicks. If desired, skim off fat and thicken pan drippings for gravy. Serve with chicken.
6 oz. cooked chicken: 599 cal., 42g fat (17g sat. fat), 191mg chol., 703mg sod., 4g carb. (3g sugars, 0 fiber), 48g pro.

SLOPPY JOE DOGS

There are so many different ways to top a hot dog, but this tasty sloppy joe version beats them all!
—Kimberly Wallace, Dennison, OH

Prep: 20 min. • **Cook:** 15 min.
Makes: 16 servings

SLOPPY JOE TOPPING

- 2 lbs. ground beef
- 2 celery ribs, chopped
- 1 small green pepper, finely chopped
- 1 small onion, chopped
- 1 can (10¾ oz.) condensed tomato soup, undiluted
- ¼ cup packed brown sugar
- ¼ cup ketchup
- 1 Tbsp. cider vinegar
- 1 Tbsp. prepared mustard
- 1½ tsp. Worcestershire sauce
- 1 tsp. pepper
- ½ tsp. salt
- ¼ tsp. garlic powder

DOGS

- 16 hot dogs
- 16 hot dog buns, split
  Optional: Warmed cheese dip and grilled onions

1. In a Dutch oven, cook the beef, celery, green pepper and onion over medium heat until the meat is no longer pink, 5-7 minutes. Crumble beef; drain. Stir in the tomato soup, brown sugar, ketchup, vinegar, mustard, Worcestershire sauce, pepper, salt and garlic powder; heat through.
2. Grill hot dogs, covered, over medium heat until heated through, 6-10 minutes, turning occasionally. Serve on buns. Top each with ¼ cup beef mixture. If desired, top with warmed cheese dip and grilled onions.

1 hot dog: 422 cal., 23g fat (9g sat. fat), 68mg chol., 959mg sod., 31g carb. (10g sugars, 1g fiber), 22g pro.

ONE-POT RED BEANS & RICE

This is a one-pot meal that's ready in about 30 minutes. It's one of my husband's favorites and uses simple ingredients, so it's been a go-to recipe in our house for years.
—Janice Conklin, Stevensville, MT

Takes: 30 min. • **Makes:** 6 servings

- 1 Tbsp. olive oil
- 2 celery ribs, sliced
- 1 medium onion, chopped
- 1 medium green pepper, chopped
- 1 pkg. (14 oz.) smoked turkey sausage, sliced
- 1 carton (32 oz.) reduced-sodium chicken broth
- 1 can (16 oz.) kidney beans, rinsed and drained
- 1¼ cups uncooked converted rice
- ⅓ cup tomato paste
- 1 bay leaf
- 1½ tsp. Cajun seasoning
- ¼ tsp. cayenne pepper
  Hot pepper sauce, optional

1. In a Dutch oven, heat oil over medium-high heat. Add celery, onion and green pepper; cook and stir until crisp-tender, 3-4 minutes. Add sausage; cook until browned, 2-3 minutes.
2. Stir in broth, beans, rice, tomato paste, bay leaf, Cajun seasoning and cayenne pepper. Bring to a boil; reduce heat. Simmer, uncovered, until rice is tender and the liquid is absorbed, 15-20 minutes, stirring occasionally. Discard bay leaf. If desired, serve with pepper sauce.

1⅓ cups: 347 cal., 6g fat (2g sat. fat), 41mg chol., 1272mg sod., 50g carb. (6g sugars, 5g fiber), 22g pro.

ALMOND CHICKEN & STRAWBERRY-BALSAMIC SAUCE

Crispy chicken with a sweet-tart sauce is served alongside wilted spinach for this special meal. I created the recipe many years ago for a contest, and it won the grand prize! It's easy to make and comes off as very elegant.
—Virginia Anthony, Jacksonville, FL

Prep: 20 min. • **Cook:** 20 min.
Makes: 4 servings

- ½ **cup panko bread crumbs**
- ⅓ **cup unblanched almonds, coarsely ground**
- ½ **tsp. salt**
- ¼ **tsp. pepper**
- 4 **boneless skinless chicken breast halves (4 oz. each)**
- 3 **tsp. canola oil, divided**
- ¼ **cup chopped shallots**
- ⅓ **cup reduced-sodium chicken broth**
- ⅓ **cup strawberry preserves**
- 3 **Tbsp. balsamic vinegar**
- 1 **Tbsp. minced fresh rosemary or 1 tsp. dried rosemary, crushed**
- 1 **pkg. (9 oz.) fresh baby spinach**

1. In a shallow dish, combine the bread crumbs, almonds, salt and pepper. Add chicken, 1 piece at a time, and turn to coat.

2. In a large nonstick skillet, cook chicken in 2 tsp. oil over medium heat for 4-5 minutes on each side or until juices run clear. Remove from pan and keep warm.

3. In the same pan, cook shallots in the remaining 1 tsp. oil until tender. Stir in broth, preserves, vinegar and rosemary. Bring to a boil. Reduce heat; simmer for 5-6 minutes or until thickened.

4. Meanwhile, in a large saucepan, bring ½ in. of water to a boil. Add spinach; cover and boil for 3-5 minutes or until wilted. Drain; serve with chicken and sauce.

1 serving: 349 cal., 13g fat (2g sat. fat), 63mg chol., 476mg sod., 31g carb. (19g sugars, 3g fiber), 29g pro.

COUNTDOWN TO THE FAIR

Ribbons aside, the real prize in 4-H is growing the skills for what President Harry S. Truman called "useful living."

STEER TAKES LEAD AT THE FARM SHOW

Every day for months, I fed, brushed and combed Scotty, a Black Angus steer. Scotty was my 4-H club project in 1947, and it's hard to describe the close ties that we formed through the daily routine on our farm in Landis Store, Pennsylvania.

At the end of that summer, Scotty and I entered the Reading Fair in Berks County, Pennsylvania. We won third place, so we were invited to the district livestock show in Lancaster. Again, we placed near the top of the show, which entitled us to participate in the big one, the Pennsylvania Farm Show, in January 1948. The show is still held today in the state capital, Harrisburg.

Everything went smoothly as we arrived at the farm show. Scotty and I prepared for the parade in the arena. He was all washed and brushed, and I was dressed in 4-H show garb, which consisted of a white shirt and white pants. As a 14-year-old, I was mindful of the many young ladies who were all around. I wrapped Scotty's halter strap around my arm and we lined up to walk

DONALD B. MOYER · BOYERTOWN, PA

Scotty practices wearing his halter for shows, top. Left, the pair's three ribbons.

into the arena. Suddenly, Scotty took off, pulling me off my feet and dragging me.

Talk about embarrassment—this rates as No. 1! My red face was a contrast with the white uniform covered in black and brown from the arena.

That day ended with the auctioning of the animals. One of the top meat companies in the U.S. at that time bought Scotty.

Though the tears flowed freely on that day over 70 years ago, I believe my experience in 4-H helped me build a strong base, which led to my many successful years as an elementary school principal.

The clover emblem was adopted in 1911 to represent young life (green) and high ideals (white). Club meetings start with the pledge to serve with head, heart, hands and health.

LUNCH CHAMP

As a 4-H beginner, I entered my "Snack and Pack" project in the county fair in 1965. I had to pack a healthful lunch and explain to the judges why it was nutritioually sound. My lunch, including radish roses I practiced to perfection, didn't fit into a standard lunchbox, so I lined a shoebox with foil and attached a small thermos with pipe cleaners. I won the grand prize.
—Candy Davis, Flornence, SC

P. 171

P. 166

P. 167

P. 168

BAKED TO PERFECTION

CHERRY DANISH

These ruby-studded pastries will be the first to disappear from your brunch table. I won an award when I first made them for a 4-H competition years ago. You can use apple pie filling with equally good results.
—Christie Cochran, Canyon, TX

Prep: 30 min. + rising • **Bake:** 15 min.
Makes: 40 pastries

- 1   pkg. (¼ oz.) active dry yeast
- ¼   cup warm water (110° to 115°)
- 1   cup warm 2% milk (110° to 115°)
- ¾   cup shortening, divided
- ⅓   cup sugar
- 3   large eggs, room temperature, divided use
- 1   tsp. salt
- ¼   tsp. each ground mace, lemon extract and vanilla extract
- 4   to 4½ cups all-purpose flour
- 1   can (21 oz.) cherry pie filling

GLAZE
- 1½   cups confectioners' sugar
- ½   tsp. vanilla extract
- 2   to 3 Tbsp. 2% milk
- ⅓   cup chopped almonds

1. In a large bowl, dissolve yeast in water. Add the milk, ¼ cup shortening, sugar, 2 eggs, salt, mace, extracts and 2 cups flour; beat until smooth. Add enough remaining flour to form a soft dough.
2. Turn onto a floured surface; knead until smooth and elastic, 6-8 minutes. Place in a greased bowl, turning once to grease top. Cover and let rise in a warm place until doubled, about 1 hour.
3. Punch dough down. On a large floured surface, roll dough out to a 24x16-in. rectangle. Dot half the dough with ¼ cup shortening; fold dough lengthwise. Fold the dough another 3 times lengthwise, then 2 times widthwise, each time dotting with some of the remaining shortening. Place dough in a greased bowl; cover and let rise 20 minutes.
4. On a floured surface, roll dough into a 16x15-in. rectangle. Cut into 8x¾-in. strips; coil each strip into a spiral shape, tucking ends underneath. Place spirals in 2 greased 15x10x1-in. baking pans. Cover and let rise in a warm place until doubled, about 1 hour.
5. Preheat oven to 375°. Beat the remaining egg. Make a depression in the center of each roll; brush with egg. Fill each depression with 1 Tbsp. pie filling. Bake 15-18 minutes or until golden brown. Cool on a wire rack. Combine confectioners' sugar, vanilla and milk; drizzle over rolls. Sprinkle with almonds.

1 pastry: 137 cal., 5g fat (1g sat. fat), 17mg chol., 70mg sod., 21g carb. (10g sugars, 1g fiber), 2g pro.

SUNFLOWER SEED & HONEY WHEAT BREAD

I've tried other bread recipes, but this one is a staple in our home. I won $50 in a baking contest with a loaf that I had stored in the freezer!
—Mickey Turner, Grants Pass, OR

Prep: 40 min. + rising • **Bake:** 35 min.
Makes: 3 loaves (12 pieces each)

- 2   pkg. (¼ oz. each) active dry yeast
- 3¼   cups warm water (110° to 115°)
- ¼   cup bread flour
- ⅓   cup canola oil
- ⅓   cup honey
- 3   tsp. salt
- 6½   to 7½ cups whole wheat flour
- ½   cup sunflower kernels
- 3   Tbsp. butter, melted

1. In a large bowl, dissolve yeast in warm water. Add the bread flour, oil, honey, salt and 4 cups whole wheat flour. Beat until smooth. Stir in sunflower kernels and enough remaining flour to form a firm dough.
2. Turn onto a floured surface; knead until smooth and elastic, 6-8 minutes. Place in a greased bowl, turning once to grease the top. Cover and let rise in a warm place until doubled, about 1 hour.
3. Punch dough down; divide it into 3 portions. Shape into loaves; place in 3 greased 8x4-in. loaf pans. Cover and let rise until doubled, about 30 minutes.
4. Bake at 350° until golden brown, 35-40 minutes. Brush with melted butter. Remove from pans to wire racks to cool.

Freeze option: Securely wrap cooled loaves in foil and then freeze. To use, thaw loaves at room temperature.

1 piece: 125 cal., 4g fat (1g sat. fat), 3mg chol., 212mg sod., 19g carb. (3g sugars, 3g fiber), 4g pro. **Diabetic exchanges:** 1 starch, 1 fat.

BLACK RASPBERRY BUBBLE RING

I first made this pretty bread years ago for a 4-H project. It helped me win grand champion for my county and took me to the Ohio State Fair. It takes some time to make, but I pull out this recipe anytime I want a breakfast or dessert that will really impress.
—Kila Frank, Reedsville, OH

....

Prep: 35 min. + rising • **Bake:** 25 min.
Makes: 1 loaf (16 pieces)

- 1 **pkg. (¼ oz.) active dry yeast**
- ¼ **cup warm water (110° to 115°)**
- 1 **cup warm 2% milk (110° to 115°)**
- ¼ **cup plus 2 Tbsp. sugar, divided**
- ½ **cup butter, melted, divided**
- 1 **large egg, room temperature**
- 1 **tsp. salt**
- 4 **cups all-purpose flour**
- 1 **jar (10 oz.) seedless
  black raspberry preserves**

SYRUP
- ⅓ **cup corn syrup**
- 2 **Tbsp. butter, melted**
- ½ **tsp. vanilla extract**

1. In a large bowl, dissolve yeast in warm water. Add the milk, ¼ cup sugar, ¼ cup butter, egg, salt and 3½ cups flour. Beat until smooth. Stir in enough remaining flour to form a soft dough.
2. Turn onto a floured surface; knead until smooth and elastic, 6-8 minutes. Place in a greased bowl, turning once to grease top. Cover and let rise in a warm place until doubled, about 1¼ hours.

3. Punch dough down. Turn onto a lightly floured surface; divide into 32 pieces. Flatten each piece into a 3-in. disk. Place about 1 tsp. preserves on center of each disk; bring edges together and seal into a rough ball shape.
4. Place 16 dough balls in a greased 10-in. fluted tube pan. Brush with half the remaining butter; sprinkle with 1 Tbsp. sugar. Top with the remaining balls, butter and sugar. Cover and let rise until doubled, about 35 minutes.
5. Bake at 350° until golden brown, 25-30 minutes. Combine the syrup ingredients; pour over warm bread. Cool for 5 minutes before inverting onto a serving plate.

1 piece: 274 cal., 8g fat (5g sat. fat), 34mg chol., 220mg sod., 46g carb. (18g sugars, 1g fiber), 4g pro.

> ### READER RAVE...
>
> *"This was delicious!!! The only thing I did different was use seedless blackberry jam. Will definitely make this again, and again, and again...YUM!"*
> —MOYER1995, TASTEOFHOME.COM

SWEET CORN MUFFINS

I love to make cornbread and corn muffins, but often the results are not moist or sweet enough for my taste. I experimented until I came up with these light, pleasant muffins. They won a blue ribbon at our county fair.
—Patty Bourne, Owings, MD

Prep: 10 min. • **Bake:** 25 min.
Makes: 1 dozen

- 1½ **cups all-purpose flour**
- 1 **cup sugar**
- ¾ **cup cornmeal**
- 1 **Tbsp. baking powder**
- ½ **tsp. salt**
- 2 **large eggs, room temperature**
- ½ **cup shortening**
- 1 **cup 2% milk, divided**

Preheat oven to 350°. Combine the dry ingredients. Add the eggs, shortening and ½ cup milk; beat for 1 minute. Add remaining ½ cup milk; beat just until blended. Fill 12 paper-lined muffin cups three-fourths full. Bake until a toothpick inserted in muffin comes out clean, 25-30 minutes.

1 muffin: 254 cal., 10g fat (3g sat. fat), 33mg chol., 241mg sod., 38g carb. (18g sugars, 1g fiber), 4g pro.

BLUE-RIBBON HERB ROLLS

These rolls have been a favorite of ours for nearly 25 years. I even baked them in an old wood stove when we lived on a farm. I developed the recipe using techniques I learned while studying the art of bread making. The recipe won a blue ribbon at our county fair.
—Mary Ann Evans, Tarpon Springs, FL

Prep: 40 min. + rising • **Bake:** 15 min.
Makes: 4 dozen

- 2 **pkg. (¼ oz. each) active dry yeast**
- 2¾ **cups warm water (110° to 115°), divided**
- ⅓ **cup canola oil**
- ¼ **cup honey or molasses**
- 1 **Tbsp. salt**
- 2 **tsp. dill weed**
- 2 **tsp. dried thyme**
- 2 **tsp. dried basil**
- 1 **tsp. onion powder**
- 1 **large egg, room temperature, beaten**
- 4 **cups whole wheat flour**
- 4 **to 4½ cups all-purpose flour**

1. In a large bowl, dissolve the yeast in ½ cup warm water. Add oil, honey, salt, dill, thyme, basil, onion powder, egg, whole wheat flour and the remaining 2¼ cup water. Beat until smooth. Stir in enough all-purpose flour to form a soft dough.

2. Turn onto a floured surface; knead until smooth and elastic, 6-8 minutes. Place in a greased bowl, turning once to grease top. Cover and let rise in a warm place until doubled, about 1 hour.

3. Punch dough down. Turn onto a lightly floured surface; divide into 6 portions. Divide each portion into 24 pieces. Shape each piece into a 1-in. ball; place 3 balls in each greased muffin cup. Cover and let rise until doubled, 20-25 minutes.

4. Bake at 375° for 12-15 minutes or until tops are golden brown. Remove from pans to wire racks.

1 roll: 94 cal., 2g fat (0 sat. fat), 4mg chol., 150mg sod., 17g carb. (2g sugars, 2g fiber), 3g pro.

SESAME WHEAT BRAIDS

When I started making this bread, my husband and our six children liked it so much that I was baking every day! I was thrilled when the judges at our county fair gave these braids both a blue ribbon and a best of show award!
—Nancy Montgomery, Hartville, OH

Prep: 30 min. + rising
Bake: 20 min. + cooling
Makes: 2 loaves (16 pieces each)

2 pkg. (¼ oz. each) **active dry yeast**
2¼ cups **warm water (110° to 115°)**
⅓ cup **sugar**
1 Tbsp. **canola oil**
1 cup **whole wheat flour**
2 **large eggs, room temperature**
1 Tbsp. **water**
1 Tbsp. **salt**
5 to 6 cups **all-purpose flour**
2 tsp. **sesame seeds**

1. In a large bowl, dissolve yeast in water. Add sugar and oil; mix well. Stir in whole wheat flour; let stand until the mixture bubbles, about 5 minutes.
2. In a small bowl, beat eggs and water. Remove 2 Tbsp. to a small bowl; cover and refrigerate. Add the remaining egg mixture and salt to batter; mix until smooth. Add 4 cups all-purpose flour and beat until smooth. Add enough remaining flour to form a soft dough.
3. Turn onto a floured surface; knead until smooth and elastic, 6-8 minutes. Place in a greased bowl, turning once to grease top. Cover and let rise in a warm place until doubled, about 1 hour. Punch dough down and divide in half. Divide each half into 3 portions.
4. Shape each portion into a rope about 15 in. long. Place 3 ropes on a greased baking sheet; braid. Pinch each end firmly and tuck under.
5. Repeat, placing second braid on the same baking sheet. Brush braids with the reserved egg mixture; sprinkle with sesame seeds. Let braids rise until doubled, about 45 minutes.
6. Bake at 350° for 20-25 minutes. Remove from baking sheet to cool on a wire rack.
1 piece: 102 cal., 1g fat (0 sat. fat), 13mg chol., 226mg sod., 20g carb. (2g sugars, 1g fiber), 3g pro.

BLUEBERRY-ORANGE MUFFINS

This recipe was given to me years ago, and I've used it often since. In fact, it is so good that it won first prize at my county fair! Blueberries are plentiful in the Midwest, and this is a fragrant and fruity way to prepare them.
—Irene Parry, Kenosha, WI

Takes: 30 min. • **Makes:** 2 dozen

- 1 cup quick-cooking oats
- 1 cup orange juice
- 1 tsp. grated orange zest
- 1 cup canola oil
- 3 large eggs, room temperature, beaten
- 3 cups all-purpose flour
- 1 cup sugar
- 4 tsp. baking powder
- 1 tsp. salt
- ½ tsp. baking soda
- 3 to 4 cups fresh blueberries

TOPPING
- ½ cup finely chopped nuts
- 3 Tbsp. sugar
- ½ tsp. ground cinnamon

1. Mix oats, orange juice and zest. Blend in oil and eggs; set aside. Stir together flour, sugar, baking powder, salt and baking soda. Add oat mixture; mix lightly. Fold in blueberries. Spoon batter into 24 paper-lined muffin tins, filling two-thirds full. Combine the topping ingredients; sprinkle over batter.
2. Bake at 400° for 15-18 minutes or until lightly browned. Let cool for 5 minutes before removing from pans to a wire rack to cool completely.
1 muffin: 228 cal., 12g fat (2g sat. fat), 27mg chol., 200mg sod., 28g carb. (13g sugars, 1g fiber), 4g pro.

BLUE-RIBBON POPPY SEED CHEESE BREAD

This bread won a blue ribbon at the Los Angeles County Fair. I usually make several batches at once to give as gifts.
—Marina Castle-Kelley, Canyon Country, CA

Prep: 20 min. • **Bake:** 45 min. + cooling
Makes: 1 loaf (16 pieces)

- ½ cup shortening
- ½ cup sugar
- 3 large eggs, room temperature
- 2 cups all-purpose flour
- 2½ tsp. baking powder
- 1 tsp. ground mustard
- ¾ tsp. salt
- 1 cup 2% milk
- 1¼ cups shredded cheddar-Monterey Jack cheese
- ½ cup chopped sweet onion
- 1 Tbsp. poppy seeds
- ⅛ tsp. paprika

1. Preheat oven to 375°. In a large bowl, cream shortening and sugar until light and fluffy, 5-7 minutes. Add eggs, 1 at a time, beating well after each addition. Combine the flour, baking powder, mustard and salt; add to the creamed mixture alternately with milk. Fold in cheese, onion and poppy seeds.
2. Transfer to a greased 9x5-in. loaf pan; sprinkle with paprika. Bake for 45-55 minutes or until a toothpick inserted in center comes out clean. Cool 10 minutes before removing from pan to a wire rack.
1 piece: 194 cal., 10g fat (4g sat. fat), 49mg chol., 248mg sod., 20g carb. (8g sugars, 1g fiber), 5g pro.

DOUBLE CHOCOLATE SCONES

Chocolate lovers will adore these moist, decadent scones that earned me a blue ribbon in a baking competition. They're perfect for a tea or brunch, and the mix of cocoa and chocolate chips makes them sweet enough for dessert.
—Stephanie Sorbie, Peoria, AZ

Prep: 15 min. • **Bake:** 20 min.
Makes: 8 scones

- 1¾ cups all-purpose flour
- ½ cup baking cocoa
- ⅓ cup sugar
- 1½ tsp. baking powder
- ½ tsp. salt
- 4 oz. cream cheese, cubed
- ¼ cup cold butter, cubed
- 2 large eggs, room temperature, divided use
- ¾ cup heavy whipping cream
- 2 tsp. vanilla extract
- ⅔ cup semisweet chocolate chips

1. Preheat oven to 375°. In a large bowl, whisk the first 5 ingredients. Cut in cream cheese and butter until mixture resembles coarse crumbs. In another bowl, whisk 1 egg, cream and vanilla; stir into the crumb mixture just until moistened. Stir in the chocolate chips.
2. Turn dough onto a floured surface; knead gently 10 times. Pat dough into a 6-in. circle. Cut into 8 wedges.
3. Place wedges on a greased baking sheet. In a small bowl, whisk remaining egg; brush over scones. Bake until a toothpick inserted into center comes out clean, 18-20 minutes. Serve warm.
1 scone: 412 cal., 25g fat (15g sat. fat), 114mg chol., 334mg sod., 42g carb. (17g sugars, 3g fiber), 8g pro.

MUENSTER BREAD

Many years ago my sister and I won blue ribbons in 4-H with this bread. The recipe makes a beautiful golden loaf with cheese peeking out of every slice.
—Melanie Mero, Ida, MI

Prep: 20 min. + rising
Bake: 40 min. + cooling
Makes: 1 loaf (16 pieces)

- 2 pkg. (¼ oz. each) active dry yeast
- 1 cup warm 2% milk (110° to 115°)
- ½ cup butter, softened
- 2 Tbsp. sugar
- 1 tsp. salt
- 3¼ to 3¾ cups all-purpose flour
- 1 large egg plus 1 large egg yolk, room temperature
- 4 cups shredded Muenster cheese
- 1 large egg white, beaten

1. In a large bowl, dissolve yeast in milk. Add the butter, sugar, salt and 2 cups flour; beat until smooth. Stir in enough remaining flour to form a soft dough.
2. Turn onto a floured surface; knead until smooth and elastic, 6-8 minutes. Place in a greased bowl, turning once to grease top. Cover and let rise in a warm place until doubled, about 1 hour.
3. In a large bowl, beat egg and yolk; stir in cheese. Punch down dough; roll into a 16-in. circle.
4. Place in a greased 10-in. cast-iron skillet or 9-in. round baking pan, letting dough drape over the edges. Spoon the cheese mixture into center of dough. Gather dough up over filling in 1½-in. pleats. Gently squeeze pleats together at top and twist to make a topknot. Let rise 10-15 minutes.
5. Brush loaf with egg white. Bake at 375° for 40-45 minutes. Cool on a wire rack for 20 minutes. Serve warm.
1 piece: 273 cal., 16g fat (9g sat. fat), 71mg chol., 399mg sod., 22g carb. (3g sugars, 1g fiber), 11g pro.

MAPLE NUT BANANA BREAD

This recipe boosts banana bread to a whole new level with maple syrup, sour cream, pecans and a cinnamon-spiced streusel. I was lucky enough to be a finalist in the Pillsbury Bake-Off.
—David Dahlman, Chatsworth, CA

Prep: 40 min.
Bake: 55 min. + cooling
Makes: 1 loaf (12 pieces)

- ½ cup butter, softened
- ½ cup packed brown sugar
- 2 large eggs, room temperature
- 1 cup mashed ripe bananas (about 2 medium)
- ½ cup sour cream
- ⅓ cup maple syrup
- 1 tsp. vanilla extract
- 2 cups all-purpose flour
- 1 tsp. baking powder
- 1 tsp. baking soda
- 1 tsp. salt
- 1 cup chopped pecans

STREUSEL

- 2 Tbsp. all-purpose flour
- 2 Tbsp. sugar
- 1 Tbsp. brown sugar
- 1 Tbsp. butter, softened
- ⅛ tsp. ground cinnamon
- 2 Tbsp. finely chopped pecans

1. Preheat oven to 350°. In a large bowl, cream butter and brown sugar until light and fluffy, 5-7 minutes. Add eggs, 1 at a time, beating well after each addition. In a small bowl, mix bananas, sour cream, maple syrup and vanilla. In another bowl, whisk flour, baking powder, baking soda and salt; add to the creamed mixture alternately with banana mixture, beating well after each addition. Fold in pecans. Transfer batter to a greased 9x5-in. loaf pan.
2. For streusel, in a small bowl, mix flour, sugars, butter and cinnamon until blended. Stir in pecans; sprinkle over the batter.
3. Bake 55-60 minutes or until a toothpick inserted in center comes

out clean. Cool in pan 10 minutes before removing to a wire rack to cool.
1 piece: 353 cal., 19g fat (8g sat. fat), 64mg chol., 416mg sod., 41g carb. (21g sugars, 2g fiber), 5g pro.
For mini loaves: Transfer batter to 4 greased 5¾x3x2-in. loaf pans; top with streusel. Bake at 350° for 30-35 minutes or until a toothpick comes out clean.
For muffins: Transfer batter to 16 greased or paper-lined muffin cups; top with streusel. Bake at 350° for 18-22 minutes or until a toothpick comes out clean.
For mini muffins: Transfer batter to 4 dozen greased or paper-lined mini-muffin cups; top with streusel. Bake at 350° for 10-12 minutes or until a toothpick comes out clean.

BRAIDED ONION LOAF

This recipe won the blue ribbon for best loaf of bread at our county fair a few years ago. One bite and you'll see why the tender, savory slices appealed to the judges.

—Linda Knoll, Jackson, MI

Prep: 30 min. + rising • **Bake:** 30 min.
Makes: 1 loaf

- 1 pkg. (¼ oz.) active dry yeast
- ¾ cup warm water (110° to 115°)
- ½ cup warm whole milk (110° to 115°)
- ¼ cup butter, softened
- 1 large egg, room temperature
- ¼ cup sugar
- 1½ tsp. salt
- 4 to 4½ cups all-purpose flour

FILLING

- ¼ cup butter, softened
- ¾ cup dried minced onion
- 1 Tbsp. grated Parmesan cheese
- 1 tsp. paprika
- 1 tsp. garlic salt, optional
  Melted butter

1. In a large bowl, dissolve yeast in warm water. Add the milk, butter, egg, sugar, salt and 2 cups flour; beat until smooth. Add enough remaining flour to form a soft dough.

2. Turn dough onto a floured surface; knead dough until smooth and elastic, 6-8 minutes. Place in a greased bowl, turning once to grease top. Cover and let rise in a warm place until doubled, about 1 hour.

3. For filling, combine the butter, onion, Parmesan cheese, paprika and garlic salt if desired; set aside.

4. Punch dough down; turn onto a lightly floured surface. Divide into thirds. Roll each portion into a 20x4-in. rectangle. Spread filling over rectangles. Roll up jelly-roll style, starting from a long side.

5. Place rolls on an ungreased baking sheet; braid. Pinch ends to seal and tuck under. Cover and let rise until doubled, about 45 minutes.

6. Bake at 350° for 30-35 minutes or until golden brown. Brush with melted butter. Remove from pan to a wire rack.

1 piece: 198 cal., 7g fat (4g sat. fat), 30mg chol., 294mg sod., 30g carb. (6g sugars, 1g fiber), 4g pro.

PINA COLADA ZUCCHINI BREAD

At my husband's urging, I entered this recipe at the Pennsylvania Farm Show—and won first place! You'll love the cakelike texture and tropical flavors.
—Sharon Rydbom, Tipton, PA

Prep: 25 min. • **Bake:** 45 min. + cooling
Makes: 3 loaves (12 pieces each)

- 4 cups all-purpose flour
- 3 cups sugar
- 2 tsp. baking powder
- 1½ tsp. salt
- 1 tsp. baking soda
- 4 large eggs, room temperature
- 1½ cups canola oil
- 1 tsp. each coconut, rum and vanilla extracts
- 3 cups shredded zucchini
- 1 cup canned crushed pineapple, drained
- ½ cup chopped walnuts or chopped pecans

1. Line the bottoms of 3 greased and floured 8x4-in. loaf pans with waxed paper and grease the paper; set pans aside. Preheat oven to 350°.
2. Combine flour, sugar, baking powder, salt and baking soda. In another bowl, whisk the eggs, oil and extracts. Stir into dry ingredients until just moistened. Fold in zucchini, pineapple and walnuts.
3. Transfer to prepared pans. Bake for 45-55 minutes or until a toothpick inserted in the center comes out clean. Cool for 10 minutes before removing from pans to wire racks. Gently remove waxed paper.
1 piece: 225 cal., 11g fat (1g sat. fat), 24mg chol., 165mg sod., 29g carb. (18g sugars, 1g fiber), 3g pro.

SPICY PUMPKIN GINGERBREAD

I have been making this delicious gingerbread for years and it's won several blue ribbons. Serve it with whipped cream and caramel sauce, or simply dust it with confectioners' sugar after it cools.
—Marina Castle-Kelley, Canyon Country, CA

Prep: 25 min. • **Bake:** 30 min. + cooling
Makes: 16 servings

- ½ cup butter, softened
- ½ cup packed dark brown sugar
- 2 large eggs, room temperature
- ½ cup canned pumpkin
- ½ cup molasses
- 2 Tbsp. grated orange zest
- 2½ cups all-purpose flour
- 1 tsp. baking soda
- 1 tsp. ground ginger
- 1 tsp. ground cinnamon
- ½ tsp. salt
- ½ tsp. ground ancho chile pepper
- ¾ cup buttermilk
- ⅓ cup shelled pumpkin seeds, chopped and toasted

Optional: Whipped cream, caramel sundae syrup or confectioners' sugar

1. Preheat oven to 325°. In a large bowl, cream butter and brown sugar until light and fluffy, 5-7 minutes. Add eggs, 1 at a time, beating well after each addition. Beat in pumpkin, molasses and orange zest (mixture will appear curdled).
2. In a small bowl, combine the flour, baking soda, ginger, cinnamon, salt and chile pepper. Add to the creamed mixture alternately with buttermilk, beating well after each addition. Stir in pumpkin seeds.
3. Pour the batter into a greased 9-in. square baking pan. Bake until a toothpick inserted in the center comes out clean, 28-32 minutes. Cool completely on a wire rack. Serve with toppings as desired.
1 piece: 209 cal., 8g fat (4g sat. fat), 39mg chol., 242mg sod., 31g carb. (15g sugars, 1g fiber), 4g pro.

BLUE-RIBBON WHITE BREAD

This recipe took first-place honors seven consecutive years at our local fair. My relatives rave about this bread and its pleasant, subtle ginger flavor.
—Pam Goodlet, Washington Island, WI

....

Prep: 15 min. + rising • **Bake:** 40 min.
Makes: 2 loaves

- 1 pkg. (¼ oz.) active dry yeast
- 2½ cups warm water (110° to 115°)
- 1 cup instant nonfat dry milk powder
- 3 Tbsp. shortening
- 2 Tbsp. sugar
- 2 tsp. salt
- ¼ tsp. ground ginger
- 6 to 7 cups all-purpose flour

1. In a large bowl, dissolve yeast in warm water. Add the milk powder, shortening, sugar, salt, ginger and 3½ cups flour. Beat until smooth. Stir in enough remaining flour to form a soft dough.
2. Turn dough onto a floured surface; knead until smooth and elastic, 6-8 minutes. Place in a greased bowl, turning once to grease top. Cover and let rise in a warm place until doubled, about 1 hour.
3. Punch dough down. Turn onto a lightly floured surface; divide in half. Shape into loaves. Place in 2 greased 8x4-in. loaf pans. Cover and let rise until doubled, about 45 minutes.
4. Bake at 350° for 40-45 minutes or until golden brown and bread sounds hollow when tapped. Remove from pans to wire racks to cool.
1 piece: 113 cal., 1g fat (0 sat. fat), 1mg chol., 168mg sod., 21g carb. (3g sugars, 1g fiber), 4g pro.

DOWN EAST BLUEBERRY BUCKLE

This buckle won a contest at my daughter's college. The prize was four lobsters, but the real reward was the smile on our daughter's face.
—Dianne van der Veen, Plymouth, MA

....

Prep: 15 min. • **Bake:** 30 min.
Makes: 9 servings

- 2 cups all-purpose flour
- ¾ cup sugar
- 2½ tsp. baking powder
- ¼ tsp. salt
- 1 large egg, room temperature
- ¾ cup 2% milk
- ¼ cup butter, melted
- 2 cups fresh or frozen blueberries

TOPPING
- ½ cup sugar
- ⅓ cup all-purpose flour
- ½ tsp. ground cinnamon
- ¼ cup butter, softened

1. Whisk flour, sugar, baking powder and salt. In another bowl, whisk egg, milk and melted butter until blended. Add to the flour mixture; stir just until moistened. Fold in blueberries. Transfer to a greased 9-in. square baking pan.
2. For topping, in a small bowl, mix the sugar, flour and cinnamon. Using a fork, stir in softened butter until mixture is crumbly. Sprinkle over batter.
3. Bake at 375° until a toothpick inserted in center comes out clean, 30-35 minutes (do not overbake). Cool in pan on a wire rack. Serve warm or at room temperature.
Note: If using frozen blueberries, use without thawing.
1 piece: 354 cal., 12g fat (7g sat. fat), 49mg chol., 277mg sod., 59g carb. (32g sugars, 2g fiber), 5g pro.

CHEESE & GARLIC BISCUITS

My biscuits won the prize for best quick bread at my county fair. One judge liked them so much, she asked for the recipe! These buttery, savory biscuits go with just about anything.
—Gloria Jarrett, Loveland, OH

Takes: 20 min. • **Makes:** 2½ dozen

2½ cups biscuit/baking mix
¾ cup shredded sharp cheddar cheese
1 tsp. garlic powder
1 tsp. ranch salad dressing mix
1 cup buttermilk

TOPPING
½ cup butter, melted
1 Tbsp. minced chives
½ tsp. garlic powder
½ tsp. ranch salad dressing mix
¼ tsp. pepper

1. In a large bowl, combine the baking mix, cheese, garlic powder and salad dressing mix. Stir in buttermilk just until moistened. Drop by tablespoonfuls onto greased baking sheets.
2. Bake at 450° until golden brown, 6-8 minutes. Meanwhile, combine the topping ingredients. Brush over biscuits. Serve warm.
1 biscuit: 81 cal., 5g fat (3g sat. fat), 11mg chol., 176mg sod., 7g carb. (1g sugars, 0 fiber), 2g pro.

LOUISIANA PECAN BACON BREAD

One Christmas, the babysitter brought gifts for my daughter and a basket of goodies, including pecan bread. When I make this bread, I remember that kind soul. This bread won a blue ribbon at the Los Angeles County Fair in 1988, and I still bake it for family and friends.
—Marina Castle-Kelley, Canyon Country, CA

Prep: 20 min. • **Bake:** 50 min. + cooling
Makes: 1 loaf (16 pieces)

- 6 **bacon strips, chopped**
- 6 **oz. cream cheese, softened**
- ⅓ **cup sugar**
- 1 **large egg, room temperature**
- 2 **cups all-purpose flour**
- 2½ **tsp. baking powder**
- ½ **tsp. salt**
- ¾ **cup 2% milk**
- 1 **cup chopped pecans**
- ¼ **cup finely chopped onion**
- ¼ **cup chopped green pepper**

1. Preheat oven to 350°. In a large skillet, cook bacon over medium-low heat until crisp, stirring occasionally. Remove with a slotted spoon; drain on paper towels. Reserve 2 Tbsp. drippings; cool slightly.

2. In a large bowl, beat cream cheese, sugar and reserved drippings until smooth. Beat in egg. In another bowl, whisk flour, baking powder and salt; add to the cream cheese mixture alternately with milk, beating well after each addition. Fold in pecans, onion, pepper and bacon. Transfer to a greased 9x5-in. loaf pan.

3. Bake until a toothpick inserted in center comes out clean, 50-60 minutes. Cool in pan 10 minutes before removing to a wire rack to cool.

1 piece: 198 cal., 12g fat (4g sat. fat), 29mg chol., 242mg sod., 18g carb. (6g sugars, 1g fiber), 5g pro.

PUMPKIN BREAD WITH GINGERBREAD TOPPING

This yummy pumpkin bread won first prize in the Acorn Pantry Bread Contest. It melts in your mouth, and the recipe easily doubles for gift-giving.
—Renee Nanez, Frederic, WI

....

Prep: 35 min. • **Bake:** 30 min. + cooling
Makes: 5 loaves (6 pieces each)

¾ cup butter, cubed
2¼ cups sugar
1½ cups canned pumpkin
3 large eggs, room temperature
2¼ cups all-purpose flour
1 tsp. ground cinnamon
1 tsp. ground nutmeg
¾ tsp. baking soda
½ tsp. baking powder
½ tsp. salt
½ cup chopped walnuts
½ cup finely chopped crystallized ginger

TOPPING
10 gingersnap cookies
⅓ cup packed brown sugar
2 Tbsp. all-purpose flour
¼ tsp. ground cinnamon
¼ tsp. ground nutmeg
6 Tbsp. cold butter
¼ cup finely chopped walnuts, optional

1. Preheat oven to 350°. In a large heavy saucepan, melt butter over medium heat. Heat 5-7 minutes or until golden brown, stirring constantly. Remove from heat and transfer to a large bowl; cool slightly. Add sugar, pumpkin and eggs; beat until well blended.
2. In another bowl, whisk the flour, cinnamon, nutmeg, baking soda, baking powder and salt; gradually beat into the pumpkin mixture. Fold in walnuts and ginger.
3. Transfer to 5 greased 5¾x3x2-in. loaf pans. Place the cookies, brown sugar, flour, cinnamon and nutmeg in a food processor; pulse until cookies are finely ground. Add butter; pulse until crumbly. Sprinkle cookie mixture and, if desired, walnuts over batter.
4. Bake for 30-35 minutes or until a toothpick inserted in center comes out clean. Cool in pans 10 minutes before removing to wire racks to cool.
1 piece: 212 cal., 9g fat (5g sat. fat), 37mg chol., 156mg sod., 32g carb. (20g sugars, 1g fiber), 2g pro.

BLUE-RIBBON TIP

To ensure even distribution of leavening and spices, it helps to whisk the dry ingredients thoroughly. For the most tender texture in quick breads, use a gentle hand when mixing the batter.

CHEDDAR CHEESE BATTER BREAD

As a dairy farmer, I like anything that calls for cheese. This golden loaf—a proven winner at our state fair—tastes wonderful either fresh from the oven or cooled and sliced.
—Jeanne Kemper, Bagdad, KY

Prep: 30 min. + rising
Bake: 25 min. + cooling
Makes: 2 loaves (16 pieces each)

- 2 pkg. (¼ oz. each) active dry yeast
- ¾ cup warm water (110° to 115°)
- 3 cups shredded cheddar cheese
- ¾ cup shredded Parmesan cheese
- 2 cups warm 2% milk (110° to 115°)
- 3 Tbsp. sugar
- 1 Tbsp. butter, melted
- 2 tsp. salt
- 6 to 6½ cups all-purpose flour
- 1 large egg white
- 1 Tbsp. water

TOPPING
- ½ cup finely shredded cheddar cheese
- 1 garlic clove, minced
- ½ tsp. sesame seeds
- ½ tsp. poppy seeds
- ½ tsp. paprika
- ¼ tsp. celery seed

1. In a large bowl, dissolve yeast in warm water. Add cheeses, milk, sugar, butter, salt and 3 cups flour. Beat on medium speed for 3 minutes. Stir in enough remaining flour to form a firm dough.
2. Do not knead. Cover and let rise in a warm place until doubled, about 1½ hours.
3. Stir dough down; transfer to 2 greased 9x5-in. loaf pans. Cover and let rise until doubled, about 30 minutes.
4. Preheat oven to 375°. In a small bowl, combine egg white and water. In another bowl, combine the topping ingredients. Brush loaves with egg white mixture; sprinkle with topping. Bake until golden brown, 25-30 minutes. Remove from pans to wire racks to cool.
1 piece: 155 cal., 5g fat (3g sat. fat), 17mg chol., 266mg sod., 21g carb. (2g sugars, 1g fiber), 7g pro.

CONTEST-WINNING BLUEBERRY QUICK BREAD

This sweet bread recipe won a blue ribbon at our state fair, perhaps because the pineapple and coconut give it a mild, unexpectedly delicious twist.
—Lois Everest, Goshen, IN

Prep: 25 min. • **Bake:** 50 min. + cooling
Makes: 2 loaves (12 pieces each)

- ⅔ cup butter, softened
- 1¼ cups sugar blend
- 2 large eggs, room temperature
- 4 large egg whites, room temperature
- 1½ tsp. lemon juice
- 3 cups all-purpose flour
- 3¾ tsp. baking powder
- ½ tsp. salt
- ½ cup fat-free milk
- 2 cups fresh or frozen blueberries
- 1 cup canned unsweetened crushed pineapple, drained
- ½ cup chopped pecans or walnuts
- ½ cup sweetened shredded coconut

1. Preheat oven to 350°. Cream butter and sugar blend until light and fluffy, 5-7 minutes. Beat in eggs, egg whites and lemon juice. Combine flour, baking powder and salt; gradually add to the creamed mixture alternately with the milk, beating well after each addition. Fold in blueberries, pineapple, pecans and coconut.
2. Transfer to two 8x4-in. loaf pans coated with cooking spray. Bake for 50-60 minutes or until a toothpick inserted in the center comes out clean. Cool for 10 minutes before removing from pans to wire racks.
1 piece: 193 cal., 8g fat (4g sat. fat), 31mg chol., 186mg sod., 27g carb. (14g sugars, 1g fiber), 3g pro.

APRICOT BUBBLE RING

Both of our daughters received ribbons for this recipe at the 4-H fair. This bubble ring is perfect for serving a crowd at breakfast.
—Lois Schlickau, Haven, KS

Prep: 25 min. + rising • **Bake:** 30 min.
Makes: 20 servings

- 1 pkg. (¼ oz.) active dry yeast
- ¼ cup warm water (110° to 115°)
- ½ cup warm whole milk (110° to 115°)
- ⅓ cup butter, melted
- ⅓ cup sugar
- 2 large eggs, room temperature
- 1 tsp. salt
- 3¾ to 4 cups all-purpose flour

FILLING
- ¾ cup sugar
- 1 tsp. ground cinnamon
- 6 Tbsp. butter, melted, divided
- ⅔ cup apricot preserves
- ¾ cup finely chopped walnuts

1. In a large bowl, dissolve yeast in warm water. Add milk, butter, sugar, eggs and salt; mix well. Add 2 cups flour; beat until smooth. Stir in enough remaining flour to form a soft dough.
2. Turn onto a floured surface; knead until smooth and elastic, 6-8 minutes. Place in a greased bowl, turning once to grease top. Cover and let rise in a warm place until doubled, about 1 hour.
3. For filling, combine the sugar and cinnamon in a shallow bowl; set aside. Punch dough down; cover and let rest for 10 minutes. Pour 2 Tbsp. melted butter into bottom of greased 10-in. fluted tube pan.
4. On a lightly floured surface, divide dough into 20 pieces and form into balls. Dip each ball into the remaining 4 tsp. melted butter, then roll in the cinnamon-sugar. Place 10 balls into prepared pan. Spoon half the apricot preserves between the balls; sprinkle with half the walnuts. Repeat. Cover and let rise until doubled, about 45 minutes.
5. Bake at 350° for 30-35 minutes or until browned. Cool in pan for 5 minutes before inverting onto a serving plate. Serve warm.

1 piece: 252 cal., 10g fat (5g sat. fat), 37mg chol., 185mg sod., 37g carb. (16g sugars, 1g fiber), 4g pro.

BLUE-RIBBON RYE BREAD

My kids once had a little bread business, selling homemade loaves to neighbors and people in the community. Many purchased this rye that won best of show at our county fair.
—Susanne Spicker, North Ogden, UT

Prep: 40 min. + rising
Bake: 20 min. + cooling
Makes: 3 loaves (12 pieces each)

- 1 pkg. (¼ oz.) active dry yeast
- 1 Tbsp. sugar
- 2¼ cups warm water (110° to 115°)
- ¼ cup packed brown sugar
- ¼ cup shortening
- ¼ cup molasses
- 1 Tbsp. caraway seeds
- 1 tsp. salt
- 1 cup rye flour
- 3½ to 4 cups all-purpose flour

1. In a large bowl, dissolve yeast and sugar in warm water. Stir in brown sugar, shortening, molasses, caraway seeds and salt. Add rye flour and 1¾ cups all-purpose flour; beat until smooth. Stir in enough remaining all-purpose flour to form a soft dough.
2. Turn the dough onto a floured surface; knead until smooth and elastic, 6-8 minutes. Place in a greased bowl, turning once to grease the top. Cover and let rise in a warm place until doubled, about 1 hour.
3. Punch dough down; shape into 3 loaves. Place on greased baking sheets. Cover and let rise until doubled, about 1 hour.
4. Bake at 350° for 20-25 minutes or until golden brown. Remove from pans to wire racks to cool.

1 piece: 81 cal., 2g fat (0 sat. fat), 0 chol., 67mg sod., 15g carb. (3g sugars, 1g fiber), 2g pro.

CONFETTI FIESTA BRAIDS

This bread is based on the winning recipe of a local contest I judged. I turned it into a double braid and added more peppers. It's not difficult, and the result is impressive. It smells glorious when baking!
—Fancheon Resler, Albion, IN

....

Prep: 1 hour + rising
Bake: 25 min. + cooling
Makes: 2 loaves (20 pieces each)

5½ to 6½ cups all-purpose flour
1 cup cornmeal
2 pkg. (¼ oz. each) active dry yeast
1 Tbsp. sugar
2 tsp. salt
1 cup buttermilk
½ cup butter, cubed
½ cup finely chopped onion
2 large eggs, room temperature
1½ cups shredded cheddar cheese
1 can (8¼ oz.) cream-style corn
½ cup finely chopped sweet red, yellow and/or orange peppers
¼ cup chopped seeded jalapeno peppers
¼ cup butter, melted

1. In a large bowl, combine 4 cups flour, cornmeal, yeast, sugar and salt. In a small saucepan, heat the buttermilk, butter and onion to 120°-130°. Add to the dry ingredients; beat just until moistened. Add the eggs; beat until smooth. Stir in the cheese, corn and peppers. Stir in enough remaining flour to form a stiff dough.
2. Turn the dough onto a floured surface; knead until smooth and elastic, 6-8 minutes. Place in a greased bowl, turning once to grease top. Cover and let rise in a warm place until doubled, about 1 hour.

3. Punch dough down. Turn onto a lightly floured surface; divide in half. Set 1 half of dough aside; divide the remaining half into 2 portions so that 1 portion is twice the size of the other. Shape the larger portion into three 16-in. ropes. Place on a greased baking sheet and braid; pinch ends to seal and tuck under.
4. Shape smaller portion into three 10-in. ropes. Braid on a lightly floured surface; tuck ends under. Brush the bottom with water and place over the larger braid. Repeat with remaining half of dough. Cover and let rise until doubled, about 45 minutes.
5. Bake at 350° for 25-30 minutes or until golden brown. Brush with melted butter. Cool on a wire rack. Refrigerate any leftovers.
Note: Wear disposable gloves when cutting hot peppers; the oils can burn skin. Avoid touching your face.
1 piece: 134 cal., 5g fat (3g sat. fat), 24mg chol., 195mg sod., 18g carb. (1g sugars, 1g fiber), 4g pro.

BLUE-RIBBON TIP

If you proofed your dough too long in the first rising (if it looks stretched across the top and if it springs back instantly when you press it with your fingertip), there's an easy fix. Just punch it down, knead it briefly and let it proof to the correct size.

BUTTERSCOTCH MUFFINS

Butterscotch pudding gives a distinctive flavor to these muffins topped with brown sugar and nuts. My son won first-place purple ribbons in a 4-H competition with these treats.
—Jill Hazelton, Hamlet, IN

Prep: 20 min. • **Bake:** 15 min.
Makes: 1½ dozen

- 2 **cups all-purpose flour**
- 1 **cup sugar**
- 1 **pkg. (3.4 oz.) instant butterscotch pudding mix**
- 1 **pkg. (3.4 oz.) instant vanilla pudding mix**
- 2 **tsp. baking powder**
- 1 **tsp. salt**
- 1 **cup water**
- 4 **large eggs, room temperature**
- ¾ **cup canola oil**
- 1 **tsp. vanilla extract**

TOPPING
- ⅔ **cup packed brown sugar**
- ½ **cup chopped pecans**
- 2 **tsp. ground cinnamon**

1. Preheat oven to 350°. In a large bowl, combine the flour, sugar, pudding mixes, baking powder and salt. Combine the water, eggs, oil and vanilla; stir into the dry ingredients just until moistened.
2. Fill greased or paper-lined muffin cups two-thirds full. Combine topping ingredients; sprinkle over batter.
3. Bake for 15-20 minutes or until a toothpick inserted in the center comes out clean. Cool for 5 minutes before removing from pans to wire racks.
1 muffin: 284 cal., 13g fat (2g sat. fat), 47mg chol., 352mg sod., 40g carb. (27g sugars, 1g fiber), 3g pro.

ORANGE ZUCCHINI BREAD

These moist mini loaves have pretty flecks of green from the zucchini. I won first place at the Ohio State Fair with this recipe!
—Pat Woolley, Jackson Center, OH

Prep: 20 min. • **Bake:** 35 min. + cooling
Makes: 4 mini loaves

- 3 **large eggs, room temperature**
- ¾ **cup canola oil**
- 1½ **cups sugar**
- 2 **tsp. grated lemon zest**
- 2 **tsp. grated orange zest**
- ½ **tsp. orange extract**
- ¼ **tsp. vanilla extract**
- 2 **cups shredded unpeeled zucchini**
- 2½ **cups all-purpose flour**
- 2 **tsp. baking powder**
- ¾ **tsp. salt**
- ½ **tsp. ground ginger**
- ¼ **tsp. baking soda**
- ½ **cup chopped walnuts**

1. Preheat oven to 350°. In a large bowl, combine the eggs and oil. Add sugar; mix well. Stir in the lemon zest, orange zest and extracts. Add zucchini; mix well. In another bowl, combine the flour, baking powder, salt, ginger and baking soda; stir into zucchini mixture just until moistened. Fold in walnuts.
2. Transfer the batter to 4 greased 5¾x3x2-in. loaf pans. Bake for 35-40 minutes or until golden brown and a toothpick inserted in the center comes out clean. Cool for 10 minutes before removing from pans to wire racks to cool completely.
1 piece: 275 cal., 14g fat (2g sat. fat), 40mg chol., 193mg sod., 35g carb. (19g sugars, 1g fiber), 4g pro.

CONTEST-WINNING POTATO PAN ROLLS

Beautiful color and a light-as-a-feather texture make these rolls our family's favorite for holiday meals. I won the reserve champion award at a 4-H yeast bread competition with this recipe.
—LeAnne Hofferichter-Tieken, Floresville, TX

Prep: 55 min. + rising
Bake: 20 min.
Makes: 2½ dozen

- 2 **medium potatoes, peeled and quartered**
- 2 **pkg. (¼ oz. each) active dry yeast**
- 1 **tsp. sugar**
- ½ **cup butter, melted**
- ½ **cup honey**
- ¼ **cup canola oil**
- 2 **large eggs, room temperature**
- 2 **tsp. salt**
- 6 **to 7 cups all-purpose flour**

1. In a large saucepan, bring potatoes and 1½ cups water to a boil. Reduce heat; cover and simmer 15-20 minutes or until tender. Drain, reserving 1 cup cooking liquid; cool liquid to 110°-115°. Mash potatoes; set aside 1 cup to cool to 110°-115° (save remaining potatoes for another use).
2. In a large bowl, dissolve yeast and sugar in the reserved potato liquid; let stand for 5 minutes. Add the reserved mashed potatoes, butter, honey, oil, eggs, salt and 1½ cups flour; beat until smooth. Stir in enough remaining flour to form a soft dough.
3. Turn onto a floured surface; knead until smooth and elastic, 6-8 minutes. Place in a greased bowl, turning once to grease top. Cover and let rise in a warm place until doubled, about 1 hour.
4. Punch dough down and turn onto a floured surface; divide into 30 pieces. Shape each piece into a ball. Place 10 balls in each of 3 greased 9-in. round baking pans. Cover and let rise until doubled, about 30 minutes.
5. Meanwhile, preheat oven to 400°. Bake until golden brown, 20-25 minutes. Remove from pans to wire racks to cool.

1 roll: 165 cal., 5g fat (2g sat. fat), 22mg chol., 193mg sod., 26g carb. (5g sugars, 1g fiber), 3g pro.

READER RAVE...

"You can use this dough for dinner rolls, cinnamon rolls or pizza dough. Amazing."
—PAMHAN, TASTEOFHOME.COM

SWEDISH LIMPA BREAD

I've entered my bread in several fairs, and it has won every single time! Orange and anise give it a subtle but wonderful flavor.
—Beryl Parrott, Franklin, MB

Prep: 30 min. + rising • Bake: 30 min.
Makes: 2 loaves (12 pieces each)

- ½ cup packed light brown sugar
- ¼ cup dark molasses
- ¼ cup butter, cubed
- 2 Tbsp. grated orange zest
- 1½ tsp. salt
- 1 tsp. aniseed, lightly crushed
- 1 cup boiling water
- 1 cup cold water
- 2 pkg. (¼ oz. each) active dry yeast
- ½ cup warm water (110° to 115°)
- 4½ cups all-purpose flour
- 3 to 4 cups rye flour
- 2 Tbsp. cornmeal
- 2 Tbsp. butter, melted

1. In a large bowl, combine brown sugar, molasses, butter, orange zest, salt, aniseed and boiling water; stir until the brown sugar is dissolved and butter is melted. Stir in cold water; let stand until mixture cools to 110°-115°.
2. Meanwhile, in a large bowl, dissolve yeast in warm water. Stir in molasses mixture; mix well. Add all-purpose flour and 1 cup rye flour. Beat on medium speed for 3 minutes. Stir in enough remaining rye flour to form a stiff dough.
3. Turn onto a floured surface; knead until smooth and elastic, 6-8 minutes. Place in a greased bowl, turning once to grease the top. Cover and let rise in a warm place until doubled, about 1 hour.
4. Punch dough down. Turn onto a lightly floured surface; divide in half. Shape dough into 2 oval loaves. Grease 2 baking sheets and sprinkle them lightly with cornmeal. Place loaves on prepared pans. Cover and let rise until doubled, about 30 minutes.
5. Preheat oven to 350°. With a sharp knife, make 4 shallow slashes across the top of each loaf. Bake 30-35 minutes or until golden brown. Remove to wire racks; brush with butter.

1 piece: 186 cal., 3g fat (2g sat. fat), 8mg chol., 172mg sod., 35g carb. (7g sugars, 3g fiber), 4g pro.

BLUE-RIBBON TIP

Bread rises quickly when first placed in the oven; scoring creates controlled weak points to release pressure and avoid a burst top.

CINNAMON CRUMB MUFFINS

When I was 13, these muffins won a blue ribbon at our state fair. Coffee really enhances the cinnamon flavor, making these tender treats quite delicious.
—Theresa Houze, Southfield, MI

Prep: 15 min. • **Bake:** 20 min.
Makes: 6 muffins

- 1   cup all-purpose flour
- ⅓   cup sugar
- 1   tsp. baking powder
- ¼   tsp. salt
- ¼   tsp. ground cinnamon
- 1   large egg, room temperature
- ⅓   cup 2% milk
- ¼   cup butter, melted
- 1¼   tsp. instant espresso powder

CRUMB TOPPING
- 4   tsp. all-purpose flour
- 2   tsp. sugar
       Pinch ground cinnamon
- 2   tsp. cold butter

1. Preheat oven to 400°. In a small bowl, combine the first 5 ingredients. Whisk the egg, milk, butter and espresso powder until espresso powder is dissolved. Stir into dry ingredients just until moistened. Fill greased or paper-lined muffin cups two-thirds full.
2. For topping, combine flour, sugar and cinnamon. Cut in butter until mixture resembles coarse crumbs. Sprinkle about 1 tsp. over each muffin.
3. Bake for 18-20 minutes or until a toothpick comes out clean. Cool for 5 minutes before removing to a wire rack. Serve warm.
1 muffin: 229 cal., 10g fat (6g sat. fat), 60mg chol., 245mg sod., 31g carb. (14g sugars, 1g fiber), 4g pro.

KAISER ROLLS

These rolls can be enjoyed plain with soup or used for sandwiches. I make them at least once a month. This recipe earned me a blue ribbon at the county fair.
—Loraine Meyer, Bend, OR

Prep: 25 min. + rising • **Bake:** 15 min.
Makes: 16 rolls

- 2 **pkg. (¼ oz. each) active dry yeast**
- 2 **cups warm water (110° to 115°), divided**
- 4 **Tbsp. sugar, divided**
- ⅓ **cup canola oil**
- 2 **tsp. salt**
- 6 **to 6½ cups all-purpose flour**
- 1 **large egg white**
- 2 **tsp. cold water**
  Poppy and/or sesame seeds

1. In a large bowl, dissolve yeast in ½ cup warm water. Add 1 Tbsp. sugar; let stand for 5 minutes. Add the oil, salt, the remaining 1½ cups warm water and 3 Tbsp. sugar, and 4 cups flour. Beat until smooth. Stir in enough remaining flour to form a soft dough.
2. Turn the dough onto a floured surface; knead until smooth and elastic, 6-8 minutes. Place in a greased bowl, turning once to grease top. Cover and let rise in a warm place until doubled, about 1 hour.
3. Punch dough down. Turn onto a lightly floured surface; divide into 16 pieces. Shape each into a ball. Place 2 in. apart on greased baking sheets. Cover and let rise until doubled, about 30 minutes.
4. Preheat oven to 400°. Beat the egg white and cold water; brush over rolls. Sprinkle with poppy and/or sesame seeds. With scissors, cut a ¼-in.-deep cross on the top of each roll.
5. Bake for 15-20 minutes or until golden brown. Remove from pans to wire racks to cool.
1 roll: 225 cal., 5g fat (1g sat. fat), 0 chol., 300mg sod., 39g carb. (4g sugars, 1g fiber), 5g pro.

WHOLE WHEAT CRESCENT ROLLS

About 20 years ago in St. Joseph County, Indiana, my fellow 4-H judges and I selected these rolls as the grand prize winner over all the advanced pies, fancy yeast breads and holiday displays. I have shared this recipe with dozens of bakers, especially 4-H members baking with yeast for the first time so that they will experience success.
—Fancheon Resler, Albion, IN

Prep: 30 min. + rising • **Bake:** 10 min.
Makes: 2 dozen

- 2 **pkg. (¼ oz. each) active dry yeast**
- ½ **cup warm water (110° to 115°)**
- 1 **cup 2% milk (110° to 115°)**
- ½ **cup butter, softened**
- 2 **large eggs, room temperature**
- 2 **cups whole wheat flour**
- 2 **cups all-purpose flour**
- 1 **cup mashed potato flakes**
- ½ **cup packed brown sugar**
- 1 **tsp. salt**
- ¼ **cup butter, melted**

1. In a large bowl, dissolve yeast in warm water. Add the milk, softened butter, eggs, whole wheat flour, 1 cup all-purpose flour, potato flakes, brown sugar and salt. Beat on medium speed for 3 minutes. Stir in enough remaining all-purpose flour to form a soft dough (dough will be sticky).
2. Turn the dough onto a floured surface; knead until smooth and elastic, 6-8 minutes. Place dough in a greased bowl, turning once to grease the top. Cover and let rise in a warm place until doubled, about 1 hour. Punch dough down.
3. Turn onto a lightly floured surface; divide into thirds. Roll each portion into a 12-in. circle; cut each circle into 8 wedges. Roll up each wedge from the wide end; place rolls point side down 2 in. apart on greased baking sheets. Curve ends to form crescents. Cover and let rise in a warm place for 1 hour or until doubled.
4. Bake at 350° for 8-10 minutes or until golden brown. Brush with melted butter. Serve warm.
1 roll: 162 cal., 7g fat (4g sat. fat), 33mg chol., 158mg sod., 23g carb. (5g sugars, 2g fiber), 4g pro.

HEATHER ELLIOTT · FLORENCE, OREGON

HEATHER ECKSTEIN · SUNMAN, INDIANA

JUDITH LIVINGSTON · DECATUR, ALABAMA

1. EXPLORING
The fair is about trying new things. This year my kids tested the pedal tractor pull. My daughter, Taylor, pulled 165 pounds and my son, Terry, pulled 195! It was fun to see how far they could go.

2. CONNECTING
My grandson, Ryan, made a new friend at the Franklin County Fair. A moment like this lasts a lifetime.

3. COMPETING
My granddaughter, Maddyx, just loves barrel riding on her horse, Boomerang. And the ribbons the pair earns are fun, too!

FINDING STRENGTH

When I was going through a second cancer treatment in 2005, I needed to do something different to keep me going. I decided to enter one of the sewing competitions at the Elizabethtown Fair.

The first year I did a Farmall tractor throw, since we had a Farmall tractor on the farm when I was growing up. The handcrafted items like my throw were on display at a church next to the fairgrounds. Hopeful entrants would bring their work on Monday, and by Tuesday evening we could all go see if we won. That first year I won a blue ribbon!

I was hooked. Over the next eight years I did different John Deere fleece throws—each earning a first-place ribbon. The ninth year I also donated the throw to the fair auction. It went for $220!

In the 10th year I entered a Farmall throw again and got third place. I donated both that and a John Deere throw for the auction. The John Deere outdid the Farmall by a few dollars. That year my husband also surprised me during the auction by buying me a commemorative fair crock with a floral arrangement inside.

I've won 20 ribbons in 10 years: 14 blue ribbons and three each for second and third place. I also entered bedspreads, curtain valances and a wall hanging during those years of recovery.

We sure had good times at the fair, getting together with friends, listening to the country music and eating the delicious fair food— especially the homemade ice cream.

I've recently finished treatments for the fourth time. I am doing well and am thankful for that. I've spent some of my time sewing throws again. I just might have to enter some of them in the fair!

P. 202
P. 200

P. 205

P. 205

WINNING JAMS, JELLIES & PRESERVES

RASPBERRY PEACH JAM

When my jam won a first-place ribbon at our local county fair, I was overjoyed—but it's not the highest compliment that recipe has received. Two girlfriends I share it with tell me if they don't hide the jam from their husbands and children, they'll devour an entire jarful in just one sitting!
—Patricia Larsen, Leslieville, AB

Prep: 35 min. • **Process:** 15 min.
Makes: 3 half-pints

2⅔ cups finely chopped
    peeled peaches
1½ cups crushed raspberries
3 cups sugar
1½ tsp. lemon juice

1. In a Dutch oven, combine all the ingredients. Cook over low heat, stirring occasionally, until sugar has dissolved and mixture is bubbly, about 10 minutes. Continue cooking until thick, 5-10 minutes. Stir mixture occasionally. Remove from the heat; skim off foam.
2. Carefully ladle hot mixture into hot half-pint jars, leaving ¼-in. headspace. Remove air bubbles, wipe the rims and adjust the lids. Process for 15 minutes in a boiling-water canner.
Note: The processing time listed is for altitudes of 1,000 feet or less. Add 1 minute to the processing time for each 1,000 feet of additional altitude.
2 Tbsp.: 33 cal., 0 fat (0 sat. fat), 0 chol., 0 sod., 8g carb. (8g sugars, 0 fiber), 0 pro.

LIME MINT JELLY

This holly-green jelly won a Best of Show at the county fair and I was so thrilled. Flavored with lime juice and zest, it's delicious on roasted meats.
—Gloria Jarrett, Loveland, OH

Prep: 10 min. • **Process:** 10 min.
Makes: 5 half-pints

4 cups sugar
1¾ cups water
¾ cup lime juice
3 to 4 drops green food coloring, optional
1 pouch (3 oz.) liquid fruit pectin
3 Tbsp. finely chopped fresh mint leaves
¼ cup grated lime zest

1. In a large saucepan, combine sugar, water and lime juice; add food coloring if desired. Bring to a rolling boil over high heat, stirring constantly. Stir in pectin, mint and lime zest. Continue to boil for 1 minute, stirring constantly.
2. Remove from heat; skim off foam. Ladle hot mixture into 5 hot half-pint jars, leaving ¼-in. headspace. Wipe rims. Center lids on jars; screw on bands until fingertip tight.
3. Place the jars into canner with simmering water, ensuring they are completely covered with water. Bring to a boil; process for 10 minutes. Remove jars and cool.
Note: The processing time listed is for altitudes of 1,000 feet or less. Add 1 minute to the processing time for each 1,000 feet of additional altitude.
2 Tbsp.: 79 cal., 0 fat (0 sat. fat), 0 chol., 1mg sod., 21g carb. (20g sugars, 0 fiber), 0 pro.

READER RAVE...

"Excellent for meats—I'll try this with fish & lamb. I used 3½ cups of sugar instead of 4."
—JOLYANNEMARCOTTE, TASTEOFHOME.COM

HOMEMADE SAUERKRAUT

Put down that jar! You need only two ingredients (and a little patience) to make fresh, zippy sauerkraut at home. Get those brats ready!
—Josh Rink, Milwaukee, WI

Prep: 45 min. + fermenting
Makes: 40 servings (about 10 cups)

- 6 **lbs. cabbage (about 2 heads)**
- 3 **Tbsp. canning salt**
  Optional: 2 peeled and thinly sliced Granny Smith apples, 2 thinly sliced sweet onions, 2 tsp. caraway seeds and 1 tsp. ground coriander

1. Quarter cabbages and remove cores; slice ⅛ in. thick. In an extra-large bowl, combine salt and cabbage. With clean hands, squeeze cabbage until it wilts and releases liquid, about 10 minutes. If desired, add optional ingredients.

2. Firmly pack cabbage mixture into a 4-qt. fermenting crock or large glass container, removing as many of the air bubbles as possible. To make brine, combine 4½ tsp. canning salt per 1 qt. of water in a saucepan; bring to a boil until salt is dissolved. Cool brine before adding to crock. (If cabbage mixture is not covered by 1-2 in. of liquid, make more brine.)

3. Place crock weight over cabbage; the weight should be submerged in the brine. (If you don't have a crock weight, use an inverted dinner plate or glass pie plate over cabbage. The plate should be slightly smaller than the container opening, but large enough to cover most of the cabbage mixture. Weigh down the plate with 2 or 3 sealed quart jars filled with water.) If using a glass container with a lid, cover the opening loosely so any gas produced by the fermenting cabbage can escape. Alternatively, you can cover the opening with a clean, heavy towel. If you are using a crock, seal according to the manufacturer's instructions.

4. Store crock, undisturbed, at 70°-75° for 3-4 weeks (bubbles will form and the aroma will change). Cabbage must be kept submerged below surface of the liquid throughout the fermentation. Check crock 2-3 times a week; skim and remove any scum that forms on the top. Fermentation is complete when the bubbling stops. Transfer sauerkraut to individual containers.

Cover and store in the refrigerator for up to 3 months.

¼ cup: 11 cal., 0 fat (0 sat. fat) 0 chol., 344mg sod., 3g carb. (1g sugars, 1g fiber), 1g pro.

BLUE-RIBBON TIP

Don't substitute salts here—canning salt doesn't contain additives, such as anti-caking agents, that may be present in other types of salt.

A fermenting vessel is worth the investment if you plan to make sauerkraut frequently, particularly because of the included weight and the water seal features. The water seal allows the gas to escape but blocks the contaminants from entering. Place the vessel in a Tupperware-style bin during fermentation as the liquid can sometimes bubble over as gas is released.

FIRE-AND-ICE PICKLES

These sweet and spicy pickles are delicious on sandwiches or all by themselves as a snack. I like to wrap a pretty ribbon around the tops of the jars and give them as gifts.
—Myra Innes, Auburn, KS

Prep: 10 min. + chilling • **Makes:** 3 pints

- 2 jars (32 oz. each) dill pickle slices or spears
- 4 cups sugar
- 1 Tbsp. hot pepper sauce
- ½ tsp. crushed red pepper flakes
- 3 garlic cloves, peeled

1. Drain and discard juice from pickles. In a large bowl, combine pickles, sugar, pepper sauce and pepper flakes; mix well. Cover and let stand 2 hours, stirring occasionally.
2. Spoon pickle mixture into 3 pint jars; add a garlic clove to each jar. Cover and refrigerate 1 week before serving. Store in the refrigerator up to 1 month.
¼ cup: 134 cal., 0 fat (0 sat. fat), 0 chol., 362mg sod., 34g carb. (33g sugars, 0 fiber), 0 pro.

CANNED BLUEBERRY JAM

Summer doesn't feel complete without at least one berry-picking trip and a batch of homemade blueberry jam. Eat atop fresh scones or biscuits for maximum enjoyment!
—Marisa McClellan, Philadelphia, PA

....

Prep: 35 min. • **Process:** 10 min./batch
Makes: 9 half-pints

8 **cups fresh blueberries**
6 **cups sugar**
3 **Tbsp. lemon juice**
2 **tsp. ground cinnamon**
2 **tsp. grated lemon zest**
½ **tsp. ground nutmeg**
2 **pouches (3 oz. each)**
   liquid fruit pectin

1. Place berries in a food processor; cover and pulse until almost fully blended. Transfer to a stockpot. Stir in sugar, lemon juice, cinnamon, lemon zest and nutmeg. Bring to a full rolling boil over high heat, stirring constantly. Stir in the pectin. Boil for 1 minute, stirring constantly.

2. Remove from heat; skim off foam. Ladle hot mixture into hot sterilized half-pint jars, leaving ¼-in. headspace. Remove air bubbles; wipe rims and adjust lids. Process for 10 minutes in a boiling-water canner.

Note: The processing time listed is for altitudes of 1,000 feet or less. Add 1 minute to the processing time for each 1,000 feet of additional altitude.

2 Tbsp.: 74 cal., 0 fat (0 sat. fat), 0 chol., 0 sod., 19g carb. (18g sugars, 0 fiber), 0 pro.

GINGERBREAD SPICE JELLY

I've made batches of this simple jelly, a winner at our county fair, to give as gifts for many years. When the jars are empty, people return them for a refill.
—Robin Nagel, Whitehall, MT

Prep: 15 min. + steeping
Process: 10 min. • **Makes:** 5 half-pints

2½ cups water
18 gingerbread spice tea bags
4½ cups sugar
½ cup unsweetened apple juice
2 tsp. butter
2 pouches (3 oz. each) liquid fruit pectin

1. In a large saucepan, bring water to a boil. Remove from heat; add tea bags. Cover and steep 30 minutes.
2. Discard tea bags. Stir in the sugar, apple juice and butter. Bring to a full rolling boil over high heat, stirring constantly. Stir in pectin. Continue to boil 1 minute, stirring constantly.
3. Remove from heat; skim off foam. Ladle hot mixture into 5 hot half-pint jars, leaving ¼-in. headspace. Wipe rims. Center lids on jars; screw on the bands until fingertip tight.
4. Place the jars into canner with simmering water, ensuring that they are completely covered with water. Bring liquid to a boil; process for 10 minutes. Remove the jars and cool. (Jelly may take up to 2 weeks to set.)

2 Tbsp.: 91 cal., 0 fat (0 sat. fat), 1mg chol., 2mg sod., 23g carb. (23g sugars, 0 fiber), 0 pro.

READER RAVE...

"I made this jelly and it is delicious. It smells and tastes like gingerbread cookies and is not too sweet. It's great for gift giving and is so easy to make that I will certainly make more.."
—EMVM, TASTEOFHOME.COM

APRICOT PINEAPPLE JAM

Dried apricots, crushed pineapple and grapefruit juice create a memorable jam. The juice is what makes the jam taste so good.
—Carol Radil, New Britain, CT

Prep: 10 min.
Cook: 1 hour 20 min. + standing
Makes: 5 cups

- 12 **oz. dried apricots**
- 1 **cup water**
- 1 **can (20 oz.) crushed pineapple, undrained**
- ½ **cup grapefruit juice**
- 3 **cups sugar**

1. In a large saucepan, bring apricots and water to a boil. Reduce heat; cover and simmer 15 minutes or until apricots are very tender. Mash. Add pineapple, grapefruit juice and sugar. Simmer, uncovered, for 1 hour or until thick and translucent, stirring frequently.
2. Rinse five 1-cup airtight containers and lids with boiling water. Dry them thoroughly. Pour the jam into containers; cool to room temperature, about 1 hour. Cover and let stand overnight or until jam is set, but no longer than 24 hours. Refrigerate up to 3 weeks or freeze up to 1 year. Thaw frozen jam in refrigerator before serving.
2 Tbsp.: 89 cal., 0 fat (0 sat. fat), 0 chol., 0 sod., 23g carb. (20g sugars, 1g fiber), 0 pro.

SPICY PICKLED GREEN BEANS

A co-worker brought these pickled beans into work one day and I was hooked after one bite! I was thrilled when a jar of my own beans won first place at the local county fair.
—Jill Darin, Geneseo, IL

Prep: 20 min. • **Process:** 10 min.
Makes: 4 pints

- 1¾ **lbs. fresh green beans, trimmed**
- 1 **tsp. cayenne pepper**
- 4 **garlic cloves, peeled**
- 4 **tsp. dill seed or 4 fresh dill heads**
- 2½ **cups water**
- 2½ **cups white vinegar**
- ¼ **cup canning salt**

1. Pack the beans into 4 hot pint jars to within ½ in. of the top. Add the cayenne, garlic and dill seed to jars.
2. In a large saucepan, bring the water, vinegar and salt to a boil.
3. Carefully ladle hot mixture over the beans, leaving ½-in. headspace. Remove air bubbles; wipe rims and adjust lids. Process for 10 minutes in a boiling-water canner.
Note: The processing time listed is for altitudes of 1,000 feet or less. For altitudes up to 3,000 feet, add 5 minutes; 6,000 feet, add 10 minutes; 8,000 feet, add 15 minutes; 10,000 feet, add 20 minutes.
8 beans: 9 cal., 0 fat (0 sat. fat), 0 chol., 83mg sod., 2g carb. (1g sugars, 1g fiber), 1g pro.

QUICK PICKLED RADISHES

This easy recipe is the perfect addition to tacos, barbecue or just about any sandwich you can dream of. Each sliced radish is just a little bit sweet, slightly crunchy and has an amazing amount of zing. You're probably going to want to have a batch in your fridge at all times!
—Colleen Delawder, Herndon, VA

Prep: 25 min. + chilling • **Makes:** 3 cups

- 1 **lb. radishes**
- ½ **cup water**
- ½ **cup cider vinegar**
- ¼ **cup sugar**
- ¼ **cup packed light brown sugar**
- 1 **Tbsp. mustard seed**
- 1 **tsp. kosher salt**
- 1 **tsp. whole peppercorns**
- 1 **to 2 bay leaves**

With a mandoline or vegetable peeler, cut radishes into very thin slices. Place in a 1-qt. jar. In a large saucepan, bring the remaining ingredients to a boil. Carefully ladle hot liquid over radishes. Cover and refrigerate overnight.
¼ cup: 11 cal., 0 fat (0 sat. fat), 0 chol., 296mg sod., 2g carb. (1g sugars, 1g fiber), 0 pro.

STRAWBERRY BASIL JAM

I make this recipe with fresh-picked strawberries and basil grown in my own herb garden. This sweet and savory jam makes a perfect gift—just add a ribbon and a gift tag! The deep red jam laced with flecks of green basil is so beautiful.
—Julie O'Neil, Two Harbors, MN

Prep: 25 min. • **Process:** 10 min./batch
Makes: 9 half-pints

- 5 **cups crushed strawberries (about 3 lbs.)**
- 1 **tsp. butter**
- 1 **pkg. (1¾ oz.) powdered fruit pectin**
- 7 **cups sugar**
- ½ **cup minced fresh basil**

1. In a Dutch oven, combine the berries and butter. Stir in pectin. Bring mixture to a full rolling boil over high heat; stir constantly. Stir in sugar; return to a full rolling boil. Boil and stir for 1 minute. Immediately stir in basil.
2. Remove from heat; skim off foam. Ladle hot mixture into 9 hot half-pint jars, leaving ¼-in. headspace. Remove air bubbles and adjust the headspace, if necessary, by adding more hot mixture. Wipe rims. Center lids on jars; screw on bands until fingertip tight.
3. Place jars into canner with simmering water, ensuring that they are completely covered with the water. Bring to a boil; process for 10 minutes. Remove the jars and cool.
Note: The processing time listed is for altitudes of 1,000 feet or less. Add 1 minute to the processing time for each 1,000 feet of additional altitude.
2 Tbsp.: 81 cal., 0 fat (0 sat. fat), 0 chol., 1mg sod., 21g carb. (20g sugars, 0 fiber), 0 pro.

GENTLEMAN'S WHISKEY BACON JAM

You can slather this smoky jam on pretty much anything. It lasts only a week in the fridge, so I freeze small amounts for a quick, tasty snack with crackers.
—Colleen Delawder, Herndon, VA

....

Prep: 15 min. • **Cook:** 30 min.
Makes: 3 cups

- 1½ lbs. thick-sliced bacon strips, finely chopped
- 8 shallots, finely chopped
- 1 large sweet onion, finely chopped
- 2 garlic cloves, minced
- 1 tsp. chili powder
- ½ tsp. paprika
- ¼ tsp. kosher salt
- ¼ tsp. pepper
- ½ cup whiskey
- ½ cup maple syrup
- ¼ cup balsamic vinegar
- ½ cup packed brown sugar
  Assorted crackers

1. In a large skillet, cook bacon over medium heat until crisp. Drain on paper towels. Discard all but 2 Tbsp. drippings. Add shallots and onion to the drippings; cook mixture over medium heat until caramelized, stirring occasionally.
2. Stir in garlic; cook 30 seconds. Add seasonings. Remove from heat; stir in whiskey and maple syrup. Increase the heat to high; bring to a boil and cook for 3 minutes, stirring constantly. Add the vinegar and brown sugar; cook another 3 minutes, continuing to stir constantly.
3. Add crumbled bacon; reduce heat to low and cook 12 minutes, stirring every few minutes. Allow jam to cool slightly. Pulse half the jam in a food processor until smooth; stir puree into remaining jam. Serve with assorted crackers.
2 Tbsp.: 112 cal., 8g fat (3g sat. fat), 10mg chol., 118mg sod., 7g carb. (5g sugars, 0 fiber), 2g pro.

BLUE-RIBBON TIP

Make prep easier by breaking the cooked bacon into chunks, freezing it and then pulsing it in the food processor until finely chopped. It's easier (and cleaner) to crumble bacon when it's frozen.

MOM'S PICKLED CARROTS

My mother is the only person I've ever known to make this recipe. When I take it to a potluck, no one has ever heard of pickled carrots. But once they try them, they want the recipe!
—Robin Koble, Fairview, PA

....

Prep: 15 min. + chilling · **Cook:** 20 min.
Makes: 6 cups

- 2 **lbs. carrots, cut lengthwise into ¼-in.-thick strips**
- 1½ **cups sugar**
- 1½ **cups water**
- 1½ **cups cider vinegar**
- ¼ **cup mustard seed**
- 3 **cinnamon sticks (3 in.)**
- 3 **whole cloves**

1. Place the carrots in a large saucepan; add water to cover. Bring to a boil. Cook, covered, until crisp-tender, 3-5 minutes. Drain. Transfer to a large bowl.
2. In another large saucepan, combine remaining ingredients. Bring to a boil. Reduce heat; simmer liquid, uncovered, 20 minutes. Pour over the carrot sticks. Refrigerate, covered, overnight.
3. Transfer to lidded jars. Refrigerate up to 1 month.

¼ cup: 30 cal., 0 fat (0 sat. fat), 0 chol., 170mg sod., 7g carb. (6g sugars, 1g fiber), 1g pro.

GINGER BLUEBERRY JAM

When I was very young, I watched my grandma make this jam in the kitchen. As I sneaked blueberries to snack on, she picked me up and told me that if I wanted any more, I'd need to learn to make this jam!
—Jill Drury, River Forest, IL

Prep: 25 min. • **Process:** 10 min.
Makes: 4 half-pints

- 3 **cups fresh blueberries**
- 4 **cups sugar**
- 1 **Tbsp. pomegranate juice**
- 1½ **tsp. lemon juice**
- 1 **pouch (3 oz.) liquid fruit pectin**
- 2 **Tbsp. finely chopped crystallized ginger**
- ½ **tsp. ground ginger**

1. In a Dutch oven, mash the blueberries. Stir in the sugar, pomegranate juice and lemon juice. Bring to a full rolling boil over high heat, stirring constantly. Stir in pectin. Return to a full rolling boil. Boil and stir for 1 full minute.

2. Remove from the heat; skim off foam. Stir in crystallized and ground ginger. Ladle hot mixture into 4 hot sterilized half-pint jars, leaving ¼-in. headspace. Remove air bubbles; wipe rims. Center lids on jars; screw on the bands until fingertip tight. Process for 10 minutes in a boiling-water canner.

Note: The processing time listed is for altitudes of 1,000 feet or less. Add 1 minute to the processing time for each 1,000 feet of additional altitude.

2 Tbsp.: 108 cal., 0 fat (0 sat. fat), 0 chol., 1mg sod., 28g carb. (27g sugars, 0 fiber), 0 pro.

DEBBIE BRIDGES · SHELBY, NORTH CAROLINA

SONIA HEIBEL · VINING, MINNESOTA

1. SAVANNAH HAD A LITTLE LAMB

My granddaughter Savannah had a ton of fun showing her lamb at the Cleveland County Fair in North Carolina. She even won a blue ribbon!

2. QUIET MOMENT

The love between my daughter, Erika, and her calf was on display after their 4-H dairy show.

3. FAMILY AFFAIR

Ethan, Katie and McKenna exhibit hogs, lambs, goats and chickens at the Huron County Fair, earning first place in showmanship and skills. Their proud parents, siblings and grandparents cheer them on.

CHERYL NOLAN · WAKEMAN, OHIO

P. 214

P. 218

P. 221

P. 226

BEST COOKIES, BARS & BROWNIES

ORIGINAL BROWN BUTTER REFRIGERATOR COOKIES

I especially like these cookies because they're quick and easy to prepare. I can mix them up in a few minutes and pop them into the refrigerator or freezer until I'm ready to bake. These won *Country Woman* magazine's first-ever recipe contest, in December 1970.
—Ione Diekfuss, Muskego, WI

Prep: 40 min. + chilling
Bake: 5 min./batch
Makes: About 10½ dozen

- 1 **cup butter, cubed**
- 2 **cups packed brown sugar**
- 2 **large eggs, room temperature**
- 3 **cups all-purpose flour**
- 1 **tsp. cream of tartar**
- 1 **tsp. baking soda**
- ¼ **tsp. salt**
- 1 **cup finely chopped pecans**

1. Heat butter in a large saucepan over medium heat until golden brown, 7-9 minutes (do not burn). Remove from heat; stir in brown sugar until blended.
2. Transfer to a large bowl, cool slightly. Whisk in eggs, 1 at a time. Combine the flour, cream of tartar, baking soda and salt; gradually add to the butter mixture and mix well. Stir in pecans.
3. Shape the dough into four 8-in. rolls; wrap each in waxed paper. Refrigerate for 8 hours or overnight.
4. Unwrap rolls and cut into ¼-in. slices. Place 2 in. apart on ungreased baking sheets. Bake at 375° just until set, 5-7 minutes. Cool for 1 minute before removing from pans to wire racks.
1 cookie: 44 cal., 2g fat (1g sat. fat), 7mg chol., 27mg sod., 6g carb. (3g sugars, 0 fiber), 1g pro.

FIVE-STAR BROWNIES

Behind these brownies is a bit of my state's history. In 1990, when I entered them at our state fair, Kansas was celebrating the 100th birthday of a famous native son, Dwight Eisenhower. So I renamed my brownies in honor of the rank he'd achieved as a general, and I cut them out with a star-shaped cookie cutter. They ended up winning a blue ribbon!
—Pam Buerki Rogers, Victoria, KS

Prep: 15 min. • **Bake:** 30 min. + cooling
Makes: 1 dozen

- 3 **large eggs, room temperature**
- 2 **cups sugar**
- 1½ **tsp. vanilla extract**
- ½ **cup butter, melted**
- ¼ **cup shortening, melted**
- 1½ **cups all-purpose flour**
- ¾ **cup baking cocoa**
- ¾ **tsp. salt**
- 1 **cup chopped nuts, optional**

1. Preheat oven to 350°. In a large bowl, beat the eggs, sugar and vanilla until blended. Beat in butter and shortening until smooth. Combine flour, cocoa and salt; gradually add to the egg mixture. Stir in nuts if desired.
2. Line a 13x9-in. baking pan with foil and grease the foil; pour batter into pan. Bake for 30 minutes or until a toothpick inserted in the center comes out clean. Cool in pan on a wire rack.
3. Using foil, lift brownies out of pan. Discard foil. Cut brownies with a 3-in. star-shaped cookie cutter or into bars.
1 brownie: 326 cal., 14g fat (6g sat. fat), 67mg chol., 227mg sod., 49g carb. (34g sugars, 1g fiber), 4g pro.

LAYERED PEANUT BUTTER BROWNIES

The combination of chocolate and peanut butter makes these brownies a real crowd pleaser. They're so good that they won a ribbon at the fair.
—Margaret McNeil, Germantown, TN

Prep: 15 min. • **Bake:** 35 min. + cooling
Makes: 2 dozen

- 3 large eggs, room temperature
- 1 cup butter, melted
- 2 tsp. vanilla extract
- 2 cups sugar
- 1¼ cups all-purpose flour
- ¾ cup baking cocoa
- ½ tsp. baking powder
- ¼ tsp. salt
- 1 cup milk chocolate chips

FILLING
- 2 pkg. (8 oz. each) cream cheese, softened
- ½ cup creamy peanut butter
- ¼ cup sugar
- 1 large egg
- 2 Tbsp. 2% milk

1. Preheat oven to 350°. In a large bowl, beat eggs, butter and vanilla until smooth. Whisk together dry ingredients; gradually add to the egg mixture. Stir in chocolate chips. Set aside 1 cup for topping. Spread remaining batter into a greased 13x9-in. baking pan.
2. For the filling, in a small bowl, beat the cream cheese, peanut butter and sugar until smooth. Beat in egg and milk on low just until combined. Carefully spread over batter. Drop reserved batter by tablespoonfuls over filling. Cut through batter with a knife to swirl.
3. Bake until a toothpick inserted in the center comes out clean, 35-40 minutes (do not overbake). Cool on a wire rack. Chill until serving.

Note: Reduced-fat peanut butter is not recommended for this recipe.

1 brownie: 321 cal., 20g fat (11g sat. fat), 72mg chol., 196mg sod., 32g carb. (24g sugars, 1g fiber), 5g pro.

BLUE-RIBBON TIP

If a brownie recipe is too cakey or too fudgy for your tastes but you otherwise love the flavor, you can make adjustments. Fudgy brownies have a higher fat-to-flour ratio than cakelike brownies. The trick to making brownies fudgier is to add more fat (in the case of this recipe, butter). Cakelike brownies have more flour and rely on baking powder for leavening.

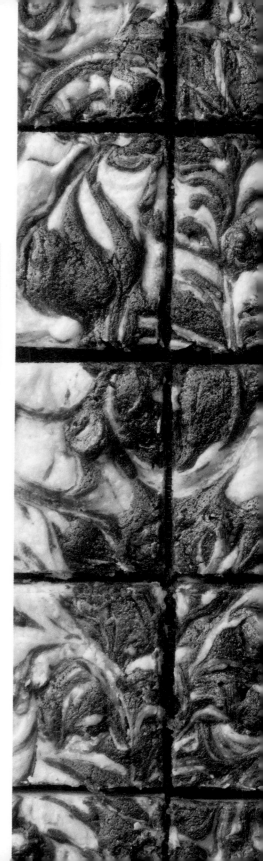

FIRST-PLACE COCONUT MACAROONS

These coconut macaroon cookies earned me a first-place ribbon at the county fair. They remain my husband's favorites—whenever I make them to give away, he always asks me where his batch is! I especially like the fact that this recipe makes a small enough batch for the two of us to nibble on.
—Penny Ann Habeck, Shawano, WI

Prep: 10 min. • **Bake:** 20 min./batch
Makes: about 1½ dozen

- 1⅓ **cups sweetened shredded coconut**
- ⅓ **cup sugar**
- 2 **Tbsp. all-purpose flour**
- ⅛ **tsp. salt**
- 2 **large egg whites, room temperature**
- ½ **tsp. vanilla extract**

1. Preheat oven to 325°. In a small bowl, combine coconut, sugar, flour and salt. Add egg whites and vanilla; mix well.
2. Drop by rounded teaspoonfuls onto greased baking sheets. Bake for 18-20 minutes or until golden brown. Cool on a wire rack.

1 cookie: 54 cal., 2g fat (2g sat. fat), 0 chol., 41mg sod., 8g carb. (7g sugars, 0 fiber), 1g pro. **Diabetic exchanges:** ½ starch, ½ fat.

PEPPERMINT BROWNIES

My grandmother encouraged me to enter these mint brownies in the county fair some years ago, and they earned top honors! They're a delicious treat to serve during the holidays.
—Marcy Greenblatt, Redding, CA

Prep: 15 min. • **Bake:** 35 min. + cooling
Makes: 2 dozen

1⅓ cups all-purpose flour
1 cup baking cocoa
1 tsp. salt
1 tsp. baking powder
¾ cup canola oil
2 cups sugar
4 large eggs, room temperature
2 tsp. vanilla extract
⅔ cup crushed peppermint candies
GLAZE
1 cup semisweet chocolate chips
1 Tbsp. shortening
2 Tbsp. crushed peppermint candies

1. Preheat oven to 350°. Line a 13x9-in. baking pan with foil and grease the foil; set pan aside.
2. In a bowl, whisk together the first 4 ingredients. In a large bowl, beat oil and sugar until blended. Add eggs, 1 at a time, beating well after each addition. Beat in vanilla. Gradually add the flour mixture; stir in peppermint candies. Spread into prepared pan.
3. Bake until a toothpick inserted in center comes out clean, 35-40 minutes. Cool in pan on a wire rack.
4. In a microwave, melt chocolate chips and shortening; stir until smooth. Spread glaze over brownies; sprinkle with candies. Cut into bars.
1 brownie: 222 cal., 11g fat (3g sat. fat), 35mg chol., 128mg sod., 31g carb. (22g sugars, 1g fiber), 3g pro.

BLUE-RIBBON CARROT CAKE COOKIES

I created this recipe because I just love carrot cake. I wanted something I could take with me anywhere, that would not need a fork. I entered my recipe in the Los Angeles County Fair, and the cookies not only won first place but were also named Best of Division.
—Marina Castle-Kelley, Canyon Country, CA

Prep: 50 min.
Bake: 10 min./batch + cooling
Makes: 4 dozen

- 1 cup butter, softened
- 1 cup packed brown sugar
- ¾ cup sugar
- 2 large eggs, room temperature
- 1½ tsp. vanilla extract
- ½ tsp. rum extract
- 3 cups all-purpose flour
- ½ cup old-fashioned oats
- 1½ tsp. ground cinnamon
- ¾ tsp. salt
- ¾ tsp. baking soda
- ½ tsp. ground ginger
- ½ tsp. ground nutmeg
- 1 cup chopped walnuts, toasted
- ¾ cup shredded carrots
- ¾ cup raisins

FILLING
- 1 pkg. (8 oz.) cream cheese, softened
- ½ cup butter, softened
- 1¼ cups confectioners' sugar
- 1 tsp. vanilla extract
- ½ cup chopped walnuts, toasted
- 2 Tbsp. crushed pineapple
  Additional confectioners' sugar

1. Preheat oven to 350°. In a large bowl, cream butter and sugars until light and fluffy, 5-7 minutes. Beat in eggs and extracts. Combine the flour, oats, cinnamon, salt, baking soda, ginger and nutmeg; gradually add to creamed mixture and mix well. Stir in the walnuts, carrots and raisins.

2. Drop dough by rounded teaspoonfuls 2 in. apart onto greased baking sheets. Flatten with a glass dipped in sugar. Bake for 9-11 minutes or until lightly browned. Remove to wire racks to cool completely.

3. In a small bowl, beat cream cheese, butter, confectioners' sugar and vanilla until light and fluffy. Stir in walnuts and pineapple. Spread over the bottoms of half the cookies; top with remaining cookies. Sprinkle both sides with additional confectioners' sugar. Store in the refrigerator.

Freeze option: Place unfilled cookies in an airtight container, separating layers with waxed paper; freeze for up to 1 month. Thaw in a single layer before filling.

1 sandwich cookie: 176 cal., 10g fat (5g sat. fat), 29mg chol., 117mg sod., 20g carb. (12g sugars, 1g fiber), 2g pro.

FROSTED CASHEW COOKIES

We savor these cookies at Christmas, but they're special year-round with coffee or tucked into a lunchbox. I won a ribbon with these cookies at my county fair.
—Sheila Wyum, Rutland, ND

Prep: 20 min.
Bake: 10 min./batch + cooling
Makes: about 3 dozen

- ½ cup butter, softened
- 1 cup packed brown sugar
- 1 large egg, room temperature
- ⅓ cup sour cream
- ½ tsp. vanilla extract
- 2 cups all-purpose flour
- ¾ tsp. each baking powder, baking soda and salt
- 1½ cups salted cashews, coarsely chopped
  BROWNED BUTTER FROSTING
- ½ cup butter, cubed
- 3 Tbsp. half-and-half cream
- ¼ tsp. vanilla extract
- 2 cups confectioners' sugar
  Additional cashew halves, optional

1. Preheat oven to 375°. In a bowl, cream butter and brown sugar. Beat in egg, sour cream and vanilla; mix well. Combine the flour, baking powder, baking soda and salt; add to creamed mixture and mix well. Stir in cashews.
2. Drop by tablespoonfuls 2 in. apart onto greased baking sheets. Bake for 8-10 minutes or until lightly browned. Cool on a wire rack.
3. Lightly brown butter in a saucepan. Remove from heat; add cream and vanilla. Beat in confectioners' sugar until thick and smooth. Frost cookies. Top with cashew halves if desired.
2 cookies: 348 cal., 19g fat (9g sat. fat), 43mg chol., 381mg sod., 40g carb. (26g sugars, 1g fiber), 5g pro.

BLUEBERRY LATTICE BARS

Since our area has an annual blueberry festival, my daughters and I are always looking for amazing new recipes to enter in the cooking contest. These lovely bars won a blue ribbon one year.
—Debbie Ayers, Baileyville, ME

Prep: 25 min. + chilling • **Bake:** 30 min.
Makes: 2 dozen

- 1⅓ cups butter, softened
- ⅔ cup sugar
- ¼ tsp. salt
- 1 large egg, room temperature
- ½ tsp. vanilla extract
- 3¾ cups all-purpose flour
  FILLING
- 3 cups fresh or frozen blueberries
- 1 cup sugar
- 3 Tbsp. cornstarch

1. Cream butter, sugar and salt until light and fluffy, 5-7 minutes; beat in egg and vanilla. Gradually beat in flour. Divide dough in half; shape each half into a 1-in.-thick rectangle. Wrap and refrigerate 2 hours or overnight.
2. Preheat oven to 375°. Place the blueberries, sugar and cornstarch in a small saucepan. Bring to a boil over medium heat, stirring frequently; cook and stir until thickened, about 2 minutes. Cool slightly.
3. Roll each portion of dough between 2 sheets of waxed paper into a 14x10-in. rectangle. Place on separate baking sheets; freeze until firm, 5-10 minutes. Place 1 rectangle in a greased 13x9-in. baking pan, pressing onto bottom and about ½ in. up the sides. Add filling.
4. Cut the remaining rectangle into ½-in. strips; freeze 5-10 minutes to firm. Arrange strips over filling in crisscross fashion. If desired, press edges with a fork to seal strips. Bake until the top crust is golden brown, 30-35 minutes. Cool on a wire rack. Cut into bars.
1 bar: 233 cal., 11g fat (7g sat. fat), 35mg chol., 109mg sod., 32g carb. (16g sugars, 1g fiber), 3g pro.

SUPER SPUD BROWNIES

These moist and cakelike brownies came from my mom's old cookbook. Mashed potatoes may seem like an unusual ingredient, but they work beautifully—this recipe took first place at a local festival.

—Marlene Gerer, Denton, MT

Prep: 15 min. • **Bake:** 25 min.
Makes: 16 servings

- ¾ **cup mashed potatoes**
- ½ **cup sugar**
- ½ **cup packed brown sugar**
- ½ **cup canola oil**
- 2 **large eggs, room temperature, lightly beaten**
- 1 **tsp. vanilla extract**
- ½ **cup all-purpose flour**
- ⅓ **cup cocoa powder**
- ½ **tsp. baking powder**
- ⅛ **tsp. salt**
- ½ **cup chopped pecans, optional Confectioners' sugar**

1. Preheat oven to 350°. In a large bowl, combine the mashed potatoes, sugars, oil, eggs and vanilla. Combine the flour, cocoa, baking powder and salt; gradually add to the potato mixture. Fold in pecans if desired. Transfer to a greased 9-in. square baking pan.
2. Bake for 23-27 minutes or until a toothpick inserted in center comes out clean. Cool on a wire rack. Dust with confectioners' sugar. Cut into bars.
1 brownie: 150 cal., 8g fat (1g sat. fat), 27mg chol., 68mg sod., 19g carb. (13g sugars, 0 fiber), 2g pro. **Diabetic exchanges:** 1½ fat, 1 starch.

BUTTER PECAN COOKIES

When my daughter was a teen, these cookies earned her blue ribbons from two county fairs. Then a few years ago, her own daughter took home a blue ribbon for the same cookie. Needless to say, these mouthwatering morsels are winners!

—Martha Thefield, Cedartown, GA

Prep: 25 min. + chilling
Bake: 10 min./batch
Makes: about 4 dozen

- 1¾ **cups chopped pecans**
- 1 **Tbsp. plus 1 cup butter, softened, divided**
- 1 **cup packed brown sugar**
- 1 **large egg, separated, room temperature**
- 1 **tsp. vanilla extract**
- 2 **cups self-rising flour**
- 1 **cup pecan halves**

1. Preheat oven to 325°. Place chopped pecans and 1 Tbsp. butter in a baking pan. Bake for 5-7 minutes or until pecans are toasted and browned, stirring frequently. Set aside to cool.
2. In a large bowl, cream brown sugar and remaining 1 cup butter until light and fluffy, 5-7 minutes. Beat in egg yolk and vanilla. Gradually add flour and mix well. Cover and refrigerate for 1 hour or until easy to handle.
3. Preheat oven to 375°. Roll dough into 1-in. balls, then roll balls in the toasted pecans, pressing nuts into dough. Place 2 in. apart on ungreased baking sheets. Beat egg white until foamy. Dip pecan halves in egg white, then gently press 1 into each ball.
4. Bake 10-12 minutes or until golden brown. Cool for 2 minutes before removing to wire racks.
Note: As a substitute for each cup of self-rising flour, place 1½ tsp. baking powder and ½ tsp. salt in a measuring cup. Add all-purpose flour to measure 1 cup.
2 cookies: 233 cal., 18g fat (6g sat. fat), 31mg chol., 208mg sod., 18g carb. (9g sugars, 1g fiber), 3g pro.

RHUBARB-FILLED COOKIES

I won a blue ribbon at our local fair for these cookies. They're so pretty with the ruby red filling peeking through the dough. Try making these tender cookies and just watch the smiles appear!
—Pauline Bondy, Grand Forks, ND

Prep: 25 min. • **Bake:** 10 min.
Makes: about 4½ dozen

- 1 **cup butter, softened**
- 1 **cup sugar**
- 1 **cup packed brown sugar**
- 4 **large eggs, room temperature**
- 4½ **cups all-purpose flour**
- 1 **tsp. baking soda**
- 1 **tsp. salt**

FILLING
- 3½ **cups chopped fresh or frozen rhubarb, thawed**
- 1½ **cups sugar**
- 6 **Tbsp. water, divided**
- ¼ **cup cornstarch**
- 1 **tsp. vanilla extract**

1. Preheat oven to 375°. Cream the butter and sugars until light and fluffy, 5-7 minutes. Add eggs, 1 at a time; beat well after each addition. Combine flour, baking soda and salt; gradually add to creamed mixture and mix well. (Dough will be sticky.)
2. For filling, combine the rhubarb, sugar and 2 Tbsp. water in a large saucepan; bring to a boil. Reduce heat; simmer, uncovered, until thickened, stirring frequently, about 10 minutes.
3. Combine cornstarch and remaining 4 Tbsp. water until smooth; stir into rhubarb mixture. Bring to a boil; cook and stir until thickened, about 2 minutes. Remove from the heat; stir in vanilla.
4. Drop dough by tablespoonfuls 2 in. apart onto ungreased baking sheets. Using the end of a wooden spoon handle, make an indentation in the center of each cookie; fill with a rounded teaspoon of filling. Top with ½ tsp. dough, allowing some filling to show. Bake until lightly browned, 8-10 minutes.
Note: If using frozen rhubarb, measure rhubarb while still frozen, then thaw completely. Drain in a colander, but do not press liquid out.
1 cookie: 129 cal., 4g fat (2g sat. fat), 23mg chol., 101mg sod., 22g carb. (13g sugars, 0 fiber), 2g pro.

BEST COOKIES, BARS & BROWNIES

CRANBERRY COOKIES WITH BROWNED BUTTER GLAZE

I won a baking contest with these chunky glazed cookies that are so easy, even novice bakers can pull them off. What makes them taste so special? Fresh cranberries.
—Laurie Cornett, Charlevoix, MI

....

Prep: 40 min.
Bake: 10 min./batch + cooling
Makes: about 4½ dozen

- ½ cup butter, softened
- 1 cup sugar
- ¾ cup packed brown sugar
- 1 large egg, room temperature
- 2 Tbsp. orange juice
- 3 cups all-purpose flour
- 1 tsp. baking powder
- ½ tsp. salt
- ¼ tsp. baking soda
- ¼ cup 2% milk
- 2½ cups coarsely chopped fresh cranberries
- 1 cup white baking chips
- 1 cup chopped pecans or walnuts

GLAZE
- ⅓ cup butter, cubed
- 2 cups confectioners' sugar
- 1½ tsp. vanilla extract
- 3 to 4 Tbsp. water

1. Preheat oven to 375°. In a large bowl, cream butter and sugars until light and fluffy, 5-7 minutes. Beat in egg and orange juice. In another bowl, whisk flour, baking powder, salt and baking soda; add to the creamed mixture alternately with milk. Stir in cranberries, baking chips and pecans.

2. Drop dough by level tablespoonfuls 1 in. apart onto greased baking sheets. Bake 10-12 minutes or until light brown. Remove from pans to wire racks to cool completely.

3. For glaze, in a small heavy saucepan, melt butter over medium heat. Heat for 5-7 minutes or until golden brown, stirring constantly. Remove from heat. Stir in confectioners' sugar, vanilla and enough water to reach a drizzling consistency. Drizzle over cookies. Let stand until set.

1 cookie: 130 cal., 5g fat (3g sat. fat), 12mg chol., 66mg sod., 19g carb. (13g sugars, 1g fiber), 1g pro.

PUMPKIN COOKIES WITH BROWNED BUTTER FROSTING

The recipe for these pleasantly spiced pumpkin cookies won a champion ribbon at our local county fair. These are a family favorite, and everyone enjoys the soft cakelike texture.
—Robin Nagel, Whitehall, MT

Prep: 25 min.
Bake: 10 min./batch + cooling
Makes: about 9 dozen

- 1½ **cups butter, softened**
- 2 **cups packed brown sugar**
- 1 **cup canned pumpkin**
- 2 **large eggs, room temperature**
- ½ **cup crystallized ginger, finely chopped**
- 5 **cups all-purpose flour**
- 2 **tsp. baking soda**
- 2 **tsp. ground cinnamon**
- 2 **tsp. ground ginger**
- ½ **tsp. salt**

FROSTING
- ⅔ **cup butter, cubed**
- 4 **cups confectioners' sugar**
- 1 **tsp. vanilla extract**
- 4 **to 5 Tbsp. 2% milk**

1. Preheat oven to 375°. In a large bowl, cream butter and brown sugar until light and fluffy, 5-7 minutes. Beat in pumpkin, eggs and crystallized ginger. In another bowl, whisk the flour, baking soda, cinnamon, ginger and salt; gradually beat into the creamed mixture.
2. Drop dough by tablespoonfuls 2 in. apart onto ungreased baking sheets. Bake 6-8 minutes or until golden brown. Remove to wire racks to cool completely.
3. For the frosting, in a small heavy saucepan, melt butter over medium heat. Heat 5-7 minutes or until golden brown, stirring constantly. Transfer to a large bowl. Gradually beat in confectioners' sugar, vanilla and enough milk to reach desired spreading consistency. Spread over cookies.
Freeze option: Freeze unfrosted cookies in freezer containers. To use, thaw in covered containers; frost as directed.
1 cookie: 93 cal., 4g fat (2g sat. fat), 14mg chol., 64mg sod., 14g carb. (9g sugars, 0 fiber), 1g pro.

CHOCOLATE TRUFFLE COOKIES

I experimented with a chocolate cookie recipe until I was satisfied with the results. I entered these cookies at our county fair and won a blue ribbon. Chocolate lovers will gobble up these sweet treats.
—Sharon Miller, Thousand Oaks, CA

Prep: 15 min. + chilling
Bake: 10 min./batch
Makes: about 5½ dozen

- 1¼ **cups butter, softened**
- 2¼ **cups confectioners' sugar**
- ⅓ **cup baking cocoa**
- ¼ **cup sour cream**
- 1 **Tbsp. vanilla extract**
- 2¼ **cups all-purpose flour**
- 2 **cups semisweet chocolate chips**
- ¼ **cup chocolate sprinkles**

1. In a large bowl, cream butter, confectioners' sugar and cocoa until light and fluffy. Beat in sour cream and vanilla. Add flour; mix well. Stir in chocolate chips. Refrigerate for 1 hour.
2. Preheat oven to 325°. Roll chilled dough into 1-in. balls; dip in chocolate sprinkles. Place, sprinkled side up, 2 in. apart on ungreased baking sheets. Bake for 10 minutes or until set. Cool 5 minutes before removing to a wire rack to cool completely.
2 cookies: 179 cal., 10g fat (6g sat. fat), 20mg chol., 72mg sod., 22g carb. (14g sugars, 1g fiber), 2g pro.

WINNING APRICOT BARS

This recipe is down-home baking at its best, and it really represents all regions of the country. It's won blue ribbons at county fairs and cookie contests in several states! It's perfect for potluck suppers, bake sales, lunchboxes or just plain snacking.
—Jill Moritz, Irvine, CA

Prep: 15 min. • **Bake:** 30 min. + cooling
Makes: 2 dozen

- ¾ **cup butter, softened**
- 1 **cup sugar**
- 1 **large egg, room temperature**
- ½ **tsp. vanilla extract**
- 2 **cups all-purpose flour**
- ¼ **tsp. baking powder**
- 1⅓ **cups sweetened**
    shredded coconut
- ½ **cup chopped walnuts**
- 1 **jar (10 to 12 oz.) apricot preserves**

1. Preheat oven to 350°. In a large bowl, cream butter and sugar until light and fluffy, 5-7 minutes. Beat in egg and vanilla. In a small bowl, whisk flour and baking powder; gradually add to creamed mixture, mixing well. Fold in coconut and walnuts.

2. Press two-thirds of dough onto the bottom of a greased 13x9-in. baking pan. Spread with preserves; crumble remaining dough over preserves. Bake 30-35 minutes or until golden brown. Cool completely in pan on a wire rack. Cut into bars.

1 bar: 195 cal., 10g fat (6g sat. fat), 23mg chol., 72mg sod., 27g carb. (16g sugars, 1g fiber), 2g pro.

BLUE-RIBBON TIP

Do you know the difference between jam and preserves? Preserves contain larger chunks—whole small fruit or big pieces of a larger fruit—suspended in a thick gelled syrup. While jams are often made with bruised or squashed fruit, because it's getting cooked anyway, preserves can showcase a perfect fruit.

SWEET & SALTY PEANUT BUTTER BITES

My son Micah and I love peanut butter cups, so we made them into a new treat. We won first place in a creative baking contest with these no-bake sweets!
—Autumn Emigh, Gahanna, OH

Prep: 20 min. • **Cook:** 5 min. + standing
Makes: about 5 dozen

- ½ **cup semisweet chocolate chips**
- 4 **peanut butter cups (¾ oz. each), chopped**
- 1⅓ **cups creamy peanut butter**
- 1 **cup sugar**
- 1 **cup light corn syrup**
- ⅛ **tsp. salt**
- 4 **cups Rice Krispies**
- 1 **cup broken pretzels**

1. Freeze chocolate chips and peanut butter cups until partially frozen, about 15 minutes. Meanwhile, in a large saucepan, combine peanut butter, sugar, corn syrup and salt. Cook and stir over low heat until blended.

2. Remove from heat; stir in the Rice Krispies and pretzels until coated. Let stand 5 minutes; gently fold in chocolate chips and peanut butter cups until just combined. Drop by tablespoonfuls onto waxed paper; let stand until set.

1 cookie: 86 cal., 4g fat (1g sat. fat), 0 chol., 67mg sod., 13g carb. (10g sugars, 0 fiber), 2g pro.

MINCEMEAT COOKIE BARS

My daughter won the grand champion title at the Alaska State Fair with these bars when she was 10 years old. The topping is delicious but a bit crumbly; for neatly edged cookies, freeze before cutting.
—Mary Bohanan, Delta, CO

Prep: 15 min. • **Bake:** 30 min. + cooling
Makes: 3 dozen

- 1 tsp. butter
- 2 cups all-purpose flour
- 1 cup sugar
- ½ tsp. baking soda
- ½ tsp. salt
- ½ cup canola oil
- ¼ cup 2% milk
- 1 jar (28 oz.) prepared mincemeat
- 1 cup chopped pecans

1. Preheat oven to 400°. Line an 8-in. square baking pan with foil; grease foil with butter. In a large bowl, whisk flour, sugar, baking soda and salt. Stir in oil and milk. Reserve 1 cup for topping; press remaining crumb mixture onto bottom of prepared pan. Spread with mincemeat.

2. Stir pecans into reserved crumb mixture; sprinkle over top. Bake for 30-35 minutes or until the topping is golden brown. Cool completely in pan on a wire rack. Cut into bars.

1 bar: 134 cal., 6g fat (1g sat. fat), 0 chol., 59mg sod., 20g carb. (13g sugars, 1g fiber), 1g pro.

LEMON BARS WITH CREAM CHEESE FROSTING

I won a baking contest at Purdue University with this recipe. I think you'll love the dreamy topping.
—Michael Hunter, Fort Wayne, IN

Prep: 20 min. • **Bake:** 20 min. + cooling
Makes: 2 dozen

- 1 **cup butter, softened**
- 2 **cups sugar**
- 4 **large eggs, room temperature**
- 2 **tsp. lemon extract**
- 1¾ **cups all-purpose flour**
- ½ **tsp. salt**
- 1 **tsp. grated lemon zest**

CREAM CHEESE FROSTING

- 4 **oz. cream cheese, softened**
- 2 **Tbsp. butter, softened**
- 2 **cups confectioners' sugar**
- 2 **tsp. lemon juice**
- 1½ **tsp. grated lemon zest**

1. Preheat oven to 350°. In a large bowl, cream butter and sugar until light and fluffy, 5-7 minutes. Beat in eggs and extract. Combine flour and salt; gradually add to creamed mixture and mix well. Stir in lemon zest.

2. Spread into a greased 13x9-in. baking pan. Bake 18-22 minutes or until center is set and edges are golden brown. Cool completely.

3. For frosting, in a large bowl, beat cream cheese and butter until fluffy. Beat in confectioners' sugar, lemon juice and zest. Frost top and cut into bars. Store in the refrigerator.

1 bar: 243 cal., 11g fat (7g sat. fat), 59mg chol., 145mg sod., 34g carb. (27g sugars, 0 fiber), 2g pro.

BLUE-RIBBON TIP

These rich bars don't use baking soda or baking powder, so it's important to beat the butter and sugar together really well to create enough air in the batter to cause the bars to rise in the oven. These bars are almost like cake; when the edges are lightly browned and pull away from the sides of the pan, the bars are ready to come out of the oven. The center will look set.

RASPBERRY NUT PINWHEELS

I won first prize in a recipe contest with these yummy swirl cookies. The flavors of the raspberry and walnuts really come through, and the pinwheels are so much fun to make!
—Pat Habiger, Spearville, KS

Prep: 20 min. + chilling
Bake: 10 min./batch
Makes: about 3½ dozen

- ½ cup butter, softened
- 1 cup sugar
- 1 large egg, room temperature
- 1 tsp. vanilla extract
- 2 cups all-purpose flour
- 1 tsp. baking powder
- ¼ cup seedless raspberry jam
- ¾ cup finely chopped walnuts

1. In a large bowl, cream butter and sugar until light and fluffy, 5-7 minutes. Beat in egg and vanilla. In another bowl, whisk flour and baking powder; gradually beat into creamed mixture.
2. Roll out dough between 2 sheets of waxed paper into a 12-in. square. Remove waxed paper. Spread dough with jam; sprinkle with nuts. Roll up tightly, jelly-roll style; cover. Refrigerate until firm, about 2 hours.
3. Preheat oven to 375°. Uncover dough roll and cut crosswise into ¼-in. slices. Place 2 in. apart on ungreased baking sheets. Bake until edges are light brown, 9-12 minutes. Remove from pans to wire racks to cool.
1 cookie: 79 cal., 4g fat (1g sat. fat), 11mg chol., 27mg sod., 11g carb. (6g sugars, 0 fiber), 1g pro.

SCOTTISH SHORTBREAD

My mother, who is of Scottish heritage, passed this recipe, along with other favorite ones, on to me. When I entered this treat at our local fair, it won a red ribbon.
—Rose Mabee, Selkirk, MB

Prep: 15 min.
Bake: 20 min./batch + cooling
Makes: about 4 dozen

- 2 cups butter, softened
- 1 cup packed brown sugar
- 4 to 4½ cups all-purpose flour

1. Preheat oven to 325°. Cream butter and brown sugar until light and fluffy, 5-7 minutes. Add 3¾ cups flour; mix well. Turn dough onto a floured surface; knead for 5 minutes, adding enough remaining flour to form a soft dough.
2. On a sheet of parchment paper, roll dough to a 16x9-in. rectangle. Transfer to a baking sheet, and cut into 3x1-in. strips. Prick each cookie multiple times with a fork. Refrigerate at least 30 minutes or overnight.
3. Separate cookies and place them 1 in. apart on ungreased baking sheets. Bake until cookies are lightly browned, 20-25 minutes. Transfer to wire racks to cool completely.
1 cookie: 123 cal., 8g fat (5g sat. fat), 20mg chol., 62mg sod., 12g carb. (5g sugars, 0 fiber), 1g pro.

LIME & GIN COCONUT MACAROONS

I took these lime and coconut macaroons to our annual cookie exchange, where we name a queen each year. These won me the crown!
—Milissa Kirkpatrick, Palestine, TX

Prep: 20 min.
Bake: 15 min./batch + cooling
Makes: about 2½ dozen

- 4 large egg whites
- ⅔ cup sugar
- 3 Tbsp. gin
- 1½ tsp. grated lime zest
- ¼ tsp. salt
- ¼ tsp. almond extract
- 1 pkg. (14 oz.) sweetened shredded coconut
- ½ cup all-purpose flour
- 8 oz. white baking chocolate, melted

1. Preheat oven to 350°. Whisk the first 6 ingredients until blended. In another bowl, toss coconut with flour; stir in egg white mixture.
2. Drop by tablespoonfuls 2 in. apart onto greased baking sheets. Bake until tops are light brown, 15-18 minutes. Remove from pans to wire racks to cool completely.
3. Dip bottoms of macaroons into melted chocolate, allowing excess to drip off. Place on waxed paper; let stand until set. Store in an airtight container.

1 cookie: 133 cal., 7g fat (6g sat. fat), 0 chol., 67mg sod., 17g carb. (15g sugars, 1g fiber), 2g pro.

COOKIE JAR GINGERSNAPS

My grandma kept two cookie jars in her pantry. One of the jars, which I now have, always had these crisp and chewy gingersnaps in it. They're still my favorite cookies. My daughter used this recipe for a 4-H fair and won a blue ribbon.
—Deb Handy, Pomona, KS

Prep: 20 min. • **Bake:** 15 min./batch
Makes: 3 dozen

- ¾ cup shortening
- 1 cup plus 2 Tbsp. sugar, divided
- 1 large egg, room temperature
- ¼ cup molasses
- 2 cups all-purpose flour
- 2 tsp. baking soda
- 1½ tsp. ground ginger
- 1 tsp. ground cinnamon
- ½ tsp. salt

1. Preheat oven to 350°. Cream shortening and 1 cup sugar until light and fluffy, 5-7 minutes. Beat in egg and molasses. In another bowl, combine the next 5 ingredients; gradually add to the creamed mixture and mix well.
2. Shape level tablespoons of dough into balls. Dip 1 side of each ball into the remaining 2 Tbsp. sugar; place 2 in. apart, sugary side up, on greased baking sheets. Bake until lightly browned and crinkly, 12-15 minutes. Remove to wire racks to cool.

1 cookie: 92 cal., 4g fat (1g sat. fat), 5mg chol., 106mg sod., 13g carb. (7g sugars, 0 fiber), 1g pro.

BLUE-RIBBON TIP

For easy cleanup, spritz the measuring cup with a little cooking spray before measuring sticky ingredients like honey and molasses.

CHERRY NO-BAKE COOKIES

I always loved my no-bake cookie recipe but was never able to place at the fair with it. So I mixed in some maraschino cherries, added almond extract and voila! I won a blue ribbon at the county fair in 2010.
—Denise Wheeler, Newaygo, MI

Prep: 30 min. + chilling
Makes: about 5½ dozen

- 2 cups sugar
- ½ cup butter, cubed
- 6 Tbsp. 2% milk
- 3 Tbsp. baking cocoa
- 1 cup peanut butter
- ½ tsp. vanilla extract
- ¼ tsp. almond extract
- 3 cups quick-cooking oats
- 1 jar (10 oz.) maraschino cherries, well drained and finely chopped

1. In a large saucepan, combine sugar, butter, milk and cocoa. Bring to a boil, stirring constantly. Cook and stir 3 minutes.
2. Remove from heat; stir in peanut butter and extracts until blended. Stir in oats and cherries. Drop mixture by tablespoonfuls onto waxed paper-lined baking sheets. Refrigerate until set. Store in airtight containers.

1 cookie: 81 cal., 4g fat (1g sat. fat), 4mg chol., 29mg sod., 11g carb. (8g sugars, 1g fiber), 2g pro.

BLUE-RIBBON TIP

Cherries are jampacked with antioxidants, vitamins and minerals. To sweeten the deal, they're low in calories, too.

JAMAICAN CHOCOLATE COOKIES WITH CARAMEL CREME

I made these for an office party cookie contest—and not a crumb was left on the platter! Sweet potatoes are the secret ingredient. Canned sweet potatoes will work, too, if you're short on time.

—Noelle Myers, Grand Forks, ND

....

Prep: 45 min. + standing
Bake: 10 min./batch + cooling
Makes: about 2½ dozen cookies

- 1 pkg. (11½ oz.) semisweet chocolate chunks, divided
- ½ cup butter, softened
- ½ cup confectioners' sugar
- ½ cup mashed sweet potatoes
- 1 tsp. minced fresh gingerroot
- ½ tsp. vanilla extract
- 1¼ cups all-purpose flour
- ¼ cup cornstarch
- 2 Tbsp. baking cocoa
- 1½ tsp. baking powder
- ¼ tsp. baking soda
- ¼ tsp. salt

FILLING
- ⅔ cup whipped cream cheese
- ⅓ cup dulce de leche
- 2 Tbsp. sweetened condensed milk
- ⅛ tsp. ground cinnamon
- ⅛ tsp. ground allspice
- ⅛ tsp. salt

1. Preheat oven to 375°. In a microwave, melt ⅔ cup chocolate chunks; stir until smooth. Cool slightly.

2. In a large bowl, cream butter and confectioners' sugar. Beat in sweet potatoes, cooled melted chocolate, ginger and vanilla. In another bowl, whisk flour, cornstarch, baking cocoa, baking powder, baking soda and salt; gradually beat into creamed mixture.

3. Shape dough into ¾-in. balls; place 2½ in. apart on parchment-lined baking sheets. Flatten slightly with bottom of a glass dipped in confectioners' sugar. Bake until edges are firm, 8-10 minutes. Remove from pans to wire racks to cool completely.

4. Meanwhile, mix filling ingredients until smooth. Spread filling on bottoms of half the cookies; cover with the remaining cookies.

5. For chocolate coating, microwave the remaining chocolate chunks; stir until smooth. Dip cookies halfway into chocolate or drizzle chocolate over the tops of cookies; let stand until set. Store between pieces of waxed paper in an airtight container in the refrigerator.

1 sandwich cookie: 134 cal., 7g fat (5g sat. fat), 12mg chol., 103mg sod., 17g carb. (10g sugars, 1g fiber), 2g pro.

SWEETHEART COOKIES

These sweet rounds filled with fruit preserves were blue-ribbon winners at the county fair two years running. A family favorite, they never last beyond Christmas!
—Pamela Esposito, Smithville, NJ

Prep: 25 min. • **Bake:** 15 min./batch
Makes: 2 dozen

- ¾ **cup butter, softened**
- ½ **cup sugar**
- 1 **large egg yolk, room temperature**
- 1½ **cups all-purpose flour**
- 2 **Tbsp. raspberry or strawberry preserves**
  Confectioners' sugar, optional

1. Preheat oven to 350°. Cream the butter and sugar until light and fluffy, 5-7 minutes. Add egg yolk; mix well. Stir in the flour by hand. On a lightly floured surface, gently knead 2-3 minutes or until thoroughly combined.
2. Roll dough into 1-in. balls. Place 2 in. apart on greased baking sheets. Using the end of a wooden spoon handle, make an indention in the center of each. Fill each with ¼ tsp. preserves.
3. Bake 13-15 minutes or until edges are lightly browned. Remove to wire racks. Dust warm cookies with confectioners' sugar if desired. Cool.

1 cookie: 102 cal., 6g fat (4g sat. fat), 23mg chol., 46mg sod., 11g carb. (5g sugars, 0 fiber), 1g pro.

GRANDMA NEIFERD'S COUNTY-FAIR-WINNING COOKIES

My grandmother Mary Katherine Neiferd was raised in the central part of Ohio, where many German immigrants settled. In fact, while she was growing up, her household spoke mostly German. This recipe is for her soft sugar cookies—the secret to the softness is real lard and whole buttermilk.

The cookies were popular at the church bazaar. Back in the '50s and '60s, before plastic was used for food storage, she would carry them in big, wide dress boxes she got from a shop downtown. She sold her cookies to the restaurants in Lima, Ohio, where Grandpa Neiferd worked at Lima Locomotive Works.

After she passed, I was the only one with the patience and knack to make her cookies. Before I moved away, some of the older church ladies who had memories of the bazaars would beg me to bring them some cookies whenever I baked them. Now, for Valentine's Day, I make big, soft heart cookies with pink icing and mail them to relatives across the country. I serve them with icing, but Grandma usually just sprinkled sugar or a few raisins on top. I even won a blue ribbon for best sugar cookie at the local county fair with this recipe.

Whenever I make these cookies, I think of Grandma watching over me and hope I am making her proud.

CANDY (NEIFERD) DAVIS · FLORENCE, SC

GRANDMA NEIFERD'S COOKIES

PREPARATION TIME _____
NUMBER OF SERVINGS _____
SOURCE OF RECIPE _____

FOR COOKIES:

2 cups sugar	1 cup buttermilk	**FOR ICING:**
1 cup lard or Crisco	4 cups flour	½ lb. powdered sugar
2 large eggs, room temp.	2 tsp. baking powder	½ stick of butter
1 tsp. baking soda	½ tsp. salt	Vanilla
	1 tsp. vanilla	A little milk

Preheat oven to 400°. Cream sugar and lard; add 2 eggs and beat again. Stir baking soda into buttermilk; let sit for 5 minutes, then mix with creamed sugar and lard. Add 2 cups flour, the baking powder, salt, and vanilla; beat until mixed, then add remaining flour. Mix well but briefly. Pat out with hands to about ¼-in. thick on floured cutting board, then cut with floured cutter. Bake 7-9 minutes on greased baking sheet until edges are brown and tops are nearly brown. For icing, mix powdered sugar, butter and vanilla while adding just enough milk to make smooth. Makes 30 big heart-shaped cookies or about 40 round cookies.

REFILL NO. 801 R

STYLECRAFT, BALTO. 30, MD.   PRINTED IN U.S.A.

P. 254

P. 245

P. 253

P. 241

BLUE-RIBBON PIES

DOUBLE PEANUT PIE

I created this recipe for a national pie contest and won second place for my state. Many peanuts are grown in Virginia, and I always look for ways to use local products.
—Vivian Cleeton, Richmond, VA

Prep: 10 min. • **Bake:** 30 min. + cooling
Makes: 8 servings

- 2 large eggs, room temperature
- ⅓ cup creamy peanut butter
- ⅓ cup sugar
- ⅓ cup light corn syrup
- ⅓ cup dark corn syrup
- ⅓ cup butter, melted
- 1 tsp. vanilla extract
- 1 cup salted peanuts
- 1 pie shell (9 in.), unbaked
  Optional: Whipped cream or ice cream

1. In a large bowl, lightly beat eggs. Gradually add the peanut butter, sugar, corn syrups, butter and vanilla until well blended. Fold in peanuts.
2. Pour into the crust. Bake at 375° for 30-35 minutes or until set. Cool. Serve with whipped cream or ice cream if desired.

1 piece: 484 cal., 30g fat (10g sat. fat), 79mg chol., 358mg sod., 48g carb. (23g sugars, 2g fiber), 10g pro.

CRANBERRY & WALNUT PIE

The ladies of the former First Baptist Church of Warrens baked hundreds of cranberry pies and served slices to visitors during the Warrens Cranberry Festival. This was the recipe they used for years.
—June Potter, Warrens, WI

Prep: 20 min. • **Bake:** 40 min.
Makes: 8 servings

- Dough for single-crust pie
- 1½ cups fresh or frozen cranberries
- ¼ cup packed brown sugar
- ¼ cup chopped walnuts
- 1 large egg
- ½ cup sugar
- ½ cup all-purpose flour
- ⅓ cup butter, melted
  Vanilla ice cream

1. Preheat oven to 375°. On a lightly floured surface, roll dough to a ⅛-in.-thick circle; transfer to a 9-in. pie plate. Trim crust to ½ in. beyond rim of plate; flute edge.
2. Spread cranberries evenly into crust; sprinkle with brown sugar and walnuts. In a bowl, beat egg on high speed until thick and pale yellow, about 5 minutes. Gradually beat in sugar. Beat in flour and melted butter (mixture will be thick). Spoon over the cranberries, spreading evenly.
3. Bake on a lower oven rack until crust is golden brown, 40-45 minutes. Cover the pie loosely with foil during the last 10-15 minutes if needed to prevent overbrowning. Remove foil. Cool on a wire rack. Serve warm with ice cream.

Dough for single-crust pie: Combine 1¼ cups all-purpose flour and ¼ tsp. salt; cut in ½ cup cold butter until crumbly. Gradually add 3-5 Tbsp. ice water, tossing with a fork until dough holds together when pressed. Shape into a disk; wrap and refrigerate 1 hour.

1 piece: 384 cal., 22g fat (13g sat. fat), 74mg chol., 227mg sod., 43g carb. (21g sugars, 2g fiber), 4g pro.

CHOCOLATE CREAM PIE

Our son, John, did lots of 4-H baking as a teenager. His favorite pie was this old-fashioned creamy chocolate pudding in a flaky crust.
—Mary Anderson, De Valls Bluff, AR

Prep: 1¼ hours + chilling
Makes: 8 servings

Dough for single-crust pie
1½ cups sugar
⅓ cup all-purpose flour
3 Tbsp. baking cocoa
½ tsp. salt
1½ cups water
1 can (12 oz.) evaporated milk
5 large egg yolks, lightly beaten
½ cup butter
1 tsp. vanilla extract
Optional: Whipped topping and baking cocoa

1. On a lightly floured surface, roll dough to a ⅛-in.-thick circle; transfer to a 9-in. pie plate. Trim to ½ in. beyond rim of plate; flute edge. Refrigerate 30 minutes. Preheat oven to 425°.

2. Line crust with a double thickness of foil. Fill with pie weights, dried beans or uncooked rice. Bake on a lower oven rack until the edge is golden brown, 20-25 minutes. Remove foil and weights; bake until bottom is golden brown, 3-6 minutes longer. Cool completely on a wire rack.

3. In a large saucepan, combine the next 6 ingredients. Cook and stir over medium-high heat until thickened and bubbly, about 2 minutes. Reduce heat; cook and stir 2 minutes longer. Remove from the heat. Whisk 1 cup hot mixture into egg yolks. Return all to the pan; bring to a gentle boil, stirring constantly.

4. Remove from the heat; stir in butter and vanilla. Cool slightly. Pour warm filling into crust. Cool for 1 hour. Chill until set. If desired, top with whipped cream and sprinkle with cocoa to serve.

Dough for a single-crust pie: Combine 1¼ cups all-purpose flour and ¼ tsp. salt; cut in ½ cup cold butter until crumbly. Gradually add 3-5 Tbsp. ice water, tossing with a fork until dough holds together when pressed. Shape into a disk; wrap and refrigerate 1 hour.

1 piece: 488 cal., 25g fat (13g sat. fat), 184mg chol., 413mg sod., 60g carb. (42g sugars, 1g fiber), 7g pro.

READER RAVE...

"When I was diagnosed with Type 2 diabetes, I could not believe that this pie, my all-time favorite, was never going to grace our table again. I put the wheels to work and subbed a non-sugar sweetener for the sugar in this recipe and then made a crust from almond flour, a bit more sweetener and butter. I can't begin to tell you how happy I am with the results! The recipe as written is the most requested pie I make. Now I make my version just so I can enjoy it again!"
—SOUTHERNMAMA, TASTEOFHOME.COM

STRAWBERRY-PECAN PIE

I stock up on locally grown berries for treats like this pie that pairs strawberries with pecans. The recipe received a ribbon from the Strawberry Festival food show in nearby Poteet.
—Becky Duncan, Leming, TX

Prep: 15 min. • **Bake:** 50 min.
Makes: 8 servings

- 1½ **cups sugar**
- ¼ **cup all-purpose flour**
- 1 **tsp. ground nutmeg**
- 1 **tsp. ground cinnamon**
- 2 **cups chopped fresh strawberries**
- 1 **cup chopped pecans**
  Dough for double-crust pie
- 1 **to 2 Tbsp. butter**

1. In a large bowl, combine the sugar, flour, nutmeg and cinnamon. Add strawberries and pecans; toss gently.
2. On a lightly floured surface, roll half the dough to a ⅛-in.-thick circle; transfer to a 9-in. pie plate. Trim crust to ½ in. beyond rim of plate. Add filling. Dot with butter.
3. Roll remaining dough to a ⅛-in.-thick circle; cut into ½-in.-wide strips. Arrange over filling in a lattice pattern. Trim and seal strips to edge of bottom crust; flute edge. Bake at 375° until crust is golden brown, 50-55 minutes. Cool on a wire rack.

Dough for double-crust pie: Combine 2½ cups all-purpose flour and ½ tsp. salt; cut in 1 cup shortening until crumbly. Gradually add 4–5 Tbsp. ice water, tossing with a fork until dough holds together when pressed. Divide in half and shape into disks; wrap and chill 1 hour.

1 piece: 529 cal., 26g fat (8g sat. fat), 14mg chol., 215mg sod., 72g carb. (41g sugars, 3g fiber), 4g pro.

ORANGE COCONUT MERINGUE PIE

I have won first place in two cream pie competitions with this recipe. It's one of my absolute favorites.
—Daisy Duncan, Stillwater, OK

Prep: 35 min. • **Bake:** 15 min. + chilling
Makes: 8 servings

- 1 cup sugar
- 3 Tbsp. cornstarch
- 3 Tbsp. all-purpose flour
- ¼ tsp. salt
- 1½ cups water
- ¾ cup orange juice
- 3 large egg yolks, lightly beaten
- ¾ cup sweetened shredded coconut
- 2 Tbsp. butter
- 1 Tbsp. grated orange zest
- 2 Tbsp. lemon juice
- 1 sheet refrigerated pie crust, baked

MERINGUE

- 3 large egg whites
- ½ tsp. vanilla extract
- ¼ tsp. cream of tartar
- 6 Tbsp. sugar

1. Preheat oven to 350°. In a large saucepan, combine sugar, cornstarch, flour and salt. Gradually stir in water and orange juice until smooth. Cook and stir over medium-high heat until thickened and bubbly. Reduce heat; cook and stir 2 minutes. Remove from heat.

2. Stir a small amount of hot filling into egg yolks; return all to the pan, stirring constantly. Bring to a gentle boil; cook and stir 2 minutes longer. Remove from heat. Stir in coconut, butter and orange zest. Gently stir in lemon juice. Pour into pie crust.

3. In a small bowl, beat the egg whites, vanilla and cream of tartar on medium speed until soft peaks form. Gradually beat in sugar, 1 Tbsp. at a time, on high until stiff glossy peaks form and sugar is dissolved. Spread evenly over hot filling, sealing edges to crust.

4. Bake 12-15 minutes or until meringue is golden brown. Cool on a wire rack for 1 hour. Refrigerate at least 3 hours before serving. Refrigerate leftovers.

1 piece: 385 cal., 15g fat (8g sat. fat), 92mg chol., 250mg sod., 60g carb. (40g sugars, 1g fiber), 4g pro.

PERSIMMON SQUASH PIE

I created this recipe for our local persimmon festival, using homegrown squash. I like to make two pies, with toffee bits and pecans for garnish.
—Betty Milligan, Bedford, IN

Prep: 25 min. • **Bake:** 40 min. + cooling
Makes: 8 servings

    Dough for single-crust pie
¼ **cup buttermilk**
½ **cup mashed cooked butternut squash**
½ **cup mashed ripe persimmon pulp**
¾ **cup sugar**
¼ **cup packed brown sugar**
3 **Tbsp. all-purpose flour**
½ **tsp. ground cinnamon**
¼ **tsp. baking powder**
¼ **tsp. baking soda**
¼ **tsp. salt**
2 **large eggs, room temperature**
¼ **cup heavy whipping cream**
¼ **cup butter, melted**
1 **tsp. vanilla extract**
CARAMEL TOPPING
30 **caramels**
2 **Tbsp. 2% milk**
⅓ **cup chopped pecans**
⅓ **cup English toffee bits or almond brickle chips**

1. On a lightly floured surface, roll dough to a ⅛-in.-thick circle. Transfer to a 9-in. pie plate; flute edge. Line unpricked crust with a double thickness of heavy-duty foil. Bake at 450° for 5-6 minutes or until lightly browned; cool on a wire rack. Reduce heat to 350°.
2. In a blender, combine the buttermilk, squash and persimmon pulp; cover and process until smooth.
3. Combine the sugars, flour, cinnamon, baking powder, baking soda and salt. Combine the eggs, cream, butter, vanilla and squash mixture; stir into the dry ingredients just until moistened. Pour into crust. Bake 40-45 minutes or until a knife inserted in center comes out clean.
4. In a small saucepan, combine the caramels and milk. Cook and stir over medium heat until melted and smooth. Pour over hot pie. Sprinkle with pecans and toffee bits. Cool completely on a wire rack. Store in the refrigerator.
Dough for single-crust pie: Combine 1¼ cups all-purpose flour and ¼ tsp. salt; cut in ½ cup cold butter until crumbly. Gradually add 3-5 Tbsp. ice water, tossing with a fork until dough holds together when pressed. Shape into a disk; wrap and refrigerate 1 hour.
1 piece: 578 cal., 27g fat (13g sat. fat), 90mg chol., 465mg sod., 82g carb. (60g sugars, 2g fiber), 6g pro.

TEXAS PECAN PIE

I won a blue ribbon for this pie at the Texas State Fair. Since I was in the military for more than 20 years, I didn't really start cooking until after I retired. Now I enjoy spending my time in the kitchen.
—Michelle Shockley, Wichita, KS

Prep: 25 min. • **Bake:** 45 min. + cooling
Makes: 8 servings

- 1 cup all-purpose flour
- ¼ tsp. salt
- ⅓ cup shortening
- 3 Tbsp. cold water

FILLING

- 1¼ cups chopped pecans
- 1 cup plus 1 Tbsp. light corn syrup
- 3 large eggs
- ½ cup plus 1 Tbsp. sugar
- 1½ tsp. vanilla extract
  Pinch salt

1. Preheat oven to 350°. In a bowl, combine the flour and salt; cut in the shortening until crumbly. Gradually add cold water, tossing with a fork until a ball forms.
2. Roll out dough to fit a 9-in. pie plate. Transfer crust to pie plate. Trim crust to ½ in. beyond edge of plate; flute the edges. Sprinkle with pecans; set aside.
3. In a small bowl, beat the corn syrup, eggs, sugar, vanilla and salt until well blended. Pour over pecans.
4. Bake for 45-50 minutes or until a knife inserted in the center comes out clean. Cool on a wire rack.
1 piece: 466 cal., 23g fat (4g sat. fat), 80mg chol., 151mg sod., 62g carb. (37g sugars, 2g fiber), 6g pro.

GOLDEN PEACH PIE

Years ago, I entered this pie in the Park County Fair in Livingston. It won a first-place blue ribbon plus a purple ribbon for best all around! Family and friends agree with the judges—it's a perfectly peachy pie.
—Shirley Olson, Polson, MT

Prep: 20 min. • **Bake:** 50 min. + cooling
Makes: 8 servings

- 2 sheets refrigerated pie crust
- 5 cups sliced peeled fresh peaches (about 5 medium)
- 2 tsp. lemon juice
- ½ tsp. grated orange zest
- ⅛ tsp. almond extract
- 1 cup sugar
- ¼ cup cornstarch
- ¼ tsp. ground nutmeg
- ⅛ tsp. salt
- 2 Tbsp. butter
  Optional: Heavy whipping cream and coarse sugar

1. Preheat oven to 400°. Line a 9-in. pie plate with 1 crust; trim, leaving a 1-in. overhang around rim. Set aside. In a large bowl, combine peaches, lemon juice, orange zest and extract. Combine sugar, cornstarch, nutmeg and salt. Add to peach mixture; toss gently to coat. Pour into crust; dot with butter.
2. Roll out the remaining crust to a ⅛-in.-thick circle; cut into strips. Arrange over filling in a lattice pattern. Trim and seal strips to bottom crust; fold overhang over and lightly press or flute edge. If desired, brush lattice with heavy cream and sprinkle with sugar. Cover the edge loosely with foil.
3. Bake for 40 minutes. Remove foil; bake until crust is golden brown and filling is bubbly, 10-15 minutes longer. Cool on a wire rack. Store in the refrigerator.
1 piece: 425 cal., 17g fat (8g sat. fat), 18mg chol., 267mg sod., 67g carb. (36g sugars, 2g fiber), 3g pro.

GOLDEN COCONUT PEACH PIE

This peaches-and-cream pie once captured the blue ribbon at the Iowa State Fair. It always disappears fast!
—Gloria Kratz, Des Moines, IA

Prep: 20 min. • **Bake:** 55 min.
Makes: 8 servings

- 4 to 4½ cups sliced fresh peaches
- ½ cup sugar
- 3 Tbsp. all-purpose flour
- ¼ tsp. ground nutmeg
- ⅛ tsp. salt
- ¼ cup orange juice
- 1 pie shell (9 in.), unbaked
- 2 Tbsp. butter
- 2 cups sweetened shredded coconut
- 1 can (5 oz.) evaporated milk
- 1 large egg, lightly beaten
- ¼ to ½ cup sugar
- ¼ tsp. almond extract

1. Preheat oven to 450°. In a large bowl, combine peaches, sugar, flour, nutmeg, salt and juice. Pour into pie shell; dot with butter. Bake for 15 minutes.
2. Meanwhile, combine remaining ingredients. Pour over hot filling. Reduce oven temperature to 350° and bake until coconut is toasted, about 40 minutes. Serve warm or chilled. Store in the refrigerator.

1 piece: 418 cal., 20g fat (13g sat. fat), 45mg chol., 252mg sod., 57g carb. (37g sugars, 3g fiber), 5g pro.

BEST EVER FRESH STRAWBERRY PIE

Next time you get a pint or two of perfectly ripe strawberries, make my favorite pie. It combines fresh berries and a lemony cream cheese layer. If you're in a hurry, use a premade pie shell.
—Janet Leach, Granger, WA

Prep: 1 hour + chilling
Cook: 10 min. + chilling
Makes: 8 servings

- 2 cups all-purpose flour
- 2 tsp. sugar
- ½ tsp. salt
- ⅔ cup shortening
- 1 Tbsp. white vinegar
- 4 to 5 Tbsp. 2% milk

FILLING
- 1 pkg. (8 oz.) cream cheese, softened
- ¾ cup confectioners' sugar
- 2 tsp. grated lemon zest
- ½ tsp. lemon extract

TOPPING
- 6 cups fresh strawberries, hulled (about 2 lbs.)
- ¾ cup sugar
- 1 Tbsp. cornstarch
- ¼ tsp. salt
- 1 cup water
- 1 pkg. (3 oz.) strawberry gelatin
- 1 tsp. butter

1. In a large bowl, mix flour, sugar and salt; cut in shortening until crumbly. Gradually add vinegar and milk, tossing with a fork until dough holds together when pressed. Shape into a disk; wrap and refrigerate 1 hour or overnight.

2. On a lightly floured surface, roll dough to a ⅛-in.-thick circle; transfer to a 9-in. deep-dish pie plate. Trim crust to ½ in. beyond rim of plate; flute edge. Refrigerate 30 minutes. Preheat oven to 425°.

3. Line crust with a double thickness of foil. Fill with pie weights, dried beans or uncooked rice. Bake on a lower oven rack 20-25 minutes or until edges are golden brown. Remove foil and weights; bake 3-6 minutes longer or until bottom is golden brown. Cool completely on a wire rack.

4. Beat cream cheese, confectioners' sugar, lemon zest and extract until blended. Spread carefully onto the bottom of crust. Refrigerate filled crust while preparing topping.

5. Place strawberries in a large bowl. In a small saucepan, mix the sugar, cornstarch, salt and water until blended; bring to a boil over medium heat, stirring constantly. Cook and stir 1-2 minutes longer or until thickened and clear.

6. Remove from heat; stir in gelatin until dissolved. Stir in butter. Pour over strawberries, tossing gently to coat. Arrange over filling. Refrigerate 4 hours or until set.

Note: Let pie weights cool before storing. Beans and rice may be reused for pie weights, but not for cooking.

1 piece: 564 cal., 27g fat (10g sat. fat), 33mg chol., 359mg sod., 75g carb. (47g sugars, 3g fiber), 7g pro.

WINNING RHUBARB-STRAWBERRY PIE

While growing up on a farm, I often ate rhubarb, so it's natural for me to use it in a pie. I prefer to use lard for the flaky pie crust and thin, red rhubarb stalks for the filling. These two little secrets helped this recipe win top honors at the 2013 Iowa State Fair.
—Marianne Carlson, Jefferson, IA

....

Prep: 50 min. + chilling
Bake: 65 min. + cooling
Makes: 8 servings

- 1   **large egg**
- 4   **to 5 Tbsp. ice water, divided**
- ¾   **tsp. white vinegar**
- 2¼ **cups all-purpose flour**
- ¾   **tsp. salt**
- ¾   **cup cold lard**

FILLING

- 1¼ **cups sugar**
- 6   **Tbsp. quick-cooking tapioca**
- 3   **cups sliced fresh or frozen rhubarb, thawed**
- 3   **cups halved fresh strawberries**
- 3   **Tbsp. butter**
- 1   **Tbsp. 2% milk**
     Coarse sugar

1. In a small bowl, whisk egg, 4 Tbsp. ice water and vinegar until blended. In a large bowl, mix flour and salt; cut in lard until crumbly. Gradually add egg mixture, tossing with a fork, until dough holds together when pressed. If mixture is too dry, slowly add additional ice water, 1 tsp. at a time, just until the dough comes together.
2. Divide dough in half. Shape each into a disk; wrap and refrigerate for 1 hour or overnight.
3. Preheat oven to 400°. In a large bowl, mix sugar and tapioca. Add rhubarb and strawberries; toss to coat evenly. Let stand 15 minutes.
4. On a lightly floured surface, roll half the dough to a ⅛-in.-thick circle; transfer to a 9-in. pie plate. Trim crust even with rim.
5. Add filling; dot with butter. Roll the remaining dough to a ⅛-in.-thick circle. Place over filling. Trim, seal and flute edge. Cut slits in top. Brush milk over top crust; sprinkle with coarse sugar. Place pie on a baking sheet; bake 20 minutes.
6. Reduce oven setting to 350°. Bake 45-55 minutes longer or until crust is golden brown and filling is bubbly. Cool on a wire rack.

Note: If using frozen rhubarb, measure rhubarb while still frozen, then thaw completely. Drain in a colander, but do not press liquid out.

1 piece: 531 cal., 25g fat (11g sat. fat), 53mg chol., 269mg sod., 73g carb. (35g sugars, 3g fiber), 5g pro.

BLUE-RIBBON TIP

There are several tricks to prevent soggy crust. First, choose a glass pie plate or a metal pie plate with a dull finish. For double-crust fruit pies, cut slits in the top crust to allow steam to escape. Finally, bake your pie in the lower third of the oven to allow the bottom crust to become crisp.

If your pie is runny, it may mean your fruit wasn't defrosted enough or there wasn't enough tapioca added.

TRIPLE-APPLE PIE

This won the blue ribbon in the Double Crust Apple Pie class at the Iowa State Fair. It's my original recipe, plus I used my homemade jelly.
—Louise Piper, Garner, IA

....

Prep: 30 min. + standing
Bake: 50 min. + cooling • **Makes:** 8 servings

5½ cups thinly sliced peeled tart apples
¼ cup apple cider or juice
⅓ cup apple jelly, melted
1 cup sugar
3 Tbsp. all-purpose flour
1 Tbsp. quick-cooking tapioca
⅛ tsp. salt
Dough for double-crust pie
2 Tbsp. butter

1. Combine the apples, cider and jelly. Combine sugar, flour, tapioca and salt; add to apple mixture and toss gently to coat. Let stand 15 minutes.

2. On a lightly floured surface, roll half the dough to a ⅛-in.-thick circle; transfer to a 9-in. pie plate. Trim crust even with edge of plate. Add filling; dot with butter. Roll out remaining dough to fit top of pie; place over filling. Trim, seal and flute edges. Cut slits in top. Cover edges with foil.

3. Bake at 400° for 20 minutes. Remove foil; bake 30-35 minutes longer or until crust is golden brown and filling is bubbly. Cool on a wire rack.

Dough for double-crust pie: Combine 2½ cups all-purpose flour and ½ tsp. salt; cut in 1 cup shortening until crumbly. Gradually add 4–5 Tbsp. ice water, tossing with a fork until dough holds together when pressed. Divide in half and shape into disks; wrap and chill 1 hour.

1 piece: 458 cal., 17g fat (8g sat. fat), 18mg chol., 267mg sod., 75g carb. (44g sugars, 2g fiber), 2g pro.

COUNTY FAIR CHERRY PIE

I'm a teacher and a Navy wife, so simplicity and quickness are both mealtime musts at my house. This cherry pie delivers on both counts.
—Claudia Youmans, Virginia Beach, VA

....

Prep: 20 min. + standing
Bake: 50 min. + cooling
Makes: 8 servings

- 1¼ cups sugar
- 2 Tbsp. cornstarch
  Dash salt
- 4 cups pitted tart cherries
  Dough for double-crust pie
  Confectioners' sugar

1. In a large saucepan, combine sugar, cornstarch and salt; stir in cherries. Let stand 30 minutes.
2. Cook and stir cherry mixture over medium heat until mixture boils and starts to thicken.
3. Preheat oven to 375°. On a lightly floured surface, roll half the dough to a ⅛-in.-thick circle; transfer to a 9-in. pie plate. Trim crust to ½ in. beyond rim of plate; flute edge. Add filling. Bake until crust is golden brown and filling is bubbly, 40-45 minutes. Cover edges during the last 20 minutes to prevent overbrowning. Cool on a wire rack.
4. Meanwhile, roll remaining dough to ⅛-in.-thick circle; cut stars using floured star-shaped cutters. Place on an ungreased baking sheet. Bake at 375° for 7-11 minutes or until golden brown. Remove to a wire rack to cool.
5. Dust stars with confectioners' sugar; place over pie. Lightly dust edges of pie with confectioners' sugar.
Dough for double-crust pie: Combine 2½ cups all-purpose flour and ½ tsp. salt; cut in 1 cup shortening until crumbly.

Gradually add 4–5 Tbsp. ice water, tossing with a fork until dough holds together when pressed. Divide in half and shape into disks; wrap and chill 1 hour.
Note: To store filling for later use, pour into jars or freezer containers, leaving ½-in. headspace. Cool. Cover with lids; refrigerate or freeze. This recipe yields 3 cups filling, enough for 1 pie.
1 piece: 511 cal., 23g fat (15g sat. fat), 60mg chol., 495mg sod., 73g carb. (39g sugars, 2g fiber), 5g pro.

HOMEMADE PEAR PIE

I entered this pie in a local baking contest and ended up winning! Bartlett pears hold up well when baked, adding a nice layer of texture.
—Darlene Jacobson, Waterford, WI

....

Prep: 40 min. + chilling
Bake: 45 min. + cooling
Makes: 8 servings

- 2 cups all-purpose flour
- 1 tsp. salt
- ¾ cup shortening
- 6 Tbsp. cold water

FILLING
- 5 cups sliced peeled fresh pears
- 1 Tbsp. lemon juice
- ⅓ cup all-purpose flour
- ½ cup plus 1 Tbsp. sugar, divided
- 1 tsp. ground cinnamon
- 2 Tbsp. butter

1. In a large bowl, mix flour and salt; cut in shortening until crumbly. Gradually add water, tossing with a fork until dough holds together when pressed. Divide dough in half, and shape each half into a disk; wrap and refrigerate 1 hour or overnight.
2. Preheat oven to 425°. In a large bowl, toss pears with lemon juice. In a small

bowl, mix the flour, ½ cup sugar and cinnamon; add to the pear mixture and toss to coat.
3. On a lightly floured surface, roll 1 disk of dough into a ⅛-in.-thick circle; transfer to a 9-in. pie plate. Trim even with rim. Add filling; dot with butter.
4. Roll the remaining dough into a ⅛-in.-thick circle. Place over filling. Trim, seal and flute edges. Cut slits in top. Sprinkle with remaining 1 Tbsp. sugar. Bake until crust is golden brown and filling is bubbly, 45-50 minutes. Cover edges loosely with foil during last 20 minutes if needed to prevent overbrowning. Remove foil. Cool on a wire rack.
1 piece: 438 cal., 21g fat (6g sat. fat), 8mg chol., 317mg sod., 58g carb. (25g sugars, 4g fiber), 4g pro.

APPLE-CHERRY CREAM CHEESE PIE

A layer of sweetened cream cheese topped with a tart fruit filling makes this pie popular with family, friends and coworkers. It won the blue ribbon at a local fair.
—Donna Rettew, Jonestown, PA

Prep: 45 min. + chilling
Bake: 45 min. + cooling
Makes: 8 servings

2¼ cups all-purpose flour
2 tsp. sugar
¾ tsp. salt
1 cup cold unsalted butter, cubed
6 to 8 Tbsp. ice water
FILLING
1 pkg. (8 oz.) cream cheese, softened
1¼ cups sugar, divided
1 tsp. vanilla extract
9 cups thinly sliced peeled McIntosh apples (about 11 medium)
½ cup all-purpose flour
1 tsp. apple pie spice
¼ tsp. salt
1 can (14½ oz.) pitted tart cherries, drained
2 Tbsp. butter

1. In a large bowl, mix flour, sugar and salt; cut in butter until crumbly. Gradually add ice water, tossing with a fork until dough holds together when pressed. Divide dough in half. Shape each half into a disk; wrap each and refrigerate 1 hour or overnight.
2. Preheat oven to 425°. For filling, in a small bowl, beat cream cheese, ¼ cup sugar and the vanilla until blended. In a large bowl, toss apples with flour, pie spice, salt and remaining 1 cup sugar. Stir in cherries.

3. On a lightly floured surface, roll half the dough to a ⅛-in.-thick circle; transfer to a 9-in. pie plate. Trim crust even with rim.
4. Spread cream cheese mixture onto bottom crust. Add apple mixture; dot with butter. Roll the remaining dough to a ⅛-in.-thick circle. Place over filling. Trim, seal and flute edge. Cut slits in top.
5. Bake 45-50 minutes or until crust is golden brown and filling is bubbly. Cover top loosely with foil during the last 10-15 minutes if needed to prevent overbrowning. Cool on a wire rack. Refrigerate leftovers.
1 piece: 713 cal., 37g fat (22g sat. fat), 97mg chol., 414mg sod., 93g carb. (55g sugars, 5g fiber), 7g pro.

READER RAVE...

"This is the best apple pie I ever made. I use 1 Tbsp. apple pie spice and a mix of mostly McIntosh with Golden Delicious and Cortland apples."
—FOXYQUEEN, TASTEOFHOME.COM

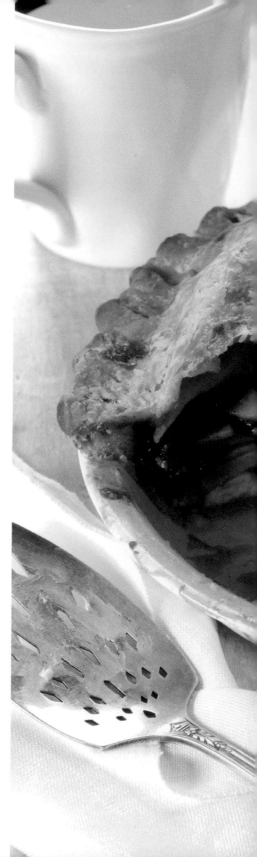

CHOCOLATE PEANUT PIE

I entered this pie in our county fair, and it was selected grand champion. Who can resist a tempting chocolate crumb crust and a creamy filling with big peanut butter taste? Be prepared to take an empty pan home when you serve this pie at your next potluck.
—Doris Doherty, Albany, OR

Prep: 20 min. + cooling
Makes: 10 servings

- 1¼ **cups chocolate cookie crumbs (20 cookies)**
- ¼ **cup sugar**
- ¼ **cup butter, melted**

FILLING
- 1 **pkg. (8 oz.) cream cheese, softened**
- 1 **cup creamy peanut butter**
- 1 **cup sugar**
- 1 **Tbsp. butter, softened**
- 1 **tsp. vanilla extract**
- 1 **cup heavy whipping cream, whipped**
  Optional: Grated chocolate or chocolate cookie crumbs

1. Preheat oven to 375°. In a small bowl, combine cookie crumbs and sugar; stir in butter. Press onto the bottom and up the sides of a 9-in. pie plate. Bake for 10 minutes. Cool on a wire rack.
2. For filling, beat the cream cheese, peanut butter, sugar, butter and vanilla in a large bowl until smooth. Fold in the whipped cream. Gently spoon into crust. Garnish with chocolate or cookie crumbs if desired. Store in refrigerator.
1 piece: 551 cal., 39g fat (18g sat. fat), 73mg chol., 349mg sod., 44g carb. (34g sugars, 3g fiber), 10g pro.

FUDGE PECAN BROWNIE TART

I love inventing my own recipes and entering contests—I won a blue ribbon at the Iowa State Fair for this one!
—Gloria Kratz, Des Moines, IA

Prep: 30 min. • **Bake:** 30 min. + cooling
Makes: 12 servings

- 1 cup all-purpose flour
- ¼ cup packed light brown sugar
- ¼ cup finely chopped pecans
- ½ cup cold butter
- 2 Tbsp. 2% milk
- 1 tsp. vanilla extract

BROWNIE FILLING
- 3 oz. unsweetened chocolate
- ½ cup chocolate chips
- ½ cup butter, cut into pieces
- 1½ cups sugar
- 3 large eggs, room temperature
- 2 tsp. vanilla extract
- ¾ cup all-purpose flour
- 1 cup chopped pecans

FUDGE FROSTING
- 1½ oz. unsweetened chocolate
- ⅔ cup sweetened condensed milk
- ¼ cup butter
- 1 large egg yolk, beaten
- ½ tsp. vanilla extract
  Optional: Whipped cream and whole pecans for garnish

1. Preheat oven to 350°. Combine the flour, brown sugar and pecans in a large bowl; cut in butter until the mixture resembles coarse meal. Mix in milk and vanilla with a fork just until blended. Pat onto bottom and up the sides of an 11-in. tart pan; set aside.

2. For filling, melt chocolate and chips in the top of a double boiler over hot water. Remove from heat and stir in the butter. Place in a large bowl and combine with sugar. Add eggs and vanilla; blend well. Gradually add flour, blending well after each addition. Add nuts. Pour over crust.

3. Bake 30-35 minutes or until the center is just set and a toothpick comes out clean. Cool on wire rack.

4. For frosting, melt chocolate in a small saucepan over low heat. Add milk, butter, yolk and vanilla. Heat, stirring vigorously, until smooth and thick, about 5 minutes. Spread over tart. Garnish with whipped cream and pecans if desired.

1 piece: 580 cal., 37g fat (17g sat. fat), 128mg chol., 236mg sod., 61g carb. (43g sugars, 3g fiber), 7g pro.

ULTIMATE CHOCOLATE CHUNK PECAN PIE

Our family hosts an annual barn party for our close friends, complete with a pie cook-off. A few years ago, this recipe won first prize!
—Janice Schneider, Kansas City, MO

Prep: 35 min. + chilling
Bake: 55 min. + chilling
Makes: 10 servings

  1¼ cups all-purpose flour
  ⅛ tsp. salt
  3 oz. cold cream cheese, cubed
  ¼ cup cold butter, cubed
  2 to 3 Tbsp. ice water
FILLING
  ⅓ cup sugar
  3 Tbsp. butter

  2 cups coarsely chopped
    semisweet chocolate, divided
  4 large eggs
  1 cup dark corn syrup
  2 tsp. vanilla extract
    Dash salt
  2½ cups pecan halves, toasted

1. In a small bowl, mix flour and salt; cut in cream cheese and butter until crumbly. Gradually add ice water, tossing with a fork until dough holds together when pressed. Shape into a disk; wrap and refrigerate 30 minutes or overnight.
2. Preheat oven to 350°. On a lightly floured surface, roll dough to a ⅛-in.-thick circle; transfer to a 9-in. pie plate. Trim to ½ in. beyond rim of plate; flute edge. Refrigerate while making filling.

3. In a small saucepan, combine sugar, butter and 1 cup chopped chocolate; stir over low heat until smooth. Cool slightly.
4. In a large bowl, whisk the eggs, corn syrup, vanilla and salt until blended. Stir in chocolate mixture. Layer the pecans and remaining 1 cup chopped chocolate in crust; pour chocolate mixture over top.
5. Bake 55-60 minutes or until set. Cool for 1 hour on a wire rack. Refrigerate 2 hours or until cold.
Note: To toast nuts, bake in a shallow pan in a 350° oven for 5-10 minutes or cook in a skillet over low heat until lightly browned, stirring occasionally.
1 piece: 650 cal., 42g fat (15g sat. fat), 115mg chol., 209mg sod., 69g carb. (35g sugars, 5g fiber), 9g pro.

WASHINGTON STATE APPLE PIE

This pie won grand champion in the Apple Pie category at the 1992 Okanogan County Fair. The pie looks traditional, but homemade filling gives it a different flair and terrific taste.
—Dolores Scholz, Tonasket, WA

....

Prep: 25 min. • **Bake:** 45 min. + cooling
Makes: 8 servings

    6 cups sliced peeled tart apples
       (about 5 to 6 medium)
    2 Tbsp. water
    1 Tbsp. lemon juice
    ½ cup sugar
    ½ cup packed brown sugar
    3 Tbsp. all-purpose flour
    1 tsp. ground cinnamon
    ¼ tsp. ground nutmeg
    ⅛ tsp. ground ginger
    ⅛ tsp. salt
       Dough for double-crust pie

1. In a large saucepan, combine the apples, water and lemon juice; cook over medium-low heat just until apples are tender. Remove from the heat and cool (do not drain).
2. Preheat oven to 450°. In a large bowl, combine the sugars, flour, cinnamon, nutmeg, ginger and salt; add apples and toss to coat.
3. On a lightly floured surface, roll half the dough into a ⅛-in.-thick circle; transfer to a 9-in. pie plate. Trim even with rim. Add the apple mixture. Roll remaining dough into a ⅛-in.-thick circle. Place over filling. Trim, seal and flute edge. Cut slits in top.
4. Bake for 10 minutes. Reduce oven setting to 350°; bake until golden brown, 35-45 minutes longer. Place on a wire rack to cool.

Dough for double-crust pie: Combine 2½ cups all-purpose flour and ½ tsp. salt; cut in 1 cup cold butter until crumbly. Gradually add ⅓–⅔ cup ice water, tossing with a fork until dough holds together when pressed. Divide dough in half. Shape each into a disk; wrap and refrigerate 1 hour.
1 piece: 496 cal., 23g fat (14g sat. fat), 60mg chol., 351mg sod., 69g carb. (35g sugars, 2g fiber), 5g pro.

CHERRY-BERRY STREUSEL PIE

I entered this delicious pie in the Oklahoma State Fair and won a ribbon. It is pretty and tastes marvelous, especially when served with a scoop of vanilla ice cream.
—Rosalie Seebeck, Bethany, OK

....

Prep: 1 hour + chilling
Bake: 55 min. + cooling
Makes: 8 servings

    2½ cups all-purpose flour
    1 Tbsp. sugar
    1 tsp. salt
    1 cup cold butter, cubed
    7 to 8 Tbsp. cold water
FILLING
    2 cans (21 oz. each) cherry pie filling
    1 cup fresh or frozen raspberries
    ¼ cup packed brown sugar
    ¼ tsp. ground cinnamon
TOPPING
    1 cup yellow cake mix
    ½ cup chopped pecans, toasted
    ½ cup sweetened shredded coconut
    ¼ cup butter, melted
    2 Tbsp. 2% milk
    2 Tbsp. sugar

1. Place the flour, sugar and salt in a food processor; cover and pulse until blended. Add butter; cover and pulse until mixture resembles coarse crumbs. While processing, gradually add water until dough forms a ball.
2. Divide dough in half so 1 portion is slightly larger than the other; wrap each half and refrigerate for 30 minutes or until easy to handle.
3. On a lightly floured surface, roll out larger portion of dough to fit a 9-in. deep-dish pie plate. Transfer to pie plate; trim to ½ in. beyond edge of plate. Combine filling ingredients; spoon into crust. Sprinkle with the dry cake mix, pecans and coconut. Drizzle with butter.
4. Roll out remaining dough to a 13-in. circle; cut into strips for a lattice top. While creating the lattice top, twist the strips for a decorative effect. Seal and flute edges of pie.
5. Brush top with milk; sprinkle with sugar. Cover edges loosely with foil. Bake at 375° for 55-65 minutes or until the crust is golden brown and filling is bubbly. Cool on a wire rack.
1 piece: 769 cal., 38g fat (21g sat. fat), 76mg chol., 659mg sod., 103g carb. (59g sugars, 4g fiber), 6g pro.

BLUE-RIBBON TIP

To make this flower pie, use a sharp paring knife to cut the top pie dough into strips of various sizes. Use a 2- or 3-in. round cookie cutter to cut a circle. Lay strips on top of the pie, sporadically overlapping them. Place circle cutout in the center. Dab water on the strips where they overlap, or brush egg wash over the finished pie. Sprinkle with coarse sugar and bake.

CONTEST-WINNING GERMAN CHOCOLATE CREAM PIE

I've won quite a few awards in recipe contests over the years, and I was truly delighted when this luscious pie sent me to the Great American Pie Show finals in Branson, Missouri.
—Marie Rizzio, Interlochen, MI

Prep: 20 min. • **Bake:** 45 min. + cooling
Makes: 8 servings

> Dough for single-crust pie
4 oz. German sweet chocolate, chopped
¼ cup butter, cubed
1 can (12 oz.) evaporated milk
1½ cups sugar
3 Tbsp. cornstarch
> Dash salt
2 large eggs, room temperature
1 tsp. vanilla extract
1⅓ cups sweetened shredded coconut
½ cup chopped pecans

TOPPING
2 cups heavy whipping cream
2 Tbsp. confectioners' sugar
1 tsp. vanilla extract

1. Preheat oven to 375°. On a lightly floured surface, roll dough to a ⅛-in.-thick circle; transfer to a 9-in. pie plate. Trim crust to ½ in. beyond rim of plate; flute edge. Refrigerate crust while preparing filling.
2. Place chocolate and butter in a small saucepan. Cook and stir over low heat until smooth. Remove from the heat; stir in evaporated milk.
3. Combine sugar, cornstarch and salt. Add eggs, vanilla and chocolate mixture; mix well. Pour into crust. Sprinkle with coconut and pecans.
4. Bake until a knife inserted in center comes out clean, 45-50 minutes. Cool completely on a wire rack.
5. For topping, in a large bowl, beat cream until it begins to thicken. Add confectioners' sugar and vanilla; beat until stiff peaks form. Spread over pie; sprinkle with additional coconut and pecans. Refrigerate until serving.

Dough for single-crust pie: Combine 1¼ cups all-purpose flour and ¼ tsp. salt; cut in ½ cup cold butter until crumbly. Gradually add 3–5 Tbsp. ice water, tossing with a fork until dough holds together when pressed. Shape into a disk; wrap and refrigerate 1 hour.

1 piece: 808 cal., 53g fat (30g sat. fat), 168mg chol., 280mg sod., 78g carb. (58g sugars, 3g fiber), 9g pro.

READER RAVE...

"I made this for Thanksgiving and everyone loved it; all that was left were a few crumbs. My mother-in-law's exact words were, 'This one is a keeper.' It fit perfectly in my pie plate (not deep dish). With my oven it took over an hour to bake, but it was well worth it."
—KNOSILLA, TASTEOFHOME.COM

CHERRY-CREAM CRUMBLE PIE

I created this yummy recipe for a cherry pie contest at the San Diego County Fair when I was first married in 1984. It won the blue ribbon. I love entering contests and have won many.
—Marian Hollingsworth, La Mesa, CA

....

Prep: 20 min. • **Bake:** 45 min. + cooling
Makes: 8 servings

- ½ cup sugar
- 3 Tbsp. all-purpose flour
- 2 cans (15 oz. each) pitted tart cherries, drained
- 1 cup sour cream
- 1 large egg, lightly beaten
- ¼ tsp. almond extract
- 1 sheet refrigerated pie crust

TOPPING

- ½ cup quick-cooking oats
- ⅓ cup all-purpose flour
- ⅓ cup packed brown sugar
- ¼ tsp. ground cinnamon
- ¼ cup cold butter
- ½ cup chopped pecans

1. Preheat oven to 400°. In a large bowl, combine sugar, flour, cherries, sour cream, egg and extract. Unroll crust into a 9-in. pie plate; flute edge. Spoon mixture into pie crust. Bake 20 minutes.
2. For the topping, combine oats, flour, brown sugar and cinnamon; cut in butter until the mixture resembles coarse crumbs. Stir in pecans. Sprinkle over filling. Cover edges of crust with foil to prevent overbrowning.
3. Bake 25-30 minutes or until topping is lightly browned. Cool on a wire rack for 1 hour. Store in the refrigerator.
1 piece: 463 cal., 24g fat (11g sat. fat), 67mg chol., 188mg sod., 56g carb. (33g sugars, 2g fiber), 6g pro.

MAPLE CREAM MERINGUE PIE

This dessert won first place in the pie category at the annual Vermont Maple Festival. It's simple to make and it uses more maple syrup than most other maple cream pies.
—Nicole Hardy, St. Albans, VT

Prep: 35 min. • **Bake:** 15 min. + chilling
Makes: 8 servings

- 1 sheet refrigerated pie crust
- 2 Tbsp. cornstarch
- ¼ cup water
- 1 cup maple syrup
- 1 cup heavy whipping cream
- 2 large egg yolks, lightly beaten
- 3 Tbsp. butter
- 3 large egg whites
- ½ tsp. vanilla extract
- ¼ tsp. cream of tartar
- 6 Tbsp. sugar

1. Preheat oven to 350°. On a lightly floured surface, roll crust to fit a 9-in. pie plate. Trim and flute edge. Line unpricked crust with a double thickness of foil. Fill with pie weights. Bake on a lower oven rack until golden brown, 15-20 minutes. Remove foil and weights; bake until the bottom is golden brown, 3-6 minutes. Cool on a wire rack.
2. In a small saucepan, combine the cornstarch and water until smooth. Stir in syrup and cream. Cook and stir over medium-high heat until thickened and bubbly, 2-3 minutes. Reduce heat to medium; cook, stirring constantly, 2 minutes longer. Remove from heat.
3. Stir a small amount of hot filling into egg yolks; return all to the pan, stirring constantly. Bring to a gentle boil; cook and stir 2 minutes longer. Remove from heat. Stir in butter. Pour into crust.
4. In a large bowl, beat egg whites, vanilla and cream of tartar on medium speed until soft peaks form. Gradually beat in sugar, 1 Tbsp. at a time, on high until stiff glossy peaks form and sugar is dissolved. Spread evenly over hot filling, sealing edges to crust.
5. Bake until meringue is golden brown, 12-15 minutes. Cool on a wire rack for 1 hour. Refrigerate for at least 3 hours before serving. Store leftovers in the refrigerator.

1 piece: 389 cal., 20g fat (11g sat. fat), 108mg chol., 138mg sod., 48g carb. (34g sugars, 0 fiber), 4g pro.

SPECIAL RAISIN PIE

When I first made this pie, I thought it was wonderful. Then I entered it at the county fair, and I guess the judges thought it was tasty, too, since it won first place.
—Laura Fall-Sutton, Buhl, ID

Prep: 40 min. • **Bake:** 35 min. + cooling
Makes: 8 servings

- 2½ cups raisins
- 2 cups water
- ⅓ cup packed brown sugar
- ⅓ cup sugar
- ⅛ tsp. salt
- 2 Tbsp. plus 1½ tsp. cornstarch
- ¼ cup cold water
- 2 Tbsp. lemon juice
- 1 Tbsp. orange juice
- 2 tsp. grated orange zest
- 1 tsp. grated lemon zest
- ½ tsp. rum extract
      Dough for double-crust pie
- 2 Tbsp. butter

1. In a small saucepan, combine the raisins and water. Bring to a boil; cook 2 minutes. Add sugars and salt; cook until sugars are dissolved. Combine cornstarch and cold water until smooth; gradually stir into the pan. Cook and stir for 2 minutes or until thickened and bubbly. Remove from the heat; stir in the juices, zests and extract.
2. Roll out half the pie dough to fit a 9-in. pie plate; transfer to pie plate. Fill with the raisin mixture. Dot with butter.
3. Roll out remaining dough; make a lattice crust. Trim, seal and flute edge. Bake at 375° for 35-40 minutes or until crust is golden brown and filling is bubbly, covering edge with foil during the last 10 minutes. Cool on a wire rack. Refrigerate leftovers.

Dough for double-crust pie: Combine 2½ cups all-purpose flour and ½ tsp. salt; cut in 1 cup cold butter until crumbly. Gradually add ⅓–⅔ cup ice water, tossing with a fork until dough holds together when pressed. Divide dough in half and shape into disks; wrap each disk and refrigerate 1 hour.
Note: To achieve the special lattice crust pictured, use additional pie dough.
1 piece: 481 cal., 17g fat (8g sat. fat), 18mg chol., 266mg sod., 82g carb. (46g sugars, 2g fiber), 3g pro.

UPSIDE-DOWN APPLE PECAN PIE

I combined two of my favorite recipes to come up with this sensational pie. It won the local apple pie contest a few years ago. I usually make two pies because we always end up wanting more.
—Becky Berger, Deerfield, IL

....

Prep: 1 hour + chilling
Bake: 1 hour + cooling
Makes: 8 servings

- 3 **cups all-purpose flour**
- 1 **Tbsp. sugar**
- 1 **tsp. salt**
- ¾ **cup cold butter, cubed**
- ⅓ **cup shortening, cubed**
- 4 **to 6 Tbsp. cold water**

PECANS
- ½ **cup packed brown sugar**
- ¼ **cup butter, melted**
- 1 **cup pecan halves**

FILLING
- 1 **cup sugar**
- ⅓ **cup all-purpose flour**
- 2 **Tbsp. butter, melted**
- ¼ **tsp. ground cinnamon**
- 8 **cups thinly sliced peeled tart apples**

1. In a food processor, combine the flour, sugar and salt; cover and pulse until blended. Add butter and shortening; pulse until the mixture resembles coarse crumbs. While processing, gradually add water until the dough forms a ball.

2. Divide dough in half so 1 portion is slightly larger than the other; wrap each portion and refrigerate for 45 minutes or until easy to handle.

3. Preheat oven to 375°. Coat a 9-in. deep-dish pie plate with cooking spray. Line bottom and sides of plate with parchment; coat paper with cooking spray and set aside.

4. In a small bowl, combine brown sugar and butter; stir in pecans. Arrange in the bottom of prepared pie plate with rounded sides of pecans facing down.

5. On a lightly floured surface, roll out larger portion of dough to fit bottom and sides of pie plate. Transfer to plate; press the crust firmly against pecans and sides of pie plate. Trim edge.

6. In a large bowl, combine the sugar, flour, butter and cinnamon. Add apples; toss to coat. Fill crust. Roll out the remaining dough to fit top of pie; place over filling. Trim and seal edges. Cut slits in crust.

7. Place a foil-lined baking sheet on a rack below the pie to catch any spills. Bake pie for 60-70 minutes or until golden brown. Carefully loosen the parchment around edge of pie; invert hot pie onto a serving plate. Remove paper. Cool for at least 15 minutes before serving.

1 piece: 791 cal., 44g fat (19g sat. fat), 68mg chol., 483mg sod., 96g carb. (53g sugars, 4g fiber), 7g pro.

1. FIRST-PRIZE PIE

After my lattice-top cherry pie won first prize at the New York State Fair in 1961, the organizers told me that I'd need to bake another pie to give to the governor the next day. With my husband and four kids off to a drive-in movie, I set to work. When I presented Gov. Nelson Rockefeller with my masterpiece, he said it was a work of art.

2. SHE'S A NATURAL

Sedona really enjoyed learning how to milk a cow at the Chelsea County Fair in Michigan.

3. JUST LIKE GRANDPA

Finn and his grandpa Randy Herrick-Stare shared toothy grins as they cheered the barrel racers at the Chaffee County Fair in Colorado. Maybe one day Finn will ride and rope in a rodeo of his own.

BLUE-RIBBON PIES

P. 276

P. 287

P. 284

P. 268

GOLD-TROPHY CAKES

MOIST LAZY DAISY CAKE

We always called this Mama's never-fail recipe. I guess the same holds true for me, since I've won contests with this cake. The tasty dessert always brings back fond memories of Mama.
—Carrie Bartlett, Gallatin, TN

Prep: 20 min. • **Bake:** 25 min.
Makes: 9 servings

- 2 large eggs, room temperature
- 1 cup sugar
- 1 tsp. vanilla extract
- 1 cup cake flour
- 1 tsp. baking powder
- ¼ tsp. salt
- ½ cup 2% milk
- 2 Tbsp. butter

FROSTING
- ¾ cup packed brown sugar
- ½ cup butter, melted
- 2 Tbsp. half-and-half cream
- 1 cup sweetened shredded coconut

1. Preheat oven to 350°. In a large bowl, beat eggs, sugar and vanilla on high until thick and lemon-colored, about 4 minutes. Combine flour, baking powder and salt; add to egg mixture. Beat on low just until combined. Heat milk and butter in a small saucepan until butter melts. Add to batter; beat thoroughly (the batter will be thin).
2. Pour into a greased 9-in. square baking pan. Bake until a toothpick inserted in center comes out clean, 20-25 minutes. Cool slightly.
3. For frosting, blend all ingredients well; spread over warm cake. Broil 4 in. from heat 3-4 minutes or until top is lightly browned.

1 piece: 405 cal., 18g fat (12g sat. fat), 78mg chol., 277mg sod., 58g carb. (46g sugars, 1g fiber), 4g pro.

CHOCOLATE CANNOLI CAKE

Hints of orange and coffee lend standout flavor in this tasty cannoli-inspired cake. A variation of this cake was a finalist in the Best Cake in Michigan contest.
—Mary Bilyeu, Ann Arbor, MI

Prep: 25 min. • **Bake:** 25 min. + cooling
Makes: 15 servings

- 1 large egg white, lightly beaten
- 1 cup reduced-fat ricotta cheese
- ¼ cup sugar
- 1 Tbsp. cold brewed coffee
- 2 tsp. grated orange zest
- ½ cup miniature semisweet chocolate chips

BATTER
- 1 cup sugar
- ½ cup cold brewed coffee
- ⅓ cup canola oil
- ⅓ cup orange juice
- 1 large egg, room temperature
- 1 large egg white, room temperature
- 1 Tbsp. cider vinegar
- 1 Tbsp. vanilla extract
- 1 cup all-purpose flour
- ½ cup whole wheat flour
- ⅓ cup baking cocoa
- 2 tsp. baking powder
- ½ tsp. salt

1. Preheat oven to 350°. In a small bowl, combine the egg white, ricotta cheese, sugar, coffee and orange zest. Stir in chocolate chips; set aside.
2. In a large bowl, combine the first 8 batter ingredients; beat until well blended. Combine the flours, cocoa, baking powder and salt; gradually beat into sugar mixture until blended.
3. Transfer to a 13x9-in. baking dish coated with cooking spray. Top with heaping tablespoons of ricotta mixture; cut through batter with a knife to swirl.
4. Bake for 25-30 minutes or until a toothpick inserted in center comes out clean. Cool on a wire rack. Refrigerate leftovers.

1 piece: 213 cal., 8g fat (2g sat. fat), 18mg chol., 160mg sod., 32g carb. (21g sugars, 1g fiber), 4g pro.

SOUR CREAM RHUBARB COFFEE CAKE

Our daughter Judy won a blue ribbon with this recipe at the New York State Fair when we were living in upstate New York. It's been a family favorite for decades.
—Arlene Vogt, Fond du Lac, WI

....

Prep: 15 min. • **Bake:** 45 min.
Makes: 15 servings

1½ **cups packed brown sugar**
½ **cup shortening**
1 **large egg, room temperature**
2 **cups all-purpose flour**
1 **tsp. baking soda**
½ **tsp. salt**
1 **cup sour cream**
1½ **cups chopped rhubarb**
   (½-in. chunks)
TOPPING
½ **cup sugar**
½ **cup chopped walnuts**
1 **tsp. ground cinnamon**
1 **Tbsp. butter, softened**

1. Preheat oven to 350°. In a bowl, cream sugar, shortening and egg. Combine flour, baking soda and salt; add to creamed mixture alternately with sour cream. Gently fold in rhubarb until evenly distributed. Spoon into a greased 13x9-in. baking pan.
2. Combine topping ingredients until crumbly; sprinkle over batter. Bake for 45-50 minutes or until a toothpick inserted in center comes out clean. Cool slightly before cutting into squares
1 piece: 298 cal., 13g fat (4g sat. fat), 26mg chol., 192mg sod., 43g carb. (29g sugars, 1g fiber), 4g pro.

SPECIAL-OCCASION CHOCOLATE CAKE

This recipe won Grand Champion at the Alaska State Fair, and with one bite, you'll see why! The decadent chocolate cake boasts a luscious ganache filling and fudge buttercream frosting.
—Cindi DeClue, Anchorage, AK

Prep: 40 min. + chilling
Bake: 25 min. + cooling
Makes: 16 servings

- 1 **cup baking cocoa**
- 2 **cups boiling water**
- 1 **cup butter, softened**
- 2¼ **cups sugar**
- 4 **large eggs, room temperature**
- 1½ **tsp. vanilla extract**
- 2¾ **cups all-purpose flour**
- 2 **tsp. baking soda**
- ½ **tsp. baking powder**
- ½ **tsp. salt**

GANACHE

- 10 **oz. semisweet chocolate, chopped**
- 1 **cup heavy whipping cream**
- 2 **Tbsp. sugar**

FROSTING

- 1 **cup butter, softened**
- 4 **cups confectioners' sugar**
- ½ **cup baking cocoa**
- ¼ **cup 2% milk**
- 2 **tsp. vanilla extract**

GARNISH

- ¾ **cup sliced almonds, toasted**

1. Preheat oven to 350°. In a small bowl, combine cocoa and water; set aside to cool completely. In a large bowl, cream butter and sugar until light and fluffy, 5-7 minutes. Add eggs, 1 at a time, beating well after each addition. Beat in the vanilla. Whisk together the flour, baking soda, baking powder and salt; add to the creamed mixture alternately with cocoa mixture, beating well after each addition.

2. Pour into 3 greased and floured 9-in. round baking pans. Bake until a toothpick inserted in the center comes out clean, 25-30 minutes. Cool for 10 minutes before removing from pans to wire racks to cool completely.

3. For ganache, place chocolate in a bowl. In a small heavy saucepan over low heat, bring cream and sugar to a boil. Pour over chocolate; whisk gently until smooth. Allow to cool until it reaches a spreadable consistency, stirring occasionally.

4. For the frosting, in a large bowl, beat the butter until fluffy. Add the confectioners' sugar, cocoa, milk and vanilla; beat until smooth.

5. Place 1 cake layer on a serving plate; spread with 1 cup frosting. Top with second layer and 1 cup ganache; sprinkle with ½ cup almonds. Top with third layer; frost top and sides of cake. Warm ganache until pourable; pour over cake, allowing some to drape down the sides. Sprinkle with remaining almonds. Refrigerate until serving.

1 piece: 736 cal., 39g fat (22g sat. fat), 125mg chol., 454mg sod., 86g carb. (63g sugars, 3g fiber), 8g pro.

Special-Occasion Mocha Cake: Add 2 Tbsp. instant coffee granules to the boiling water-cocoa mixture. In the frosting, substitute Kahlua for the milk.

BUTTERSCOTCH SWIRL CAKE

I was tickled when my swirled dessert took first place and best of division at the Los Angeles County Fair. People hovered over it, commenting on how pretty it looked. I was basking in all the attention.

—Marina Castle-Kelley,
Canyon Country, CA

....

Prep: 30 min. • **Bake:** 65 min. + cooling
Makes: 12 servings

- 1 **cup butter, softened**
- 2 **cups sugar**
- 6 **large eggs, room temperature**
- 3 **tsp. rum extract**
- 1 **tsp. vanilla extract**
- 3 **cups all-purpose flour**
- 1 **tsp. baking soda**
- 1 **tsp. baking powder**
- 1 **cup sour cream**
- 1 **pkg. (3.4 oz.) instant butterscotch pudding mix**
- ¾ **cup butterscotch ice cream topping**

BUTTERSCOTCH GLAZE

- ¼ **cup butter, cubed**
- ¼ **cup packed brown sugar**
- 2 **Tbsp. 2% milk**
- 1 **cup confectioners' sugar**
- 1 **tsp. vanilla extract**
- ¼ **cup chopped pecans**

1. Preheat oven to 350°. In a large bowl, cream butter and sugar until light and fluffy, 5-7 minutes. Add 5 eggs, 1 at a time, beating well after each addition. Stir in extracts. Combine flour, baking soda and baking powder; gradually add to creamed mixture alternately with sour cream, beating well after each addition.

2. Transfer 2 cups of batter to another large bowl; beat in the pudding mix, butterscotch topping and remaining egg until well blended. Pour half the plain batter into a greased and floured 10-in. fluted tube pan. Top with half the butterscotch batter; cut through with a knife to swirl. Repeat layers and swirl.

3. Bake for 65-70 minutes or until a toothpick inserted in center comes out clean. Cool 10 minutes before removing from pan to a wire rack to cool completely.

4. For the glaze, in a small saucepan, combine butter, brown sugar and milk. Bring to a boil. Remove from heat; add confectioners' sugar and vanilla. Beat until smooth and creamy. Drizzle over cake; sprinkle with pecans.

1 piece: 650 cal., 27g fat (15g sat. fat), 171mg chol., 573mg sod., 94g carb. (67g sugars, 1g fiber), 8g pro.

RASPBERRY LEMON CAKE

Want a change from chocolate cake? Try this elegant cake packed with refreshing lemon flavor, from the cake to the homemade lemon curd and creamy frosting. It won a blue ribbon at the Alaska State Fair and it's definitely a winner with me.
—Shirley Warren, Thiensville, WI

....

Prep: 1¼ hours + chilling
Bake: 20 min. + cooling
Makes: 12 servings

 3 **large eggs**
 ¾ **cup sugar**
 ½ **cup lemon juice**
 ¼ **cup butter, cubed**
 1 **Tbsp. grated lemon zest**
CAKE
 1 **pkg. (3 oz.) lemon gelatin**
 ½ **cup boiling water**
 ½ **cup butter, softened**
 ½ **cup canola oil**
 1¾ **cups sugar, divided**
 4 **large eggs, room temperature**
 ½ **cup lemon juice**
 4 **tsp. grated lemon zest**
 1 **tsp. lemon extract**
 1 **tsp. vanilla extract**
 2½ **cups all-purpose flour**
 2½ **tsp. baking powder**
 ½ **tsp. salt**
 ½ **cup evaporated milk**
 ¾ **cup thawed lemonade concentrate**
FROSTING
 6 **oz. cream cheese, softened**
 6 **Tbsp. butter, softened**
 3¾ **to 4 cups confectioners' sugar**
 4½ **tsp. lemon juice**
 1½ **tsp. grated lemon zest**
 ¾ **tsp. vanilla extract**
 ¾ **cup seedless raspberry jam**
    Fresh raspberries, optional

1. For lemon curd, in a heavy saucepan, beat eggs and sugar. Stir in lemon juice, butter and lemon zest. Cook and stir over medium-low heat for 15 minutes or until the mixture is thickened and reaches 160°. Cool for 10 minutes. Press plastic wrap onto the surface of the curd and chill for 1½ hours or until thickened.

2. For cake, preheat oven to 350°. In a small bowl, dissolve gelatin in boiling water; set aside to cool.

3. In a large bowl, cream butter, oil and 1½ cups sugar until blended, about 5 minutes. Add eggs, 1 at a time, beating well after each addition. Beat in gelatin mixture, lemon juice, lemon zest and extracts. Combine the flour, baking powder and salt; add to the butter mixture alternately with milk, beating well after each addition.

4. Pour batter into 3 greased and floured 9-in. round baking pans. Bake until a toothpick inserted in the center comes out clean, 20-25 minutes.

5. In a microwave-safe bowl, combine lemonade concentrate and remaining ¼ cup sugar. Microwave, uncovered, on high for 2 minutes or until sugar is dissolved, stirring occasionally. Poke holes in warm cake layers with a fork; pour lemonade mixture over tops. Cool 10 minutes before removing from pans to wire racks to cool completely.

6. For frosting, beat cream cheese and butter until fluffy. Add confectioners' sugar, lemon juice, lemon zest and vanilla; beat until blended.

7. To assemble, place 1 cake layer on a serving plate; spread with 6 Tbsp. raspberry jam. Repeat. Top with the remaining cake layer. Spread about ½ cup lemon curd over top of cake (save remaining curd for another use).

8. Spread frosting over sides of cake and pipe a shell border along the top and bottom edges. Garnish with raspberries if desired. Chill 1 hour.

1 piece: 792 cal., 32g fat (15g sat. fat), 148mg chol., 386mg sod., 122g carb. (97g sugars, 1g fiber), 8g pro.

ALMOND-TOPPED PUMPKIN CHEESECAKE

You really must try this luscious cheesecake that my family requests for every holiday dinner. I won a blue ribbon when I entered it at the state fair a few years ago.

—Carmel Mooney, Dobbins, CA

Prep: 30 min. • **Bake:** 70 min. + chilling
Makes: 12 servings

1½ cups graham cracker crumbs
⅓ cup finely chopped almonds
1 Tbsp. sugar
¼ tsp. pumpkin pie spice
¼ cup butter, melted
FILLING
3 pkg. (8 oz. each) cream cheese, softened
¾ cup sugar
1 cup canned pumpkin
¼ cup eggnog
3 Tbsp. all-purpose flour
2 Tbsp. maple syrup
½ tsp. each ground ginger, cinnamon and nutmeg
3 large eggs, lightly beaten
TOPPING
1 cup sour cream
3 Tbsp. sugar
¼ tsp. vanilla extract
¼ cup sliced almonds

1. Preheat oven to 325°. Place a greased 9-in. springform pan on a double thickness of heavy-duty foil (about 18 in. square). Securely wrap foil around pan.

2. In a small bowl, combine the cracker crumbs, almonds, sugar and pumpkin pie spice; stir in butter. Press onto the bottom of prepared pan. Place on a baking sheet. Bake for 10 minutes. Cool on a wire rack.

3. In a large bowl, beat the cream cheese and sugar until smooth. Beat in pumpkin, eggnog, flour, syrup and spices. Add eggs; beat on low speed just until combined. Pour over crust.

4. Place springform pan in a large baking pan; add 1 in. hot water to larger pan. Bake for 55-60 minutes or until center is almost set. Let stand for 5 minutes.

5. Combine the sour cream, sugar and vanilla; spread over the top of the cheesecake. Sprinkle with almonds. Bake 15-18 minutes longer or until the almonds are toasted.

6. Remove springform pan from water bath. Cool on a wire rack for 10 minutes. Carefully run a knife around edge of pan to loosen; cool 1 hour longer. Refrigerate overnight. Remove sides of pan.

1 piece: 329 cal., 19g fat (10g sat. fat), 101mg chol., 188mg sod., 33g carb. (23g sugars, 2g fiber), 6g pro.

CONTEST-WINNING CHOCOLATE POTATO CAKE

I won grand champion honors in a potato festival baking contest with this moist cake. The icing recipe can be doubled if you have a real sweet tooth.
—Catherine Hahn, Winamac, IN

Prep: 40 min. • **Bake:** 25 min. + cooling
Makes: 12 servings

- 1 cup butter, softened
- 2 cups sugar
- 2 large eggs, room temperature
- 1 cup cold mashed potatoes (without added milk and butter)
- 1 tsp. vanilla extract
- 2 cups all-purpose flour
- ½ cup baking cocoa
- 1 tsp. baking soda
- 1 cup whole milk
- 1 cup chopped walnuts or pecans

CARAMEL ICING

- ½ cup butter, cubed
- 1 cup packed brown sugar
- ¼ cup evaporated milk
- 2 cups confectioners' sugar
- ½ tsp. vanilla extract

1. In a large bowl, cream butter and sugar until light and fluffy, 5-7 minutes. Add eggs, 1 at a time, beating well after each addition. Add potatoes and vanilla. Combine the flour, cocoa and baking soda; gradually add to creamed mixture alternately with milk, beating well after each addition. Stir in nuts.
2. Pour into 2 greased and floured 9-in. round baking pans. Bake at 350° until a toothpick inserted in the center comes out clean, 25-30 minutes. Cool for 10 minutes before removing from pans to wire racks to cool completely.
3. For icing, in a saucepan over low heat, cook butter and brown sugar until butter is melted and the mixture is smooth. Stir in evaporated milk; bring to a boil, stirring constantly. Remove from the heat; cool to room temperature. Stir in the confectioners' sugar and vanilla until smooth. Spread between layers and over top of cake.

1 piece: 671 cal., 31g fat (15g sat. fat), 101mg chol., 374mg sod., 94g carb. (71g sugars, 2g fiber), 8g pro.

READER RAVE...

"This is the exact recipe that my grandmother used to make for all of my birthdays when I was a girl in school. I recommend this cake and can't think of any changes that would make it better. Five stars!"

—PATRASIOR, TASTEOFHOME.COM

BLUE-RIBBON RED VELVET CAKE

This two-layer beauty features a striking red interior. It calls for more cocoa than most red velvet cakes, making it extra chocolaty. Feel free to change the color of the food coloring to suit the occasion. This recipe won a blue ribbon in the holiday cake division at the 2006 Alaska State Fair. I think this cake will be a winner in your house, too!
—Cindi DeClue, Anchorage, AK

Prep: 35 min. • **Bake:** 25 min. + cooling
Makes: 16 servings

- 1½ cups canola oil
- 1 cup buttermilk
- 2 large eggs, room temperature
- 2 Tbsp. red food coloring
- 1 tsp. white vinegar
- 2½ cups all-purpose flour
- 1½ cups sugar
- 3 Tbsp. baking cocoa
- 1 tsp. baking soda

FROSTING

- 1 pkg. (8 oz.) cream cheese, softened
- ½ cup butter, softened
- 2 tsp. vanilla extract
- 3¾ cups confectioners' sugar

1. Preheat oven to 350°. Line the bottoms of 2 greased 9-in. round pans with parchment; grease parchment. Beat the first 5 ingredients until well blended. In another bowl, whisk together flour, sugar, baking cocoa and baking soda; gradually beat into the oil mixture.

2. Transfer batter to prepared pans. Bake until a toothpick inserted in center comes out clean, 25-30 minutes. Cool in pans 10 minutes before removing to wire racks; carefully remove the parchment. Cool completely.

3. For the frosting, beat the cream cheese, butter and vanilla until blended. Gradually beat in confectioners' sugar until smooth. Using a long serrated knife, trim tops of cakes; set tops aside. Place 1 cake layer on a serving plate. Spread with ¾ cup frosting. Top with remaining layer, bottom side up. Frost top and sides with remaining frosting.

4. Break cake tops into pieces. Pulse in a food processor until fine crumbs form. Decorate cake with crumbs as desired.

1 piece: 559 cal., 33g fat (8g sat. fat), 53mg chol., 208mg sod., 64g carb. (48g sugars, 1g fiber), 4g pro.

PINEAPPLE CHIFFON CAKE

I was looking for an unusual recipe to enter in a competition at the local county fair, since it seemed unusual cakes and pies won. I searched through my mother's old recipes and found this. I thought I would give it a try because I love pineapple. It was a big hit with my husband and brought me a blue ribbon at the fair!
—Cheryl Tichenor, Elgin, IL

Prep: 25 min. • **Bake:** 55 min. + cooling
Makes: 12 servings

- 2¼ cups cake flour
- 1½ cups sugar
- 3 tsp. baking powder
- ½ tsp. salt
- 5 large egg yolks,
  room temperature
- ⅔ cup unsweetened pineapple juice
- ½ cup canola oil
- 2 tsp. grated lemon zest
- 8 large egg whites,
  room temperature
- ½ tsp. cream of tartar

GLAZE
- 2 cups confectioners' sugar
- 2 Tbsp. butter, melted
- 2 to 3 Tbsp. unsweetened
  pineapple juice

1. Preheat oven to 325°. In a large bowl, combine the flour, sugar, baking powder and salt. In a small bowl, whisk the egg yolks, pineapple juice, oil and lemon zest. Add to dry ingredients; beat until well blended.

2. In another bowl, beat the egg whites and cream of tartar until stiff peaks form; fold into batter. Gently spoon into an ungreased 10-in. tube pan. Cut through the batter with a knife to remove air pockets.

3. Bake on the lowest oven rack for 55-60 minutes or until the top springs back when lightly touched. Immediately invert pan; cool completely, about 1 hour.

4. Run a knife around side and center tube of pan. Remove cake to a serving plate. Combine the confectioners' sugar, butter and enough pineapple juice to achieve a glaze consistency. Drizzle over top of cake, allowing some glaze to drape down the sides.

1 piece: 408 cal., 13g fat (3g sat. fat), 90mg chol., 253mg sod., 68g carb. (46g sugars, 1g fiber), 6g pro.

SUNSHINE CAKE

I took this cake to the county fair for 4-H and easily brought home a purple ribbon. For a quicker lemon filling, use a cup of lemon curd from a jar.
—Leah Will, Bel Aire, KS

....

Prep: 1 hour + chilling
Bake: 25 min. + cooling
Makes: 16 servings

- 1 cup butter, softened
- 1⅔ cups sugar
- 4 large eggs, room temperature
- 1½ tsp. vanilla extract
- 1½ tsp. each grated lemon, orange and lime zest
- 2¾ cups all-purpose flour
- 3 tsp. baking powder
- ¾ tsp. salt
- 1 cup 2% milk

FILLING
- ½ cup sugar
- ¼ cup cornstarch
- ¼ tsp. salt
- ¾ cup water
- 2 large egg yolks
- 2 Tbsp. butter
- ⅓ cup lemon juice

FROSTING
- ½ cup butter, softened
- 3¾ cups confectioners' sugar
- ¼ cup light corn syrup
- 3 Tbsp. orange juice
- 1 tsp. vanilla extract
- ½ tsp. grated orange zest
  Dash salt
- 3 drops yellow food coloring
- 1 drop red food coloring
  Assorted lollipops, unwrapped

1. Preheat oven to 350°. Line bottom of a greased 15x10x1-in. jelly-roll pan with parchment; grease paper.

2. In a large bowl, cream butter and sugar until light and fluffy, 5-7 minutes. Add eggs, 1 at a time, beating well after each addition. Beat in the vanilla and citrus zest. In another bowl, whisk the flour, baking powder and salt; add to creamed mixture alternately with milk, beating well after each addition.

3. Transfer to prepared pan. Bake for 25-30 minutes or until a toothpick inserted in center comes out clean. Cool in pan 5 minutes before removing to a wire rack; carefully remove the paper. Cool completely.

4. For filling, in a small saucepan, combine sugar, cornstarch and salt. Whisk in water. Cook and stir over medium heat until thickened and bubbly. Remove from heat.

5. In a small bowl, whisk a small amount of hot mixture into egg yolks; return all to pan, whisking constantly. Bring to a gentle boil; cook and stir 2 minutes. Remove from heat. Stir in butter. Gently stir in lemon juice. Press plastic wrap onto surface of filling; cool slightly. Refrigerate until cold.

6. For the frosting, in a large bowl, cream the butter until fluffy. Beat in the confectioners' sugar, corn syrup, orange juice, vanilla, orange zest and salt until smooth. Tint orange with yellow and red food coloring.

7. Trim edges of cake; cut crosswise into thirds. Place 1 cake layer on a serving plate; spread with half the filling. Repeat layers. Top with remaining cake layer. Frost top and sides of cake with frosting. Insert lollipops in top for flowers. Refrigerate leftovers.

1 piece: 533 cal., 22g fat (12g sat. fat), 129mg chol., 394mg sod., 82g carb. (58g sugars, 1g fiber), 5g pro.

To make window box: Press about 28 cream-filled wafer cookies against sides of cake. Tie 2 pieces of shoestring licorice together to make a longer strand. Wrap and tie 3 longer strands around window box.

To make flowers: Cut Fruit Roll-Ups with flower-shaped cutters. Sandwich 2 cutouts around each unwrapped lollipop, moistening edges with water. For stems and leaves, insert drinking straws in cake. Top with the lollipop flowers. Cut leaves from green licorice twists and insert in cake.

READER RAVE...

"Tasty and fun to make. I used a 9x13 pan and cut it in half to make two layers. My kids had a lot of fun making the flowers. We added Peeps on top to play on a spring theme."
—AUG-95, TASTEOFHOME.COM

COASTAL COCONUT CREAM CAKE

This is my son's county fair cake. He was awarded a top-10 prize, and he auctioned the coconut cream cake for big bucks!
—Amy Freeze, Avon Park, FL

....

Prep: 45 min. + chilling
Bake: 35 min. + cooling
Makes: 16 servings

- 1 **cup butter, softened**
- 2 **cups sugar**
- 4 **large eggs, room temperature**
- 1½ **tsp. coconut extract**
- 3 **cups all-purpose flour**
- 1½ **tsp. baking soda**
- 1½ **tsp. baking powder**
- 1 **tsp. salt**
- 1 **cup canned coconut milk**
- ½ **cup cream of coconut**
- ¼ **cup sweetened shredded coconut**

FILLING

- 1 **cup sugar**
- 6 **Tbsp. cornstarch**
- 1 **can (20 oz.) unsweetened crushed pineapple, undrained**
- 2 **Tbsp. butter**

FROSTING

- 3¾ **cups confectioners' sugar**
- 1 **cup shortening**
- ½ **cup butter, softened**
- 1½ **tsp. meringue powder**
- ¾ **tsp. coconut extract**
- ¼ **tsp. salt**
- 2 **to 3 Tbsp. canned coconut milk**
- 2 **cups sweetened shredded coconut, toasted**

1. Preheat oven to 350°. Line bottoms of 2 greased 9-in. round baking pans with parchment; grease paper.

2. In a large bowl, cream butter and sugar until light and fluffy, 5-7 minutes. Add eggs, 1 at a time, beating well after each addition. Beat in extract. In another bowl, whisk flour, baking soda, baking powder and salt; add to the creamed mixture alternately with the coconut milk, beating well after each addition. Fold in the cream of coconut and the shredded coconut.

3. Transfer to prepared pans. Bake until a toothpick inserted in center comes out clean, 35-40 minutes. Cool in pans 10 minutes before removing to wire racks; remove paper. Cool completely.

4. For filling, in a large saucepan, mix the sugar and cornstarch. Whisk in the pineapple and butter. Cook and stir over medium heat until thickened and bubbly. Reduce the heat to low; cook and stir 2 minutes longer. Remove from heat; cool completely.

5. For frosting, in a large bowl, beat the confectioners' sugar, shortening, butter, meringue powder, extract, salt and enough coconut milk to reach desired consistency.

6. To assemble cake, using a long serrated knife, cut each cake in half horizontally. Place 1 cake layer on a serving plate; spread with a third of the filling. Repeat twice. Top with remaining cake layer. Frost top and sides of cake with frosting. Gently press toasted coconut into frosting on the sides of the cake. Refrigerate at least 4 hours before serving.

Note: Meringue powder is available from Wilton Brands. Call 800-794-5866 or visit wilton.com.

1 piece: 788 cal., 41g fat (23g sat. fat), 96mg chol., 560mg sod., 103g carb. (81g sugars, 2g fiber), 5g pro.

HOMEMADE CHOCOLATE ANGEL FOOD CAKE

I developed this cake using my mother's angel food cake recipe because my husband and three daughters all love chocolate. It won first place at our county and state fairs, as well as best of class at the state fair!
—Lois Bayles, Hastings, NE

Prep: 30 min. • **Bake:** 45 min. + cooling
Makes: 16 servings

- 1½ **cups plus ⅓ cup sugar, divided**
- 1¼ **cups sifted cake flour**
- ¼ **cup baking cocoa**
- 2 **cups egg whites (about 14), room temperature**
- 1 **tsp. vanilla extract**
- ½ **tsp. chocolate flavoring**
- 1½ **tsp. cream of tartar**
- ½ **tsp. salt**
  Optional: Ice cream and fudge sauce

1. Preheat oven to 350°. Sift together 1½ cups sugar with flour and cocoa; set aside.
2. In a large bowl, beat egg whites, vanilla and chocolate flavoring until foamy. Combine cream of tartar, salt and remaining sugar; add a little at a time to egg mixture. Beat until very stiff but not dry peaks form. Gradually fold in flour mixture; do not over mix. Pour into an ungreased 10-in. tube pan.
3. Bake for 45 minutes. Remove from oven and invert pan; allow to cool completely before removing from pan. Serve with ice cream and fudge sauce if desired.
1 piece: 148 cal., 0 fat (0 sat. fat), 0 chol., 124mg sod., 32g carb. (23g sugars, 0 fiber), 4g pro.

BLUE-RIBBON APPLE CAKE

A friend from New Hampshire gave me this recipe for her cake, which took a blue ribbon at the county fair.
—Jennie Wilburn, Long Creek, OR

....

Prep: 15 min. • **Bake:** 55 min. + cooling
Makes: 16 servings

- 3   cups all-purpose flour
- 2¼ cups sugar, divided
- 1   Tbsp. baking powder
- ½   tsp. salt
- 4   large eggs, room temperature
- 1   cup canola oil
- ⅓   cup orange juice
- 2½ tsp. vanilla extract
- 4   medium tart apples, peeled and thinly sliced
- 2   tsp. ground cinnamon
      Confectioners' sugar

1. Preheat oven to 350°. In a large bowl, combine flour, 2 cups sugar, the baking powder and salt. Combine eggs, oil, orange juice and vanilla. Add to flour mixture; mix well. In a bowl, toss apples with cinnamon and remaining sugar.
2. Spread a third of the batter into a greased 10-in. tube pan. Top with half the sliced apples. Repeat the layers. Carefully spread the remaining batter over the apples.

3. Bake until a toothpick inserted in the center comes out clean, 55-65 minutes. Cool 15 minutes before removing from pan to a wire rack; cool. Dust with confectioners' sugar.
1 piece: 353 cal., 15g fat (2g sat. fat), 53mg chol., 165mg sod., 51g carb. (32g sugars, 1g fiber), 4g pro.

BLUE-RIBBON TIP

We recommend using any tart apple. Some of our favorite apples to bake with are Gravenstein, Rome Beauty and Northern Spy.

APRICOT, PINEAPPLE & ALMOND COFFEE CAKE

I created this recipe for a contest at the Los Angeles County Fair in the 1980s. My kids were very proud of me when my name was called for first place. The cake would be the perfect partner for morning coffee or it'd be a delightful dessert with a scoop of ice cream.
—Marina Castle-Kelley, Canyon Country, CA

Prep: 30 min. • **Bake:** 1 hour + cooling
Makes: 12 servings

- ½ cup unsalted butter, softened
- 1 cup superfine sugar
- 2 large eggs, room temperature
- ½ tsp. almond extract
- 1½ cups all-purpose flour
- ½ cup almond flour
- ½ tsp. baking powder
- ½ tsp. baking soda
- ½ tsp. kosher salt
- 1 cup sour cream
- ¾ cup pineapple preserves
- ¾ cup apricot preserves
- ½ cup sliced almonds
  Confectioners' sugar, optional

1. Preheat oven to 350°. In a large bowl, beat butter and sugar until crumbly, about 2 minutes. Add eggs, 1 at a time, beating well after each addition. Beat in extract. In another bowl, whisk flour, almond flour, baking powder, baking soda and salt; add to creamed mixture alternately with sour cream, beating well after each addition.

2. Transfer half the batter to a greased 10-in. springform pan. Mix pineapple and apricot preserves; drop by tablespoonfuls over batter. Carefully top with remaining batter. Sprinkle with almonds. Bake until a toothpick inserted in center comes out clean, 60-65 minutes. Cool on a wire rack 10 minutes. Loosen sides from pan with a knife. Cool completely. Remove rim from the pan. Sprinkle with the confectioners' sugar if desired.

1 piece: 389 cal., 17g fat (8g sat. fat), 56mg chol., 182mg sod., 57g carb. (39g sugars, 1g fiber), 5g pro.

SANDY'S CHOCOLATE CAKE

Years ago, I drove 4½ hours to a cake contest, holding my entry on my lap the whole way. But it paid off. One bite and you'll see why this velvety beauty was named the best chocolate cake recipe and won first prize.
—Sandy Johnson, Tioga, PA

Prep: 30 min. • **Bake:** 30 min. + cooling
Makes: 16 servings

- 1 **cup butter, softened**
- 3 **cups packed brown sugar**
- 4 **large eggs, room temperature**
- 2 **tsp. vanilla extract**
- 2⅔ **cups all-purpose flour**
- ¾ **cup baking cocoa**
- 3 **tsp. baking soda**
- ½ **tsp. salt**
- 1⅓ **cups sour cream**
- 1⅓ **cups boiling water**

FROSTING
- ½ **cup butter, cubed**
- 3 **oz. unsweetened chocolate, chopped**
- 3 **oz. semisweet chocolate, chopped**
- 5 **cups confectioners' sugar**
- 1 **cup sour cream**
- 2 **tsp. vanilla extract**

1. Preheat oven to 350°. Grease and flour three 9-in. round baking pans.
2. In a large bowl, cream butter and brown sugar until light and fluffy, 5-7 minutes. Add eggs, 1 at a time, beating well after each addition. Beat in vanilla. In another bowl, whisk flour, cocoa, baking soda and salt; add to creamed mixture alternately with sour cream, beating well after each addition. Stir in water until blended.
3. Transfer batter to prepared pans. Bake until a toothpick comes out clean, 30-35 minutes. Cool in pans 10 minutes; remove to wire racks to cool completely.
4. For frosting, in a metal bowl over simmering water, melt the butter and chocolates; stir until smooth. Cool slightly.
5. In a large bowl, combine the confectioners' sugar, sour cream and vanilla. Add chocolate mixture; beat until smooth. Spread frosting between layers, and over top and sides of cake. Refrigerate leftovers.

1 piece: 685 cal., 29g fat (18g sat. fat), 115mg chol., 505mg sod., 102g carb. (81g sugars, 3g fiber), 7g pro.

STREUSELED ZUCCHINI BUNDT CAKE

Inspired by an abundance of zucchini, I created this spiced and lightly sweet cake. It even won a blue ribbon at our county fair! Fat-free plain yogurt replaces some of the oil and helps make this cake tender and moist.
—Regina Stock, Topeka, KS

Prep: 25 min. • **Bake:** 55 min. + cooling
Makes: 14 servings

- 2 **cups shredded zucchini, patted dry**
- 1⅓ **cups fat-free plain yogurt**
- ¾ **cup sugar**
- 2 **large egg whites, room temperature**
- ⅓ **cup canola oil**
- 1 **large egg, room temperature**
- 4 **tsp. vanilla extract, divided**
- 3 **cups all-purpose flour**
- 1½ **tsp. baking powder**
- 1 **tsp. baking soda**
- ½ **tsp. salt**
- 1 **Tbsp. dry bread crumbs**
- ⅓ **cup packed brown sugar**
- ⅓ **cup chopped walnuts**
- ⅓ **cup raisins**
- 1 **Tbsp. ground cinnamon**
- ½ **tsp. ground allspice**
- ¾ **cup confectioners' sugar**
- 2 **to 3 tsp. fat-free milk**

1. Preheat oven to 350°. In a large bowl, beat the zucchini, yogurt, sugar, egg whites, oil, egg and 3 tsp. vanilla until well blended. Combine the flour, baking powder, baking soda and salt; gradually beat into zucchini mixture until blended.

2. Coat a 10-in. fluted tube pan with cooking spray; sprinkle with bread crumbs. Pour a third of the batter into pan. Combine brown sugar, walnuts, raisins, cinnamon and allspice; sprinkle half over batter. Top with another third of the batter. Sprinkle with the remaining brown sugar mixture; top with the remaining batter.

3. Bake for 55-65 minutes or until a toothpick inserted in the center comes out clean. Cool for 10 minutes before removing from pan to a wire rack to cool completely.

4. Combine the confectioners' sugar, remaining vanilla and enough milk to achieve desired consistency; drizzle over cake.

1 piece: 287 cal., 8g fat (1g sat. fat), 14mg chol., 259mg sod., 49g carb. (26g sugars, 2g fiber), 6g pro.

GRANDMA'S BLACKBERRY CAKE

A lightly seasoned spice cake lets the wonderful flavor of blackberries shine through in this delectable treat.
—Diana Martin, Moundsville, WV

Prep: 15 min. • **Bake:** 45 min.
Makes: 9 servings

- 1 cup fresh blackberries
- 2 cups all-purpose flour, divided
- ½ cup butter, softened
- 1 cup sugar
- 2 large eggs, room temperature
- 1 tsp. baking soda
- 1 tsp. ground cinnamon
- 1 tsp. ground nutmeg
- ½ tsp. salt
- ¼ tsp. ground cloves
- ¼ tsp. ground allspice
- ¾ cup buttermilk
  Optional: Whipped cream and confectioners' sugar

1. Preheat the oven to 350°. Toss the blackberries with ¼ cup flour; set aside. In a large bowl, cream butter and sugar until light and fluffy, 5-7 minutes. Beat in eggs. Combine baking soda, cinnamon, nutmeg, salt, cloves, allspice and remaining 1¾ cups flour; add to creamed mixture alternately with buttermilk, beating well after each addition. Fold in blackberries.
2. Pour into a greased and floured 9-in. square baking pan. Bake until a toothpick inserted in center comes out clean, 45-50 minutes. Cool on a wire rack. If desired, serve with whipped cream and top with confectioners' sugar and additional fresh blackberries.
1 piece: 312 cal., 12g fat (7g sat. fat), 75mg chol., 410mg sod., 47g carb. (24g sugars, 2g fiber), 5g pro.

CLASSIC CARROT CAKE

I entered this moist cake in a Colorado Outfitters Association dessert contest, and it took first place.
—Cheri Eby, Gunnison, CO

Prep: 30 min. • **Bake:** 35 min. + cooling
Makes: 15 servings

- 1 can (8 oz.) unsweetened crushed pineapple
- 4 large eggs, room temperature
- 2 cups shredded carrots (about 4 medium)
- 1 cup sugar
- 1 cup packed brown sugar
- 1 cup canola oil
- 2 cups all-purpose flour
- 2 tsp. baking soda
- 2 tsp. ground cinnamon
- ¼ tsp. salt
- ¾ cup chopped walnuts
FROSTING
- 2 pkg. (8 oz. each) cream cheese, softened
- ¼ cup butter, softened
- 2 tsp. vanilla extract
- 1½ cups confectioners' sugar

1. Preheat oven to 350°. Grease a 13x9-in. baking dish. Drain pineapple, reserving 2 Tbsp. juice (discard the remaining juice or save for another use). In a large bowl, beat the eggs, carrots, sugars, oil, drained pineapple and reserved juice until well blended. In another bowl, whisk together the flour, baking soda, cinnamon and salt; gradually beat into carrot mixture until blended. Stir in the walnuts. Transfer to prepared dish.
2. Bake until a toothpick inserted in center comes out clean, 35-40 minutes. Cool completely on a wire rack.
3. For the frosting, in a large bowl, beat cream cheese and butter until smooth. Beat in vanilla. Gradually beat in confectioners' sugar. Spread over cake.
1 piece: 555 cal., 34g fat (10g sat. fat), 88mg chol., 361mg sod., 59g carb. (44g sugars, 2g fiber), 6g pro.
Coconut Carrot Cake: Omit walnuts. Fold 1 cup flaked coconut into batter.
Cranberry Carrot Cake: Omit walnuts. Fold 1 cup dried cranberries into batter.

ORANGE GROVE CAKE

A few years ago, I won best in show in the Western Idaho State Fair for this citrusy cake with a luscious filling and creamy frosting. It bursts with fantastic orange flavor.
—Amanda Bowyer, Caldwell, ID

....

Prep: 55 min. + chilling
Bake: 20 min. + cooling
Makes: 16 servings

1 cup butter, softened
1¾ cups sugar
4 large eggs, room temperature
⅓ cup orange juice
2 tsp. grated orange zest
3 cups cake flour
2½ tsp. baking powder
½ tsp. salt
⅔ cup 2% milk
FILLING
½ cup sugar
1 Tbsp. plus 2 tsp. cornstarch
⅔ cup orange juice
2 Tbsp. water
3 large egg yolks, beaten
2 Tbsp. lemon juice
1 tsp. grated orange zest
⅛ tsp. salt
SYRUP
½ cup sugar
⅓ cup water
¼ cup orange juice
1 tsp. orange extract
FROSTING
1 cup butter, softened
4 cups confectioners' sugar
3 Tbsp. heavy whipping cream
1 tsp. grated orange zest
1 tsp. orange extract
¼ tsp. salt

1. Preheat oven to 350°. In a large bowl, cream butter and sugar until light and fluffy, 5-7 minutes. Add eggs, 1 at a time, beating well after each addition. Beat in orange juice and zest. Combine flour, baking powder and salt; add to the creamed mixture alternately with milk, beating well after each addition.

2. Transfer to 2 greased and floured 9-in. round baking pans. Bake for 20-25 minutes or until a toothpick inserted in the center comes out clean. Cool for 10 minutes before carefully removing from pans to wire racks to cool completely.

3. For filling, in a small saucepan, combine the sugar and cornstarch. Stir in the orange juice and water until smooth. Bring to a boil; cook and stir for 1 minute or until thickened. Remove from the heat. Stir a small amount of hot mixture into egg yolks; return all to the pan, stirring constantly. Bring to a gentle boil; cook and stir 1 minute longer. Remove from the heat; gently stir in the lemon juice, orange zest and salt. Cool to room temperature without stirring. Refrigerate for 1 hour.

4. For syrup, in a small saucepan, bring the sugar, water and orange juice to a boil. Reduce heat; simmer, uncovered, for 10 minutes or until reduced to about ½ cup. Remove from the heat; stir in extract. Cool.

5. For the frosting, beat butter until light and fluffy. Add the remaining ingredients; beat until smooth.

6. Cut each cake horizontally into 2 layers. Place bottom layer on a serving plate; brush with 2 Tbsp. syrup and spread with ⅓ cup filling. Repeat layers twice. Top with the remaining cake layer; brush with remaining syrup. Frost top and sides of cake.

1 piece: 602 cal., 26g fat (16g sat. fat), 156mg chol., 379mg sod., 88g carb. (65g sugars, 1g fiber), 5g pro.

BEST OF SHOW

I was always involved with 4-H as a kid, and I especially enjoyed the annual competition at the county fair.

That hasn't changed. The fair is still a big event each year, and now my obsession of sorts has become entering things to be judged. I especially love the canning, baked goods and home categories. I always try to win for my baked goods, and one year I managed to get the elusive best of show for my carrot layer cake. I was so excited. To this day I have my rosette on my memory board.

I look forward to the years ahead—entering wonderful things to be judged at the fair.

SARAH HEASTON · NEW PHILADELPHIA, OHIO

KATHY MCMILLEN · GRANVILLE, OHIO

1. FAMILY AFFAIR

Our four grandkids—Cole, Skylar, Craig and Sierra—earned first-place finishes with their feeder calves at our local fair. A happy day!

2. RODEO KIDS

Kaleb shows his little cousin William the ropes at the rodeo while they wear the chaps their grandpa made for them.

PATRICIA BIGALK · WHITE BEAR LAKE, MINNESOTA

P. 294

P. 298

P. 301

P. 305

GRAND-PRIZE DESSERTS, SWEETS & TREATS

BLUEBERRY FRUIT COBBLER

I was raised on a farm in southeast Georgia, and tobacco was our main crop. Nowadays in our small town, we grow blueberries. This recipe was a recent winner at our blueberry festival.
—Evelyn Dunlap, Nicolls, GA

Prep: 20 min. • **Bake:** 40 min.
Makes: 15 servings

- 6 **cups fresh or frozen blueberries**
- 1½ **cups sugar**
- ¼ **cup water**
- CRUST
- ¾ **cup butter, softened**
- 1½ **cups plus 2 Tbsp. sugar, divided**
- 3 **large eggs, room temperature**
- 1 **tsp. vanilla extract**
- 1½ **cups all-purpose flour**
- 1 **tsp. baking powder**
- ½ **tsp. salt**
- ¼ **cup butter, melted**
  Vanilla ice cream, optional

1. Place blueberries in a greased 13x9-in. baking dish; set aside. In a small saucepan, bring sugar and water to a boil; cook and stir until sugar is dissolved. Pour over berries.
2. In a large bowl, cream butter and 1½ cups sugar until light and fluffy, 5-7 minutes. Add eggs, 1 at a time, beating well after each addition. Beat in vanilla. Combine flour, baking powder and salt; add to the creamed mixture. Spread over berry mixture. Drizzle with butter; sprinkle with remaining sugar.
3. Bake at 350° for 40-45 minutes or until golden brown. Serve warm, with ice cream if desired.
1 serving: 362 cal., 13g fat (8g sat. fat), 74mg chol., 206mg sod., 60g carb. (48g sugars, 2g fiber), 3g pro.

COUNTY FAIR TOFFEE

I don't live in the country, but I love everything about it—especially good old-fashioned home cooking! Every year, you'll find me at our county fair, entering a different recipe contest. This toffee is a family favorite!
—Kathy Dorman, Snover, MI

Prep: 25 min. • **Cook:** 15 min. + chilling
Makes: 32 pieces

- 2 **cups unblanched whole almonds**
- 11 **oz. milk chocolate, chopped**
- 1 **cup butter, cubed**
- 1 **cup sugar**
- 3 **Tbsp. cold water**

1. Preheat oven to 350°. In a shallow baking pan, toast almonds until golden brown, 5-10 minutes, stirring occasionally. Cool. Pulse chocolate in a food processor until finely ground (do not overprocess); transfer to a bowl. Pulse almonds in food processor until coarsely chopped. Sprinkle 1 cup almonds over bottom of a greased 15x10x1-in. pan. Sprinkle with 1 cup chocolate.
2. In a heavy saucepan, combine butter, sugar and water. Cook over medium heat until a candy thermometer reads 290° (soft-crack stage), stirring occasionally.
3. Immediately pour the mixture over almonds and chocolate in pan. Sprinkle with remaining chocolate and almonds. Refrigerate until set; break into pieces.
Note: We recommend that you test your candy thermometer before each use. To do this, bring water to a rolling boil; the thermometer should read 212°. Adjust your recipe temperature up or down based on your test.
1 oz.: 177 cal., 13g fat (6g sat. fat), 17mg chol., 51mg sod., 14g carb. (12g sugars, 1g fiber), 3g pro.

CHOCOLATE CARAMEL CANDY

This treat tastes like a Snickers bar but has homemade flavor beyond compare. When I entered it in a recipe contest at our harvest festival, it won five ribbons, including grand prize and the judges' special award.
—Jane Meek, Pahrump, NV

Prep: 45 min. + chilling
Makes: about 8 dozen

- 2 tsp. butter
- 1 cup milk chocolate chips
- ¼ cup butterscotch chips
- ¼ cup creamy peanut butter

FILLING
- ¼ cup butter
- 1 cup sugar
- ¼ cup evaporated milk
- 1½ cups marshmallow creme
- ¼ cup creamy peanut butter
- 1 tsp. vanilla extract
- 1½ cups chopped salted peanuts

CARAMEL LAYER
- 1 pkg. (14 oz.) caramels
- ¼ cup heavy whipping cream

ICING
- 1 cup (6 oz.) milk chocolate chips
- ¼ cup butterscotch chips
- ¼ cup creamy peanut butter

1. Line a 13x9-in. pan with foil; grease foil with 2 tsp. butter and set aside.
2. In a small saucepan, combine milk chocolate chips, butterscotch chips and peanut butter; stir over low heat until melted and smooth. Spread into prepared pan. Refrigerate until set.
3. For filling, in a small heavy saucepan, melt butter over medium heat. Add sugar and milk; bring to a gentle boil. Reduce heat to medium-low; cook and stir 5 minutes. Remove from heat; stir in marshmallow creme, peanut butter and vanilla until smooth. Add the peanuts. Spread over the first layer. Refrigerate until set.
4. For caramel layer, in a small heavy saucepan, combine the caramels and cream; stir over low heat until melted and smooth. Cook and stir 4 minutes. Spread over filling. Refrigerate until set.
5. For the icing, in another saucepan, combine chips and peanut butter; stir over low heat until melted and smooth. Pour over caramel layer. Refrigerate at least 4 hours or overnight.
6. Remove from refrigerator 20 minutes before cutting. Remove from pan and cut into 1-in.-wide strips, then into squares. Store in an airtight container.
1 piece: 86 cal., 5g fat (2g sat. fat), 4mg chol., 41mg sod., 10g carb. (9g sugars, 0 fiber), 2g pro.

READER RAVE...

"I have made this recipe for years. It's always a hit and one of my hubby's favorites. I don't make it often enough for him! I use a little less cream in my caramel mixture so it is not as runny."
—RENA 55, TASTEOFHOME.COM

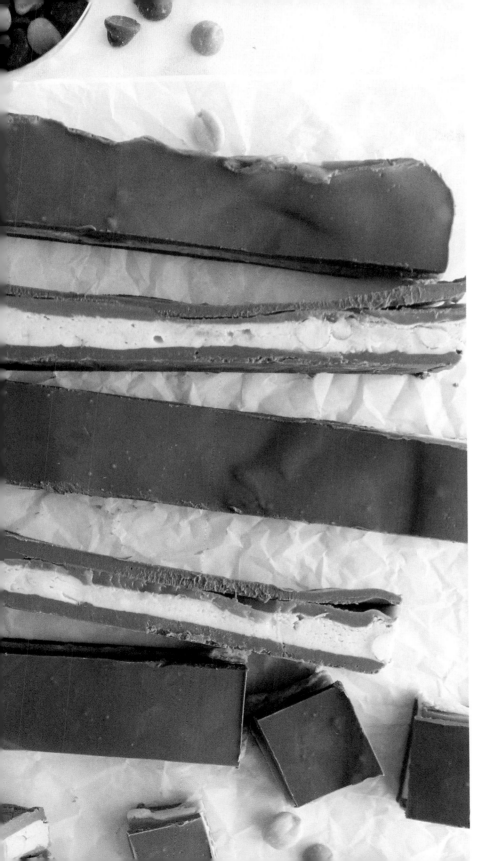

CRANBERRY WALNUT WHITE FUDGE

A visit to several Oregon cranberry farms inspired my unusual fruit-flavored white fudge. I make it for family and friends at holidays and for special occasions. I was thrilled when the recipe earned first place at our county fair.
—Wanda Green, Woodland, CA

Prep: 25 min. + cooling • **Makes:** 3 lbs.

- 1 tsp. plus ½ cup butter, divided
- 2 cups sugar
- ¾ cup sour cream
- 1 pkg. (10 to 12 oz.) vanilla or white chips
- 1 jar (7 oz.) marshmallow creme
- 1 tsp. vanilla extract
- 3 cups coarsely chopped walnuts
- 1 cup dried cranberries, coarsely chopped

1. Line an 8-in. square pan with foil and butter foil with 1 tsp. butter; set aside. In a heavy saucepan, bring the sugar, sour cream and remaining butter to a boil over medium heat. Cook and stir until a candy thermometer reads 234° (soft-ball stage), about 15 minutes.
2. Remove from heat. Stir in the chips, marshmallow creme and vanilla until smooth. Fold in the chopped walnuts and cranberries. Pour into prepared pan. Let stand at room temperature until cool.
3. Using foil, lift the fudge out of the pan. Discard foil; cut fudge into 1-in. squares. Store in an airtight container in the refrigerator.

1 piece: 632 cal., 36g fat (12g sat. fat), 36mg chol., 124mg sod., 74g carb. (50g sugars, 2g fiber), 10g pro.

APPLE COBBLER CHEESECAKE

I call this combination of two classic desserts my lucky recipe. It won top honors when I entered the baking contest in my hometown's annual apple festival.
—Jay Hoover, The Villages, FL

Prep: 50 min.
Bake: 1¼ hours + cooling
Makes: 16 servings

  2 **cups graham cracker crumbs**
  ¼ **cup sugar**
  ½ **cup butter, melted**

COBBLER LAYER

  1 **cup butter, softened**
  1 **cup sugar**
  2 **large eggs**
  2 **cups all-purpose flour**
  2 **Tbsp. baking powder**
  2 **medium tart apples, peeled and thinly sliced**

  1 **jar (12 oz.) hot caramel ice cream topping, divided**

CHEESECAKE LAYER

  3 **pkg. (8 oz. each) cream cheese, softened**
  1 **cup sugar**
  ¼ **cup all-purpose flour**
  ¼ **cup water**
  3 **large eggs, room temperature, lightly beaten**
      Whipped cream

1. Preheat oven to 325°. In a small bowl, mix cracker crumbs and sugar; stir in butter. Press onto bottom and 1 in. up sides of a greased 10-in. springform pan. Place on a 15x10x1-in. baking pan.

2. For cobbler layer, in a large bowl, cream butter and sugar until light and fluffy, 5-7 minutes. Add eggs, 1 at a time, beating well after each addition. In a small bowl, whisk flour and baking powder; add to creamed mixture. Drop half the dough by tablespoonfuls into crust. Top with half the apple slices; drizzle with ⅓ cup caramel topping.

3. For cheesecake layer, in a large bowl, beat cream cheese and sugar until smooth. Beat in flour and water. Add eggs; beat on low speed just until combined. Pour over the caramel. Repeat cobbler layer with remaining dough, apple and an additional ⅓ cup caramel topping.

4. Bake 1¼-1½ hours or until the cheesecake layer no longer jiggles when moved. Cool on a wire rack for 30 minutes.

5. Serve warm or refrigerate overnight, covering when completely cooled, and serve cold. Loosen sides of cheesecake with a knife. Remove the rim from pan. Warm the remaining caramel topping. Serve caramel with cheesecake; top with whipped cream.

1 piece: 800 cal., 46g fat (28g sat. fat), 211mg chol., 742mg sod., 89g carb. (45g sugars, 2g fiber), 11g pro.

BUTTERSCOTCH FUDGE

Lovers of butterscotch and fudge will agree—this award-winning recipe is a match made in heaven! Special add-ins like walnuts and marshmallow take this treat to a whole new level.
—Virginia Hipwell, Fenwick, ON

Prep: 20 min. + standing
Makes: about 1½ lbs.

- 1 **tsp. plus 2 Tbsp. butter, divided**
- 1⅔ **cups sugar**
- ⅔ **cup evaporated milk**
- ½ **tsp. salt**
- 2 **cups miniature marshmallows**
- 1 **pkg. (10 to 11 oz.) butterscotch chips**
- ½ **cup chopped walnuts, toasted**
- 1 **tsp. maple flavoring**

1. Line an 8-in. square pan with foil and grease the foil with 1 tsp. butter; set aside.
2. In a large saucepan, combine the sugar, milk, salt and remaining 2 Tbsp. butter; cook and stir over medium heat until the mixture comes to a boil. Boil for 5 minutes, stirring constantly.
3. Remove mixture from heat; add the marshmallows, chips, nuts and maple flavoring. Stir until marshmallows and chips are melted. Spoon into prepared pan. Let stand until set.
4. Using foil, lift the fudge out of pan. Discard foil; cut fudge into 1-in. squares. Store in an airtight container at room temperature.
1 serving: 64 cal., 2g fat (2g sat. fat), 2mg chol., 29mg sod., 10g carb. (9g sugars, 0 fiber), 1g pro.

BLUE-RIBBON TIP

If your fudge ends up too hard, it could be because it was overcooked or it didn't cool down properly (fudge is finicky that way). Next time, mix a cup of water with the fudge mixture in a saucepan at low heat. Stir until the water dissolves, then boil. Wash off the sides of the saucepan to prevent sugar crystals from forming. Once complete, follow the recipe's baking and cooling instructions.

CARAMEL CHOCOLATE TRIFLE

A highlight of our annual family reunion is the dessert competition. The judges take their jobs very seriously! Last year's first-place winner was this tempting trifle.
—Barb Hausey, Independence, MO

Prep: 20 min. • **Bake:** 20 min. + cooling
Makes: 16 servings

- 1 pkg. (9 oz.) devil's food cake mix
- 2 pkg. (3.9 oz. each) instant chocolate pudding mix
- 1 carton (12 oz.) frozen whipped topping, thawed
- 1 jar (12¼ oz.) caramel ice cream topping
- 1 pkg. (7½ or 8 oz.) English toffee bits or almond brickle chips

1. Prepare and bake cake according to the package directions for an 8-in. square baking pan. Cool on a wire rack. Prepare chocolate pudding according to package directions.
2. Cut cake into 1½-in. cubes. Place half the cubes in a 3-qt. trifle bowl or large glass serving bowl; lightly press down to fill in gaps. Top cake with half each of the whipped topping, pudding, caramel topping and toffee bits; repeat layers. Cover and refrigerate until serving.
1 serving: 349 cal., 11g fat (7g sat. fat), 21mg chol., 533mg sod., 61g carb. (29g sugars, 1g fiber), 3g pro.

NO-FRY FRIED ICE CREAM

This ice cream has a crispy cinnamon coating just like the fried ice cream served at Mexican restaurants, but minus the oily mess. Make ahead of time and freeze until serving.
—Tim White, Windsor, ON

Prep: 20 min. + freezing
Makes: 8 servings

- 1 qt. vanilla ice cream
- ¼ cup packed brown sugar
- 1 Tbsp. butter, melted
- 1 tsp. ground cinnamon
- 2 cups crushed cornflakes
  Optional: Whipped cream and caramel ice cream topping

1. Preheat oven to 350°. Using a ½-cup ice cream scoop, place 8 scoops of ice cream on a baking sheet. Freeze until firm, about 1 hour. Meanwhile, combine the brown sugar, butter and cinnamon. Stir in cornflakes. Transfer mixture to an ungreased 15x10x1-in. baking pan. Bake until lightly browned, 4-6 minutes. Cool completely.
2. Roll ice cream balls in the crumb mixture. Cover and freeze until firm, at least 1 hour. If desired, serve with the toppings.
½ cup: 216 cal., 8g fat (5g sat. fat), 32mg chol., 168mg sod., 33g carb. (20g sugars, 1g fiber), 3g pro.

APPLE ROLY-POLY

My grandmother's apple dessert is genuine regional fare. With 13 children plus the men at Grandpa's sawmill, she had to do lots of cooking each day!
—Megan Newcombe, Cookstown, ON

Prep: 25 min. • **Bake:** 35 min.
Makes: 12 servings

- 1¾ cups all-purpose flour
- ¼ cup sugar
- 4 tsp. baking powder
- ½ tsp. salt
- ¼ cup shortening
- ¼ cup cold butter
- ⅔ cup sour cream

FILLING
- ¼ cup butter, softened
- 1 cup packed brown sugar
- 2 tsp. ground cinnamon
- 6 medium Granny Smith apples, peeled and coarsely shredded (about 5 cups)

TOPPING
- 2½ cups water
- 2 Tbsp. brown sugar
- 1 tsp. ground cinnamon
- ½ cup half-and-half cream

1. In a bowl, combine flour, sugar, baking powder and salt. Cut in shortening and butter until crumbly. Add sour cream and blend until a ball forms.
2. Roll out on a floured surface into a 15x10-in. rectangle. Spread with the softened butter; sprinkle with the remaining filling ingredients.
3. Roll up, jelly-roll style, starting with a long side. Cut into 12 slices. Place slices, cut side down, in a 13x9-in. baking pan.
4. For topping, combine water, brown sugar and cinnamon in a saucepan. Bring to a boil; remove from the heat. Stir in the cream.

5. Carefully pour hot topping over the dumplings. Bake, uncovered, at 350° for 35 minutes or until bubbly. (Center will jiggle when dumplings are hot out of the oven but will set as dumplings stand for a few minutes.) Serve warm.
1 serving: 336 cal., 15g fat (8g sat. fat), 34mg chol., 329mg sod., 48g carb. (32g sugars, 2g fiber), 3g pro.

PEPPERMINT TAFFY

For a fun afternoon activity, get the kids or friends involved in an old-fashioned taffy pull. This soft, chewy taffy has a minty flavor, and it won't stick to the wrapper. Feel free to change up the flavor with almond or spearmint oil.
—Elaine Chichura, Kingsley, PA

Prep: 1¾ hours + cooling • **Makes:** 1¾ lbs.

- 2½ cups sugar
- 1½ cups light corn syrup
- 4 tsp. white vinegar
- ¼ tsp. salt
- ½ cup evaporated milk
- ¼ tsp. peppermint oil
  Red food coloring

1. Butter a 15x10x1-in. pan; set aside. In a heavy large saucepan, combine the sugar, corn syrup, vinegar and salt. Cook and stir over low heat until sugar is dissolved. Bring to a boil over medium heat. Slowly add the milk; cook and stir until a candy thermometer reads 248° (firm-ball stage).
2. Remove from heat; stir in peppermint oil and food coloring, keeping face away from mixture, as odor is very strong. Pour into prepared pan. Let stand for 8 minutes or until cool enough to handle.
3. With well-buttered fingers, quickly pull the candy until firm but pliable (color will become light pink). Pull into a ½-in. rope; cut into 1-in. pieces. Wrap each in waxed paper.
2 pieces: 174 cal., 0 fat (0 sat. fat), 2mg chol., 66mg sod., 44g carb. (37g sugars, 0 fiber), 0 pro.

MAPLE NUT BALLS

I created these chocolate-dipped delights a few years ago, and they quickly became a seasonal favorite with my friends and family members. The creamy confection also won a blue ribbon at our state fair.
—Kathryn Jackson, Benson, NC

Prep: 25 min. + chilling
Makes: about 3½ dozen

- ½ cup butter, softened
- 2 tsp. maple flavoring
- 3½ cups confectioners' sugar
- 1 cup finely chopped pecans
- 1 pkg. (11½ oz.) milk chocolate chips
- 2 tsp. shortening

1. In a large bowl, cream butter and maple flavoring until light and fluffy. Gradually add confectioners' sugar and mix well. Stir in pecans. Shape into 1-in. balls. Cover and refrigerate for 1½ hours or until firm.
2. In a microwave, melt chocolate chips and shortening; stir until smooth. Dip balls in chocolate mixture; allow excess to drip off. Place on waxed paper until set. Store in the refrigerator.

1 serving: 119 cal., 7g fat (3g sat. fat), 7mg chol., 22mg sod., 15g carb. (14g sugars, 0 fiber), 0 pro.

READER RAVE...

"If you love maple sugar candy as much as I do, these little balls of sappy-sweet heaven will be right up your alley."
—CARLYFACE, TASTEOFHOME.COM

DOUBLE-LAYER PUMPKIN CHEESECAKE

I thought cheesecake and pumpkin pie would be amazing together. This creamy combo won a prize in our local pie contest, so I guess the judges agreed!
—Noel Ferry, Perkasie, PA

Prep: 25 min. • **Bake:** 55 min. + cooling
Makes: 10 servings

- 1½ **cups crushed gingersnap cookies (about 30 cookies)**
- ¾ **cup chopped pecans, toasted**
- 1 **Tbsp. sugar**
- ⅛ **tsp. salt**
- ¼ **cup butter, melted**

CHEESECAKE LAYER
- 1 **pkg. (8 oz.) cream cheese, softened**
- ⅓ **cup sugar**
- 1 **large egg, room temperature, lightly beaten**
- 1 **tsp. vanilla extract**

PUMPKIN LAYER
- 2 **large eggs, room temperature, lightly beaten**
- 1⅓ **cups canned pumpkin**
- ½ **cup sugar**
- 1 **tsp. pumpkin pie spice**
- ⅛ **tsp. salt**
- ⅔ **cup heavy whipping cream**
  Optional: Sweetened whipped cream and toasted chopped pecans

1. Preheat oven to 325°. Pulse the first 4 ingredients in a food processor until ground. Add the butter; pulse to blend. Press mixture onto bottom and up sides of an ungreased 9-in. deep-dish pie plate. Refrigerate while preparing the filling.

2. For cheesecake layer, beat all ingredients until smooth. For pumpkin layer, whisk together eggs, pumpkin, sugar, pie spice and salt; gradually whisk in cream. Spread cheesecake mixture onto crust; cover with the pumpkin mixture.

3. Bake on a lower oven rack until the filling is set, 55-65 minutes. Cool at least 1 hour on a wire rack; serve or refrigerate within 2 hours. If desired, top with whipped cream and pecans.

Note: To toast nuts, bake in a shallow pan in a 350° oven for 5-10 minutes or cook in a skillet over low heat until lightly browned, stirring occasionally.

1 piece: 422 cal., 28g fat (13g sat. fat), 115mg chol., 313mg sod., 40g carb. (25g sugars, 2g fiber), 6g pro.

Double-Layer Pumpkin Cheesecake Squares: Press crumb mixture onto bottom of an ungreased 8-in. square baking pan. Prepare and add layers as directed; bake in a preheated 325° oven until filling is set, 55-65 minutes. Cool as directed. Cut into squares.

BLUE-RIBBON TIP

When making cheesecake, using room temperature cream cheese and eggs is absolutely critical. Room temp ingredients blend smoothly so you don't have a lumpy cake.

STRAWBERRY TRIFLE

I won first prize in a dairy recipe contest with this tasty strawberry trifle. You can double the recipe and make two for large groups.
—Norma Steiner, Monroe, WI

Prep: 20 min. + chilling
Makes: 10 servings

- 1 cup 2% milk
- 1 cup sour cream
- 1 pkg. (3.4 oz.) instant vanilla pudding mix
- 1 tsp. grated orange zest
- 2 cups heavy whipping cream, whipped
- 8 cups cubed angel food cake
- 4 cups sliced fresh strawberries

1. In a large bowl, beat the milk, sour cream, pudding mix and orange zest on low speed until thickened. Fold in whipped cream.
2. Place half the cake cubes in a 3-qt. glass bowl. Arrange a third of the strawberries around sides of bowl and over cake; top with half the pudding mixture. Repeat layers once. Top with the remaining berries. Refrigerate for 2 hours before serving.

1 serving: 376 cal., 23g fat (14g sat. fat), 62mg chol., 360mg sod., 38g carb. (30g sugars, 2g fiber), 6g pro.

BLUE-RIBBON TIP

Angel food cake is light and airy, so it's easy to squish when cutting it into cubes. To avoid this, freeze the cake overnight, then cut it with a serrated knife, using a gentle back-and-forth motion.

FRENCH KISS TRUFFLES

My truffles are so impressive that they won first place at the Wisconsin State Fair. These two-tone creamy candies combine an orange-flavored white chocolate with milk chocolate.
—Gerry Cofta, Milwaukee, WI

Prep: 45 min. + chilling
Makes: about 2½ dozen

- 8 oz. white baking chocolate, chopped
- ⅔ cup heavy whipping cream, divided
- ½ tsp. grated orange zest
- ¼ tsp. orange extract
- 8 oz. milk chocolate, chopped

COATING

- 12 oz. semisweet chocolate, chopped
  Additional milk and white baking chocolates, melted

1. Place white chocolate in a small bowl. In a small saucepan, bring ⅓ cup cream just to a boil. Pour over white chocolate; whisk until smooth. Stir in orange zest and extract.
2. Place milk chocolate in another small bowl. In the same saucepan, bring the remaining cream just to a boil. Pour the cream over milk chocolate; whisk until smooth. Cool both mixtures to room temperature, stirring occasionally. Refrigerate until firm.
3. To form centers, take 1½ tsp. of each chocolate mixture and shape into a 2-tone ball, about 1 in. round. Place on waxed paper-lined baking sheets; cover and refrigerate at least 1 hour.
4. In a double boiler or metal bowl over simmering water, whisk semisweet chocolate until smooth. Dip truffles in chocolate; allow excess to drip off. Return to baking sheets; drizzle with additional chocolate as desired. Refrigerate until set. Store in an airtight container in the refrigerator.

Note: *Ganache* is a French term referring to a smooth mixture of chocolate and cream used as cake fillings or glazes and in candy-making. Traditionally, ganache is made by pouring hot cream over chopped chocolate and stirring until the mixture is smooth. Flavorings can be added, as well as corn syrup to give a shiny finish. The proportions of cream to chocolate vary depending on the use.

1 truffle: 145 cal., 10g fat (6g sat. fat), 10mg chol., 9mg sod., 15g carb. (13g sugars, 1g fiber), 2g pro.

HONEY-ROASTED FIGS IN PUFF PASTRY

I created this special recipe for a national honey contest and won third place! I was thrilled, and you will be, too, when you try these tasty but elegant desserts.
—Kelly Williams, Forked River, NJ

Prep: 45 min. + chilling • **Bake:** 25 min.
Makes: 8 servings

- **4 oz. cream cheese, softened**
- **2 tsp. dark brown sugar**
- **½ tsp. vanilla extract**
- **1 vanilla bean**
- **¼ cup spun or regular honey**
- **½ tsp. balsamic vinegar**
- **8 fresh figs**
- **1 pkg. (17.3 oz.) frozen puff pastry, thawed**

EGG WASH

- **1 large egg**
- **1 Tbsp. water**
- **¼ cup pistachios, chopped**

1. In a small bowl, mix cream cheese, brown sugar and vanilla. Divide into 8 small mounds. Refrigerate for 30 minutes or until firm.
2. Meanwhile, preheat oven to 400°. Split vanilla bean lengthwise. Using the tip of a sharp knife, scrape seeds from the center; place in a small microwave-safe bowl. Add the honey and balsamic vinegar. Microwave, uncovered, at 80% power for 20 seconds; stir to mix.
3. Slice each fig lengthwise into 6 slices; place on a parchment-lined 15x10x1-in. baking pan. Drizzle with 2 Tbsp. honey sauce. Roast 8-10 minutes or until softened. Cool the figs on pan on a wire rack.
4. Unfold 1 sheet of puff pastry. On a lightly floured surface, roll out pastry just enough to smooth surface. Cut into 4 equal pieces; trim off corners to round. Cut about halfway from each rounded corner in toward center. Place a cream cheese mound in the center of each pastry. Top with 6 slices cooled roasted figs; drizzle tops with ¼ tsp. honey sauce.
5. In a small bowl, whisk egg with water; brush pastry with egg wash. Fold up 1 petal of dough wrapping around filling. Wrap the second petal around first petal from the opposite side, lightly pressing ends to stick. Continue with other 2 petals. Tuck the last 2 points under rose, and cup in hand gently to round the base.
6. Place on parchment-lined baking sheet. Repeat with remaining puff pastry sheets. Use excess corner trimmings to make leaves, and place slightly under and next to roses. Brush the outside of pastries with egg wash. Bake 25-30 minutes or until golden brown. Remove pastries to a cooling rack. Place roses on a serving plate; drizzle with re-warmed remaining honey sauce. Top with pistachios; serve warm.

1 serving: 446 cal., 24g fat (7g sat. fat), 38mg chol., 273mg sod., 54g carb. (17g sugars, 6g fiber), 7g pro.

MOLASSES TAFFY

When I was growing up, we'd have taffy pulling parties. The more experienced taffy pullers could make the long strips of shiny candy pop as they worked it into rope-like streamers.
—Sherrill Bennett, Rayville, LA

Prep: 2 hours + cooling
Makes: about 12½ dozen

- **7 Tbsp. butter, softened, divided**
- **2 cups molasses**
- **1 cup sugar**
- **¾ cup water**
- **½ tsp. vanilla extract**
- **⅛ tsp. baking soda**

1. Butter a 15x10x1-in. pan with 3 Tbsp. butter; set aside. In a heavy saucepan over medium heat, bring the molasses, sugar and water to a boil. Cook and stir until a candy thermometer reads 245° (firm-ball stage), stirring occasionally.
2. Add the vanilla, baking soda and remaining butter. Cover and cook for 3 minutes. Uncover and cook until the thermometer reads 260° (hard-ball stage), stirring occasionally. Remove from the heat; pour into prepared pan. Cool on a wire rack for 15 minutes or until cool enough to handle.
3. With buttered fingers, quickly pull half the taffy until firm but pliable. Pull and shape into a ½-in. rope; cut into 1¼-in. pieces. Repeat with remaining taffy. Wrap each piece in foil, colored candy wrappers or waxed paper.

2 pieces: 43 cal., 1g fat (1g sat. fat), 3mg chol., 16mg sod., 9g carb. (8g sugars, 0 fiber), 0 pro.

RHUBARB RASPBERRY CRISP

Every time I've entered our Boone County Bake-Off, I've won a blue ribbon. Last summer, when the category was rhubarb, this recipe was the grand champion! The orange juice and zest give it a real zip. See if your family thinks it's a winner, too.
—Mabeth Shaw, Lebanon, IN

Prep: 15 min. • **Bake:** 45 min.
Makes: 9 servings

- 4 **cups chopped fresh rhubarb (1-in. pieces)**
- ⅔ **cup sugar**
  Juice and zest of 1 orange
- 1 **cup all-purpose flour**
- ½ **cup packed brown sugar**
- ½ **tsp. ground cinnamon**
- ½ **cup chilled butter, cut into small pieces**
- ½ **cup rolled oats**
- ¼ **cup chopped pecans**
- ½ **pint fresh raspberries**

Preheat oven to 350°. In a large bowl, combine rhubarb, sugar, orange juice and zest. In another bowl, combine the flour, brown sugar and cinnamon; cut in butter as for pastry. Add oats and pecans; mix well. Place the rhubarb mixture in an 8-in. square baking pan. Sprinkle evenly with fresh raspberries and cover with the crumb topping. Bake for 45 minutes or until topping is browned.

1 serving: 306 cal., 13g fat (7g sat. fat), 27mg chol., 110mg sod., 46g carb. (30g sugars, 3g fiber), 3g pro.

NEAPOLITAN CHEESECAKE

This rich, creamy cheesecake is a crowd-pleasing standout. It has won first-place ribbons at numerous fairs and is my family's favorite dessert. It's an indulgence sure to elicit oohs and aahs when served to guests.
—Sherri Regalbuto, Carp, ON

Prep: 35 min. • **Bake:** 70 min. + chilling
Makes: 14 servings

- 1 **cup chocolate wafer crumbs (18 wafers)**
- 3 **Tbsp. butter, melted**

FILLING
- 3 **pkg. (8 oz. each) cream cheese, softened**
- ¾ **cup sugar**
- ¼ **cup heavy whipping cream**
- 3 **large eggs, room temperature, lightly beaten**
- 1 **tsp. vanilla extract**
- 2 **oz. semisweet chocolate, melted and cooled**
- 2 **oz. white baking chocolate, melted and cooled**
- ⅓ **cup mashed frozen sweetened sliced strawberries, well-drained Red liquid food coloring, optional**

TOPPING
- 3 **oz. semisweet chocolate, chopped**
- 2 **Tbsp. butter**
- 2 **tsp. shortening, divided**
- 1 **oz. white baking chocolate**

1. In a bowl, combine wafer crumbs and butter. Press onto the bottom of an ungreased 9-in. springform pan. Place pan on a baking sheet. Bake at 350° for 10 minutes. Cool on a wire rack. Reduce heat to 325°.

2. In a large bowl, beat cream cheese until smooth. Gradually beat in sugar and cream. Add eggs and vanilla; beat on low just until combined. Divide batter into thirds. Add the melted semisweet chocolate to a third. Spread over crust. Add melted white chocolate to another third. Spread over semisweet layer. Stir strawberries and, if desired, a few drops of food coloring into remaining portion. Spread over white chocolate layer. Place pan on a double thickness of heavy-duty foil (about 18 in. square). Securely wrap foil around pan.

3. Place the springform pan in a large baking pan. Fill larger pan with 1 in. hot water. Bake at 325° for 70-75 minutes or until center is just set. Remove springform pan from water bath. Cool on a wire rack for 10 minutes. Remove foil. Carefully run a knife around the edge of pan to loosen; cool for 1 hour longer. Refrigerate overnight.

4. For the topping, melt semisweet chocolate, butter and 1 tsp. shortening in a heavy saucepan or microwave; stir until smooth. Cool 5 minutes. Remove sides of pan. Pour melted chocolate mixture over cheesecake. Melt white chocolate with remaining shortening. Drizzle over cheesecake. Refrigerate until chocolate is firm. Refrigerate any leftovers.

1 piece: 265 cal., 18g fat (10g sat. fat), 82mg chol., 157mg sod., 25g carb. (18g sugars, 1g fiber), 4g pro.

LEMON CREME BRULEE

After being disappointed in this recipe the first time I tried it, I experimented. When I felt it was fit for competition, the judge was impressed, too—I won a blue ribbon and an Award of Excellence.
—Sara Scheler, Pewaukee, WI

Prep: 15 min. • **Bake:** 45 min. + chilling
Makes: 5 servings

- **3 cups heavy whipping cream**
- **6 large egg yolks, room temperature**
- **½ cup plus 5 tsp. sugar, divided**
- **½ tsp. salt**
- **2 Tbsp. grated lemon zest**
- **½ tsp. lemon extract**

1. Preheat oven to 325°. In a large saucepan, heat cream until bubbles form around sides of pan; remove from heat. In a large bowl, whisk egg yolks, ½ cup sugar and salt until blended but not foamy. Slowly stir in hot cream. Stir in lemon zest and extract.
2. Place five 6-oz. broiler-safe ramekins in a baking pan large enough to hold them without touching. Pour the egg mixture into ramekins. Place pan on oven rack; add very hot water to pan to within ½ in. of tops of ramekins. Bake until a knife inserted in center of creme brulee comes out clean (centers will still be soft), 45-50 minutes.
3. Immediately remove the ramekins from water bath to a wire rack; cool 10 minutes. Refrigerate until cold.
4. To caramelize topping with a kitchen torch, sprinkle the custards evenly with the remaining sugar. Hold torch flame about 2 in. above custard surface and rotate it slowly until the sugar is evenly caramelized. Refrigerate 30-60 minutes before serving.
5. To caramelize topping in a broiler, preheat broiler and place ramekins on a baking sheet; let stand at room temperature 15 minutes. Sprinkle custards evenly with remaining sugar. Broil 3-4 in. from heat until sugar is caramelized, 2-3 minutes. Refrigerate 30-60 minutes before serving.
1 serving: 652 cal., 57g fat (35g sat. fat), 384mg chol., 285mg sod., 29g carb. (28g sugars, 0 fiber), 7g pro.

ALMOND TOFFEE

After trying a coworker's fabulous toffee, I had to have the recipe! It's now a regular on my Christmas cookie tray. I also entered it at our county fair and received best in show.
—Sue Gronholz, Beaver Dam, WI

Prep: 50 min. + standing
Makes: about 1½ lbs.

- **1 Tbsp. plus 2 cups butter, divided**
- **2 cups sugar**
- **1 cup slivered almonds**
- **¼ cup water**
- **1 tsp. salt**
- **1 tsp. vanilla extract**
- **1 pkg. (11½ oz.) milk chocolate chips, divided**
- **½ cup finely chopped almonds**

1. Grease a 15x10x1-in. pan with 1 Tbsp. butter; set pan aside. In a large heavy saucepan, melt remaining butter. Add sugar, slivered almonds, water and salt; cook and stir over medium heat until a candy thermometer reads 295° (approaching hard-crack stage). Remove from heat; stir in vanilla.
2. Quickly pour into prepared pan. Let stand at room temperature until cool, about 1 hour.
3. In a microwave, melt 1 cup chocolate chips; spread over toffee. Refrigerate for 45 minutes or until set. Invert onto an ungreased large baking sheet. Melt remaining chips; spread over toffee. Sprinkle with chopped almonds. Let stand 1 hour. Break into bite-sized pieces. Store in an airtight container.
1 oz.: 325 cal., 24g fat (13g sat. fat), 46mg chol., 218mg sod., 28g carb. (26g sugars, 1g fiber), 3g pro.

CONTEST-WINNING PEACH COBBLER

Canned peaches make this cobbler quick to assemble. The tender topping pairs nicely with the sweet fruit filling and warm butterscotch sauce.
—Ellen Merick, North Pole, AK

Prep: 20 min. + standing
Bake: 50 min. + cooling
Makes: 12 servings

- 2 cans (29 oz. each) sliced peaches
- ½ cup packed brown sugar
- 6 Tbsp. quick-cooking tapioca
- 1 tsp. ground cinnamon, optional
- 1 tsp. lemon juice
- 1 tsp. vanilla extract

TOPPING
- 1 cup all-purpose flour
- 1 cup sugar
- 1 tsp. baking powder
- ½ tsp. salt
- ¼ cup cold butter, cubed
- 2 large eggs, room temperature, lightly beaten

BUTTERSCOTCH SAUCE
- ½ cup packed brown sugar
- 2 Tbsp. all-purpose flour
- ⅛ tsp. salt
- ¼ cup butter, melted
- 2 Tbsp. lemon juice
  Vanilla ice cream, optional

1. Drain peaches, reserving ½ cup syrup for the sauce. In a large bowl, combine the peaches, brown sugar, tapioca, cinnamon if desired, lemon juice and vanilla. Transfer to an ungreased 11x7-in. baking dish. Let the peach mixture stand for 15 minutes.
2. In a large bowl, combine the flour, sugar, baking powder and salt; cut in butter until mixture resembles coarse crumbs. Stir in eggs. Drop by spoonfuls onto peach mixture; spread evenly. Bake at 350° until the filling is bubbly and a toothpick inserted in topping comes out clean, 50-55 minutes. Cool cobbler for 10 minutes.
3. For butterscotch sauce, in a small saucepan, combine the brown sugar, flour, salt, butter and reserved peach syrup. Bring to a boil over medium heat; cook and stir until thickened, 1 minute. Remove from the heat; add lemon juice. Serve cobbler with warm sauce and, if desired, ice cream.

½ cup: 352 cal., 9g fat (5g sat. fat), 51mg chol., 248mg sod., 67g carb. (51g sugars, 1g fiber), 2g pro.

BRANDY ALEXANDER FUDGE

At Christmastime, we indulge in this marbled fudge inspired by the popular brandy drink. My sister-in-law won first place with this recipe at the county fair.
—Debbie Neubauer, Pine City, MN

Prep: 30 min. **Cook:** 15 min. + chilling
Makes: about 3 lbs. (64 pieces)

- 1 tsp. plus ¾ cup butter, divided
- 3 cups sugar
- 1 can (5 oz.) evaporated milk
- 1 jar (7 oz.) marshmallow creme
- 1 cup semisweet chocolate chips
- 2 Tbsp. brandy
- 1 cup white baking chips
- 2 Tbsp. creme de cacao or Kahlua (coffee liqueur)

1. Line an 8-in. square pan with foil and grease the foil with 1 tsp. butter; set aside. In a large heavy saucepan, combine the sugar, milk and remaining butter. Bring to a full boil over medium heat, stirring constantly; cook and stir for 4 minutes. Remove from the heat and set aside.
2. Divide marshmallow creme between 2 small heat-resistant bowls. Pour half the sugar mixture into each bowl. To 1 bowl, stir in the semisweet chips until melted; stir in the brandy. Into the remaining bowl, stir in white chips until melted; stir in creme de cacao.
3. Working quickly, spread the chocolate mixture into prepared pan. Top with the white mixture; cut through with a knife to swirl. Cool to room temperature. Chill until the fudge is set completely.
4. Using foil, lift the fudge out of the pan. Discard foil; cut fudge into 1-in. squares. Store in an airtight container in the refrigerator.

1 piece: 85 cal., 3g fat (2g sat. fat), 7mg chol., 22mg sod., 13g carb. (13g sugars, 0 fiber), 0 pro.

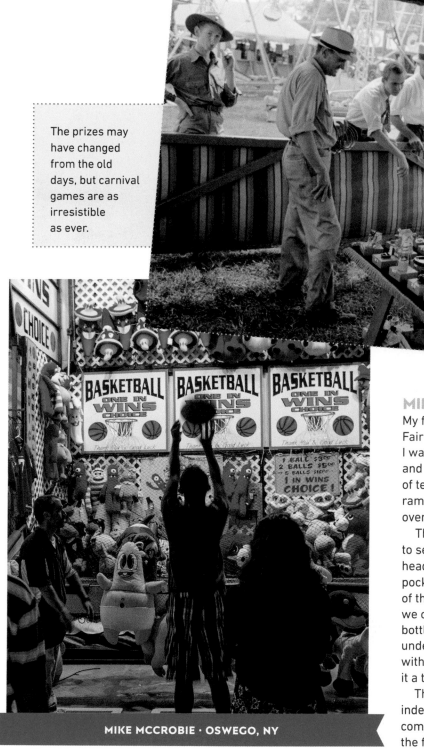

The prizes may have changed from the old days, but carnival games are as irresistible as ever.

MIKE McCROBIE · OSWEGO, NY

MIDWAY GAMES

My first trip to the Great New York State Fair in Syracuse was in the early '70s, when I was 14. I went with a bunch of my buddies, and I'm pretty sure we were like the packs of teenagers who roam the fair today—loud, rambunctious and irritating to everyone over 50.

Then, as now, the midway barkers loved to see groups of unsupervised teenagers heading their way. With some cash in our pockets, we were fresh meat for the sharks of the carnival. We fell for every challenge we came across. Toss a ring onto a Coke bottle? Sure. Shoot a basketball at an undersized hoop? Why not? Ring a bell with the sledgehammer? "We'll give it a try!"

The feelings of camaraderie and independence that we enjoyed that day come flooding back to me each year when the fair rolls around.

1. BLUE-RIBBON WINNER

My granddaughter Cheyenne, then 6, won a county fair blue ribbon for her Hereford calf. The animal loves Cheyenne and even head-butts anyone who tries to play with her.

2. COWBOY KID

I ran into this little cowboy at the state fair. I visited with him while he practiced his roping, and I learned all about how involved he is in his family's ranch.

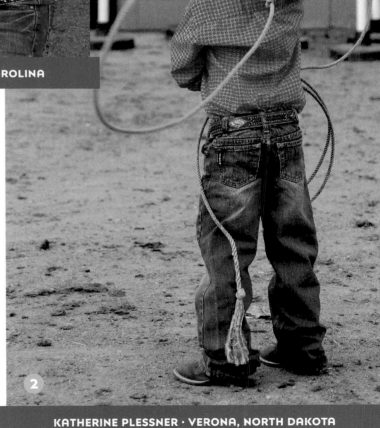

INDEX